Chemical Heroes

Global Insecurities

A Series Edited by Catherine Besteman and Darryl Li

ANDREW BICKFORD

Chemical Heroes
Pharmacological Supersoldiers in the US Military

Duke University Press | *Durham and London* | 2020

Library of Congress Cataloging-in-Publication Data
Names: Bickford, Andrew, [date] author.
Title: Chemical heroes : pharmacological supersoldiers in the US Military / Andrew Bickford.
Other titles: Global insecurities.
Description: Durham : Duke University Press, 2020. | Series: Global insecurities | Includes
bibliographical references and index.
Identifiers: LCCN 2020018849 (print) | LCCN 2020018850 (ebook)
ISBN 9781478009726 (hardcover)
ISBN 9781478011354 (paperback)
ISBN 9781478010302 (ebook)
Subjects: LCSH: United States. Army—Safety measures. | United States. Army—Medical care. |
Military art and science—Technological innovations. | Soldiers—Protection—United States. |
Soldiers—Performance—United States. | Biological warfare—Research—United States. |
Pharmaceutical industry—Military aspects.
Classification: LCC U42.5 .B535 2020 (print) | LCC U42.5 (ebook) | DDC 355.3/45—dc23
LC record available at https://lccn.loc.gov/2020018849
LC ebook record available at https://lccn.loc.gov/2020018850

Cover art: Design and illustration by Matthew Tauch

For Arwen

Heroism is endurance for one moment more.

» **George F. Kennan**, Letter to Henry Munroe Rogers,
 July 25, 1921

It is impossible to strive for the heroic life. The title of hero
is bestowed by the survivors upon the fallen, who themselves know nothing of heroism.

» **Johan Huizinga**, *The Spirit of the Netherlands*, 1968

Death is but a moment; cowardice is a lifetime of affliction.

» **Steve Coogan**, *The Trip*

Contents

Part III. Imagining the Modern US Supersoldier

Terms and Abbreviations

AFRICOM	United States Africa Command
AIT	Advanced Individual Training
AMEDD C&S	Army Medical Department Center and School
API	active pharmaceutical ingredient
ARCIC	Army Capabilities Integration Center
ARL	Army Research Laboratory
ASA (ALT)	Assistant Secretary of the Army (Acquisition, Logistics and Technology)
ASTMP	*Army Science and Technology Master Plan*
BAR	Browning Automatic Rifle
BDU	Battle Dress Uniform
Bio-MOD	Biologically Derived Medicines on Demand (DARPA program)
BRICS	Biological Robustness in Complex Settings (DARPA program)
BTO	Biological Technologies Office (DARPA)
C4ISR	Command, Control, Communications, Computers, Intelligence, Surveillance, and Reconnaissance
CBRN	Chemical, Biological, Radiological, and Nuclear
CCCRP	Combat Casualty Care Research Program
CHPPM	Center for Health Promotion and Preventive Medicine
CIA	Central Intelligence Agency
COMFUT	Combatiente del Futuro (Spanish military, enhanced soldier system)
CRISPR	clustered regularly interspaced short palindromic repeats
CWM	Chemical Warfare Material

DARPA	Defense Advanced Research Projects Agency
D-IX	World War II German experimental military performance enhancement drug
DoD	Department of Defense
DSO	Defense Sciences Office (DARPA)
F2025B	Force 2025 and Beyond (US Army)
FCS	Future Combat System
FELIN	Fantassin à Équipements et Liaisons Intégrés (French military, enhanced soldier system)
FFW	Future Force Warrior
F-INSAS	Futuristic Infantry Soldier as System (Indian military, enhanced soldier system)
FIST	Future Integrated Soldier Technology (United Kingdom, enhanced soldier system)
FOB	Forward Operating Base
FRAMR	Feedback Regulated Automatic Molecular Release (DARPA)
GI	Government Issue (US soldier)
Gladius/IdK	Infanterist der Zukunft (German military, "Future Soldier" system)
Go Pills	US military term for dextroamphetamines
HPOE	Human Performance Optimization and Enhancement
HD	Human Dimension
IED	improvised explosive device
IFF	Identification Friend or Foe
IMESS	Integrated and Modular Engagement System for the Swiss Soldier
ISIS	Islamic State of Iraq and Syria
IVN	In Vivo Nanoplatforms (DARPA program)
IVN:Dx	In Vivo Diagnostics (DARPA program)
IVN:Tx	In Vivo Therapeutics (DARPA program)
JBAIDS	Joint Biological Agent Identification and Detection System
LSD	lysergic acid diethylamide
LW	Land Warrior
MDB	Multi-Domain Battle
MIA	missing in action
MIPOE	medical intelligence preparation of the operational environment

MOAB	Massive Ordnance Air Bomb
MOMRP	Military Operational Medicine Research Program
MOOTW	Military Operations Other than War
MOS	Military Occupational Specialty
MPE	military performance enhancement
NAAFI	Navy, Army, Air Force Institutes (United Kingdom)
NATO	North Atlantic Treaty Organization
NAVMED	Navy Medicine
NBC	nuclear, biological, chemical
NCO	Noncommissioned Officer
NHGRI	National Human Genome Research Institute
No-Go Pills	US military term for sleep aids
NORMANS	NORwegian Modular Arctic Network Soldier (Norwegian military, enhanced soldier system)
NSRDEC	US Army Natick Soldier Research, Development, and Engineering Center
NPY	neuropeptide Y
NVA	Nationale Volksarmee (East German National People's Army)
OFW	Objective Force Warrior
PB pills	pyridostigmine bromide
Pervitin	World War II German methamphetamine
PoD	Pharmacy on Demand (DARPA program)
PTSD	post-traumatic stress disorder
PX	Post Exchange
Ratnik	Warrior (Russian military, enhanced soldier program)
RDECOM	Research, Development and Engineering Command (renamed in 2019 as Combat Capabilities Development Command)
RMA	Revolution in Military Affairs
RPG	rocket-propelled grenade
RT-PSM	real-time physiological status monitor
S&T	science and technology
SBCT	Stryker Brigade Combat Team
SOCOM	Special Operations Command
SS	Schutzstaffel
TALOS	Tactical Assault Light Operator Suit
TFF	Total Force Fitness
TICS/TIMS	toxic industrial chemicals / toxic industrial materials

TRADOC	United States Army Training and Doctrine Command
TRL	technology readiness level
UCMJ	Uniform Code of Military Justice (United States)
USACHPPM	United States Army Center for Health Promotion and Preventive Medicine
USAMRD-A	US Army Medical Research Directorate-Africa
USAMRIID	US Army Medical Research Institute of Infectious Diseases
USAMRMC	United States Army Medical Research and Materials Command
USARIEM	United States Army Research Institute for Environmental Medicine
WRAIR	Walter Reed Army Institute of Research

Acknowledgments

A number of people helped out and lent support to make this book possible. I'd like to extend a special thanks to Catherine Besteman for her interest, encouragement, and support for my project, and for inviting me to submit my manuscript to the Global Insecurities series at Duke University Press. It's amazing what a conversation by the escalator in the lobby at an association meeting can turn into. And thanks as well to Daniel Goldstein and Darryl Li for their shepherding of the Global Insecurities series.

Research support for this project was made possible by a residential fellowship at the Woodrow Wilson International Center for Scholars in 2014–2015. As a fellow at the Wilson Center in the Science and Technology Innovation Program, I was able to dive into the project and have the time to read deeply in the relevant literatures, think, and write. It was wonderful experience, and I am very thankful for my time there. I'd like to thank David Rejeski, Philippa Strum, Kimberly Connor, the staff of the Science and Technology Innovation Program, the Woodrow Wilson Center Library staff, and my fantastic interns Kayla Tyler and Julian Haley.

I was fortunate to be invited to take part in the Wenner-Gren "Cultures of Militarism" symposium organized by Catherine Besteman and Hugh Gusterson, and held in Sintra, Portugal, in 2017. The weeklong symposium was a fantastic opportunity to engage in intense and fruitful discussions about militarism, war, and violence with some of the leading thinkers in the field, and to present my ideas about military performance enhancement. I am grateful to Catherine and Hugh, Leslie Aiello, Laurie Obbink, Danilyn Rutherford, and the Wenner-Gren Foundation for inviting me to take part. And a huge thank you to all who took part in the symposium for your comments, questions, ideas, and suggestions.

A 2017 faculty fellowship at the Summer Institute for Museum Anthropology (SIMA), codirected by Joshua Bell and Candace Greene at the Smithsonian National Museum of Natural History, proved to be very helpful in thinking about the materiality of military biotechnology research, and pushed me to think in new and productive ways about performance enhancement technologies. I can't speak highly enough about SIMA and what I learned from Joshua and Candace, and I thank them both for the chance to take part in SIMA.

Joshua Bell also organized and invited me to speak at "The Cultural Politics of Breakdown and Repair" symposium of the Potomac Center for the Study of Modernity in 2018. Many thanks to Joshua and to Joshua Shannon, the director of the Potomac Center. The symposium helped me think through issues of repair, which informed my thinking about enhancement technologies.

At the 2018 American Anthropological Association meeting, Roger Lancaster and I organized a panel on cowardice. The papers and insights offered by the participants helped me think through and refine some of my ideas and arguments around heroism and cowardice. Thanks to Belinda Straight, Jon Marks, Augustin Fuentes, Alisse Waterston, Nancy Scheper-Hughes, Hugh Gusterson, and Roger.

Chuck Crowell at Notre Dame invited me to take part in the "Technology-Enhanced Warfare: Perspectives from Ethics and Social Science" symposium at the University of Notre Dame, Rome, Italy, in 2017. This was a chance to present my work to researchers in a wide variety of fields, and hear different perspectives on US military enhancement projects, military medicine, and ethics. I'm grateful to have had the opportunity to take part in the symposium.

Drawing from my time at the Wilson Center, and from my participation in the Cultures of Militarism symposium, some of the ideas and discussions in chapter 5 appeared in *Comparative Studies in Society and History* 60, no. 4, October 2018, and portions of chapter 8 appeared in the Wenner-Gren symposium "Cultures of Militarism" special issue of *Current Anthropology* 60, supplement 19, February 2019.

I'd like to thank my friends and colleagues in the Department of Anthropology and 308 Car Barn at Georgetown University, Denise Brennan, Susan Terrio, Gwendolyn Mikell, Amrita Ibrahim, Mubbashir Rizvi, Laurie King, Sylvia Önder, Laura Chippeaux, and Colva Weissenstein, for their help and support with my project, and for reading and listening to early parts of my manuscript. I'd also like to say a special thanks to the undergraduate research assistants in the Department of Anthropology whose help has made this a much stronger book: Thomas Mukundan, Avery Rodriquez, Rachel Weinman, Marie-Ann Wells, and Jenny Xu.

At Duke University Press, I would like to thank my wonderful editor, Gisela Fosado, for her interest in my project and support along the way, and for her generous help at all stages of the publishing process. I'd also like to thank my project editor, Annie Lubinsky, for all of her help during the production, design, and copyediting of the project, and Alejandra Mejia for all of her help with the nuts and bolts of the submission phase. I'd also like to thank my copyeditor, Sheila McMahon, for her very helpful edits and suggestions, and Matthew Tauch for his book design.

Over the years, my thinking and research have been enriched by conversations with a number of friends who generously offered ideas, inspiration, and support; this project is much stronger because of them. Special thanks to Roger Lancaster, Sarah Wagner, Hugh Gusterson, David Price, Richard Grinker, Joshua Bell, Lesley Gill, Paige West, J. C. Salyer, Janine Wedel, Seth Messinger, Jamon Halvaksz, G. S. Quid, Jeffrey Mantz, Bhavani Arabandi, Amy Best, James Snead, Katrina Schwartz, Rashmi Sadana, Roberto Gonzalez, Cynthia Pierce, Rob Marlin-Curiel, Stephanie Marlin-Curiel, Ken Mayer, Jerry Mayer, Kristin English, and Susan South.

And most important of all, I'd like to thank my family, Gabrielle and Arwen, for their love, support, and ridiculous humor.

Prologue

Supersoldier Bob Writes Home

What follows is a fictionalized letter included in a 2001 United States military report titled *Objective Force Warrior: "Another Look—The Art of the Possible . . . A Vision,"* written by scientists and researchers at the Oak Ridge National Laboratory (National Security Directorate Oak Ridge National Laboratory 2001, 28–31; see also Stouder 2002). The Objective Force Warrior program was a US military supersoldier program designed to internally and externally armor soldiers and improve their combat performance. The letter lays out how military researchers and designers imagined the new supersoldier, his capabilities, and the potential threats—medical, environmental, and enemy—the new soldier would face and overcome through the application of internal and external technologies. It is a crystallized version of a particular kind of military imagination and vision of technology, anticipation, protection, and violence.

OCTOBER 30, 2007

Dear Mom & Dad,

Yesterday I finished my last technical school and was fitted for my new uniform. It's an OFW mark 3, that's Army lingo for an Objective Force Warrior Battle Dress, third version. They won't let me send you a picture of it for some security reasons, but I can tell you what it looks like and the many things it does. I know you were hurt when I joined the Army, especially after you told me about my great uncle Jack who died on the beach at Normandy, and my uncle Fred who died in a rice paddy in Vietnam, and my older brother Bill who was injured in Afghanistan. But they didn't have technology working for them like I do. I understand the risks I'm taking, a soldier is supposed to get in harm's way, and many soldiers will still be injured and killed protecting our freedoms. But with the OFW Mark 3, I will have lots of advantages that Jack, Fred, and Bill didn't have.

My suit has the ability to stop a rifle bullet. It is made of a material that is as flexible as my football jersey, but gets hard as steel when a bullet or knife is pushed into it. The material has some kind of chemical in it that lets fresh air pass through it, but stops and destroys chemical warfare agents. The material is also filled with some kind of foam that cools me on hot days and warms me on cold nights. If I do get injured the suit automatically inflates over the wound, stopping the bleeding and applying medicine to the injury until our medic can come help me.

The medicine and medical care provided by the medic is part of the OFW Mark 3 too. It somehow measures my health and notifies my squad leader when I need to take a rest or get a drink. Remember when I got all those muscle cramps in the 3rd quarter [of] each football game? That doesn't happen now because the suit and my leaders look out for my electrolytes.

Remember how you used to tell me that playing all those videogames wouldn't get me anywhere in life? You have to see my helmet to believe it, it's like an IMAX movie right before my eyes. All I have to do is whisper "show me my battery reserves" and a little gas gauge is projected in front of me and I can see that my power pack has 2 more days of energy in it. I can ask how much ammo I have and the number of rounds [is] projected on my visor. If I see the enemy my visor tells me how far away the target is and the probability that my first shot will kill him. There are special modules that I plug into the side of my helmet that gives me other capabilities. A laser can shine on the enemy and if he has chemical weapons protective clothes on he shows up in my visor with a green glow around him. Remember the depression Bill had when he had to kill the women in Afghanistan because they all looked alike, but under their long dresses and hoods they had RPGs? Well, mistakes like that can still happen, but my visor outlines anyone who has gun cleaning oil or CWM clothing on and it gives me a chance to sort out the refugees from the terrorists. If Bill had this technology, he would know if those women were terrorists or friendlies in the wrong place.

When Bill was faced with danger he didn't have any options, he had to shoot to kill and he had to shoot a bunch of rounds because with little time to aim he had to just cover the vicinity with lead. My OFW Mark 3 rifle has steerable bullets which means any target I look at I hit the first time, even if it's moving. And, I have the option of using nonlethal bullets. I just ask my helmet, "What is the probability that the person in my sights wants to kill me?" The battle computer compares the images from the video, laser, microwave and acoustic sensors and recommends the safest action for me. Some of the microwave sensors on my helmet can see guns and knives under someone's clothes, and the laser can measure the gun cleaning fluids and gunpowder that gets on your clothes when you shoot a gun. If these are present, my visor recommends that a lethal round be chambered. If I Say "Yes" my rifle is loaded and the target range and velocity is downloaded into the bullet. . . .

My helmet has night vision enhancement, on a totally dark night I can see by star light just as well as if it was mid-day. The infrared detector makes the animals and people and machines all show up as white outlines because they give off heat. It's like the heads-up display on Dad's car, except I can look at anything and ask my helmet "What is this thing?" and the battle computer will display what the image most likely is. It can actually tell me, in total darkness if it is a Toyota pickup truck or a Ford F-150. This could be important information if our spies have told us that the terrorists have been seen in a Toyota pickup, and the nuns drive an old F-150. . . .

Next year they will issue me an OFW Mark 4. It's supposed to have some mechanical assist machine built in that will let me jump 7 feet up, run at 20 mph and carry over 200 pounds of equipment. It will be an improvement because as nifty as the Mark 3 is, it is a little cumbersome, and it's impossible to lift a wounded soldier because he weighs too much in the Mark 3. The Mark 4 will have a better fuel cell power pack, making more electricity and weighing less. The suit is supposed to have some elementary camouflage capability. I saw one in Tech School. The suit looks behind you and then changes the fabric colors on your front side to look like what's behind you. From a distance if you don't move, you really disappear into the weeds. It's like the rope oversuits the snipers wear, up close it looks like a person in a rope suit, but at 50 yards you totally miss the sniper and only see the leaves and weeds. The camouflage suit takes a lot of power which is why it isn't on my Mark 3, my power unit is too small. The new OFW Mark 4 also sends and receives battle information to the officers who are watching the battle and changing the strategy. The Mark 4 also has special "TAGS" on it so the artillery guys won't target us—if the incoming round sees our TAG, it won't arm itself. This should reduce the number of "friendly fire" accidents we used to have! I've heard that the Mark 4 can also support the new directed energy weapons that fire laser bursts and microwaves to disable or kill the enemy. It's sort of like a Star Trek phaser on "stun"; it makes your brain stop working. The new directed energy weapons make it possible to engage the enemy further away with more accuracy.

Well, I have to go to dinner now. We get special meals for several days before a mission so we will have the stamina to wear the Mark 3 for 2 or 3 days straight. I'll call when I get back from wherever we're going.

Give my love to my sister and grandma.

Love,
Bob

Chemical Heroes

We do not know what the body can do.

» **Baruch Spinoza**, 1677

The component man is the one that fails most often.

» **Marion B. Sulzberger**, "Progress and Prospects
in Idiophylaxis," 1962

A military is about making soldiers—that is, "bodies"—do things: fight, think (or not), sit still, stand up, walk, run, march up and down the square, sleep, work, mow the lawn, pull up weeds, paint rocks, collect cigarette butts, get a haircut, iron uniforms, mop the barracks, clean toilets, kill, wound, survive, die. Michel Foucault (1979) riffed on this in *Discipline and Punish*, examining how soldiers are to be compelled to act and "be" according to new ideas and needs of the body by the state. Indeed, military service is a long act of compulsion. But the first act in this line of compulsion is making sure soldiers are ready to be compelled. Bodies of soldiers will be made to do things in accordance with plans and policies, strategies and tactics, necessity and contingency, and will have to react to the other side's attempts to make their bodies and "our" bodies do things. Before any deployment or battle, the military must ask: What can our soldiers do, what can they withstand, and for how long? Is their training sufficient, and, perhaps more importantly, are they medically prepared for the upcoming battle? These are practical questions of great importance, as the backbone of a military—the soldier—needs to be manipulated and made ready, suitable, and pliable for the task at hand. But the fact is, militaries think soldiers are never quite up to the tasks at hand and are liable to fail at any moment.

When I entered United States Army Basic Training in 1984—like everyone else there, having volunteered for college money; a stable paycheck; a chance to learn a skill; a way to take care of a family; to protect freedom and the US against the Soviets, the Cubans, and the Nicaraguans; or simply as a way to escape something—one of the first things done to me was a series of vaccinations. Heads freshly shaved, and standing in line in our T-shirts, we were shuffled along between two lines of medics. Each medic had a hypodermic injection gun, and we were ordered to march between the medics to our right and left, roll up our T-shirt sleeves, and stand still while they gave us an injection in each arm (see figure I.1). This was designed to make the immunizations go as quickly and efficiently as possible, but as I have thought about it over the years, there was much more going on than I imagined at the time.

Ideally, the medics would have each pulled the trigger and given us the injections in our arms at the same time, but each time we moved forward, one pulled before the other, causing us to jerk to either our right or our left, just as the other medic was pulling the trigger on his inoculator. This caused small gashes in each arm, and by the time it was done (we received ten inoculations in the space of about one minute), all of us were bleeding—some more, some less—from our arms. While we were getting the shots, the medics kept telling us, "This will protect you—it's dangerous over there, and you never know what you'll catch" (this is something I heard again when I received another round of vaccinations prior to being sent to Berlin in 1986). We were then marched outside and given two small pieces of gauze to staunch the bleeding. We stood mutely in a parking lot outside the medical facility, arms crossed, holding the gauze to our arms to soak up the blood, already slightly dizzy from the vaccines beginning to course through our bodies.

In the space of a minute or two, our "health" had been protected from the dangers lurking "over there"—an unidentified but deadly and diseased place—and protected against specific but unknown threats, threats we might encounter based on predictions and past experiences to protect us for fighting in the future. We had also been enhanced in order to make us deployable, and the military had put its stamp on our bodies. This banal ritual transformation of our bodies and group bloodletting, the first step in a rite of passage that was to transform us from civilian to soldier, was also an initial exposure to mass protection and mass wounding (albeit on a very minor scale) that was to demonstrate that our health was no longer our own concern. Mass vaccinations dramatically make the point to the

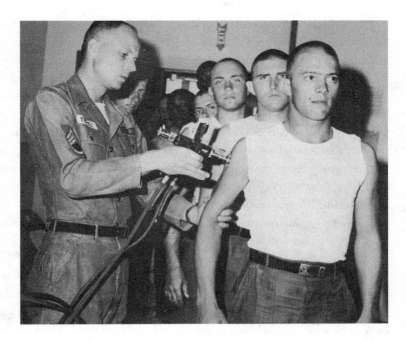

Figure I.1 Soldier enhancement via hypodermic jet injection gun, 1960s–1970s.

new recruits that the military will alter their bodies—internally and externally—to fit the needs of the military for combat. Vaccinations make the soldier militarily useful and enhance the soldier's ability to engage in combat. As mundane as it was, it was nonetheless quite remarkable: we had taken the first steps in being enhanced to fight and survive.

In *Chemical Heroes*, I examine the US military's attempts to imagine and design new kinds of biomedically enhanced and protected soldiers—soldiers who are commonly thought of and imagined in popular culture as "supersoldiers." These new soldiers will be more than they were before they entered the military, be able to do things and survive things normal soldiers cannot, and address the military's anxiety around future conflict, cowardice, and performance. And if the military is successful in its visioning and design, these new soldiers may very well prove to be kill-proof. Imagined and designed in the present, these new soldiers represent a kind of "armored" life protected against imagined future threats, a new kind of life on the battlefield that will preserve itself while more easily taking the lives of its enemies.

Chemical Heroes is an analysis of US military performance enhancement technologies, the militarization of biotechnology and pharmacology, and attempts to make the pharmacological "supersoldier," based on unclassified, open-source materials. Analyzing military performance enhancement (which I will sometimes refer to as MPE) requires a series of questions: What exactly is military performance enhancement? How does the military determine which attributes need to be enhanced? How are the US military and its various governmental and private research branches and partners going about creating new forms of enhancement technologies or modifying existing technologies? What are the operational and technological "stressors" that shape the contexts for imagining enhancements and new kinds of soldiers? And how do they imagine and design protective technologies that will allow the soldier to survive war and emerge unscathed or at least still useful?

In *Chemical Heroes*, I pay close attention to what the US military hopes to achieve through performance enhancement technologies. If we look at the supersoldier as a completely constructed entity, the question becomes: to what end? (Hacking 1999). We can lose focus when we lose sight of what the military actually wants from these technologies and from attending to their intentions instead of ours. The goals and intentions of this kind of research speak volumes about how we think about soldiers, the body, war, violence, biotechnology, and ethics. For example, much of the focus of current US military biomedical performance enhancement programs is on the impact of environmental threats and infectious disease on US soldiers, and how soldiers break down due to these stressors; the military increasingly views the battlefield as a dangerous pharmacological environment, with a focus on chemical and biological stressors and the need for "sensing the battlefield environment" (National Research Council 2001, 16–25). Analyses of soldiers and the military often do not take into account the nexus of medical and environmental threats, military medicine and prevention, and operational planning. We need to examine how the military is thinking about and planning for the emerging pharmacological battlefield of future warfare; we generally do not think of war as competing pharmacological regimes or a contest of pharmacological technologies, but increasingly, this is a possibility and concern for military planners. Biological warfare or chemical warfare is just part of the issue; we now need to consider how the US military is planning for the use of performance enhancing drugs to make soldiers "better," coming up with ways to degrade enemy forces through pharmacological means (pharmacological landmines, etc.), and the potential for warfare to become a molecular contest.

All militaries try to develop a winning edge in warfare. More often than not, these attempts focus on new weapons systems and weapons platforms, on new ways of maximizing the offensive capabilities of soldiers and a military through firepower. These attempts can also involve a focus on the training and development of soldiers, of coming up with enhancements to make soldiers fight better, longer, and smarter than the enemy. But soldiers are fragile, and if there is one thing that the history of warfare shows us, it is that military commanders, planners, researchers—and soldiers themselves—know this. Soldier-authors who glorified warfare in the early twentieth century—Ernst Jünger in Germany, Filippo Tommaso Marinetti in Italy, and Nikolai S. Gumilev in Russia—discuss the fragility of the body-in-combat, even as they spin out dreams and fantasies of internally armored bodies and the beauty of war and destruction (Bickford 2010; Gumilev [1916] 1972; Jünger [1920] 2003; Marinetti 1971; Rainey, Poggi, and Wittman 2009; Segel 1998; Theweleit 1987–89). From a military planning and implementation standpoint, the stress point of all military operations is the soldiers themselves. Throughout the history of warfare, groups and nation-states have attempted to develop superior warriors to meet these demands, to armor their soldiers against the enemy and their own fears and weakness. Soldiers are supposed to be made into, and then embody and project, an ideal of steely resolve and fortitude, an ideal of unwavering bravery and compliance.

In *On War*, Carl von Clausewitz glosses these qualities as "boldness" and discusses how "the noble capacity to rise above the most menacing of dangers" is an important factor in the fortunes of war (1976, 190). "Boldness" is a way to think about combat and how militaries and states imagine soldiers who can be "made" bold in a predictable and reliable fashion. The opposite of boldness is timidity, weakness, and fragility. What is important to understand is how exactly militaries go about trying to solve the problem of fragile soldiers—of fragile humans—who are never quite up to the dreams of 100 percent certainty and 100 percent performance demanded by those in charge, soldiers who mentally and physically "break" in combat from wounds, trauma, and illness. In *On War*, Clausewitz also writes, "All war presupposes human weakness and seeks to exploit it" (256; see also Singer 2008). This can be read as exploiting the weakness of your enemy. However, what if the weakness you want to identify and exploit is not simply the weakness of your enemy but that of your own soldiers, in order to turn them into the warriors you want? What if you can develop novel technologies to locate, exploit, and overcome weaknesses in the body of the soldier in order to protect them, extract more combat power and labor from them, and make them more readily deployable? These concerns have long held the interest of the US military (Ford and Glymour 2014; Singer 2008; Tracy and Flower 2014).

War has always changed soldiers: the rapid advances in firepower and operational tempo in warfare demand new ways of enabling soldiers to keep up and fight better, stronger, faster, and longer, and drugs and medicines have long played a role in sustaining soldiers in combat. They also play a role in internally armoring soldiers for the battlefield—and after. Whether through war magic or technology, those concerned with warfare and violence have tried to devise ways to make their soldiers or warriors better than their enemies, or at least make their soldiers or warriors think they are better armed and armored than their enemies. Tellingly, one of the founding myths of the West—Homer's *Iliad*—is about a warrior, Achilles, dipped at birth into the river Styx by his mother, Thetis, in order to protect him in combat and allow him to fight and perform as a hero, to endure the rigors and stresses of war (see Burgess 1995 for a full discussion of Achilles's birth). We can think of Achilles as perhaps the first chemical hero (see figure I.2).

Just as mythology and folklore bring us tales of men and women made seemingly invincible through the application of magic or enchantment, the US military also trades in ideas and portrayals of the mythic warrior and hero but now protected through biomedicine and biotechnology. For example, a US Marine Corps recruiting video in the late 1980s portrayed a medieval knight, wielding a sword and fighting an array of evil chess pieces, ultimately defeating the evil king and then morphing into a modern US Marine, and a Marine recruiting ad from 1998 showed a young man defeating a lava monster with a sword and then turning into a US Marine.

As such, these attempts are comments on the relationship between the body and war, conflict and fragility, technology and protection, and all speak to issues of embodiment and representation, to the somatization and portrayal of strength and invincibility. As the history of warfare shows, groups, cultures, and nation-states have attempted to develop superior warriors or "supersoldiers," to better train and armor their soldiers against the enemy, and to make them more resilient and useful. We can think about the history of weapons and armaments as a reciprocal history of defense and armor. "Armor" comes in many forms: material, ideological,

Figure I.2 Peter Paul Rubens, *Thetis Dipping the Infant Achilles into the River Styx*, ca. 1630–35.

psychological, and, increasingly in the US military, biomedical (Bickford 2008, 2011, 2018). While others have looked at the experience of wearing external body armor (MacLeish 2012; Scharre and Fish 2018)—a "skin-out solution" to soldier protection in US military medical parlance—I examine a kind of armor embedded in the body, not worn on the body, a kind of biomedical armor that in a sense "makes" the military body and is always with the soldier. This "belief armor" is often unseen and "built-in."

US military biomedical and psychopharmacological research programs are tasked with developing built-in armor for the soldier via new forms of medicines, immunizations, and performance enhancements. In *Chemical Heroes*, I trace the development of unseen and built-in biotechnical and pharmacological armor by the US military. This is not an analysis of the science behind the idea of the supersoldier per se, but an analysis of the sociocultural implications of military performance enhancement, how soldiers are imagined and designed based on anticipation, and an inquiry into the political economy of military biotechnology and psychopharmacology. At play are conceptions and linkages between technology and health, between material advantage, ideological/psychological motivation, and physical preparedness for combat; the latter two are concerned directly with the body and health of the soldier and the increasing manipulation of both in order to gain advantage in war. I look at US military research projects, programs, and policies focused on combat enhancement through military medicine, biotechnologies, psychopharmacology, synthetic biology, and other forms of technology designed to improve and enhance soldiers' combat capabilities and ability to resist trauma, both during and after combat.

The US Military and Biotechnology

An increasing number of scholars are focusing their attention on war and the embodied experiences of military service, violence, and trauma (Chua 2018; Dyvik and Greenwood 2016; Finley 2011; Hautzinger and Scandlyn 2014; Howell 2014, 2015; MacLeish 2015; McSorley 2012, 2014; Messinger 2010; Terry 2017; Wool 2015). But that is not exactly what I am interested in here. Rather, my focus is on what happens *before* embodiment, on how "embodiment" is imagined, planned, and designed: military planners and researchers might not know what a body can do, but they can very easily imagine what they would like it to be able to do.

Preparing the body for war is a biomedical, biopolitical process of research, imagination, history, and ethics, of thinking through what the soldier will have to be able to withstand and respond to. Military medicine and biotechnologies are key components of this planning and imagining, of trying to ensure that the "component man" does not fail.

Biomedical innovations allow for areas of the body to be exploited in ways that were previously considered impossible or barely feasible. The soldier can (possibly) be made to do things and withstand things previously unimaginable, and can do so in a (hopefully) controlled, predictable, and survivable way. For the military, the "body" is not necessarily an existential or philosophical problem to solve. It is a material problem rooted in the needs of war and combat. Fundamentally, the military's "body problem" is a labor issue: how can the military extract as much labor power—or "combat capability"—from the soldier as possible without actually harming the soldier?

My focus in *Chemical Heroes* is on some of the past, recent, and current military research projects focused on imagining and designing "super-soldiers," programs that are designed to use biotechnology, psychopharmacology, and other forms of technology for this purpose, such as Robert B. Rigg's "Soldier of the Futurarmy" of the 1950s, Marion B. Sulzberger's "Idiophylactic Soldier" of the 1960s, and more recent and current projects like the US military's "Land Warrior," "Objective Force Warrior," "Future

Force Warrior," and "Future Combat Systems" programs, and DARPA's "Inner Armor" program of 2007 (see table I.1). All of these programs can be seen as an interplay between imagination, anxiety, anticipation, biotechnology, and concerns with the inherent weakness of soldiers in and out of combat.

The US military takes a "nuts and bolts" approach to defining and imagining biotechnology. An early report on the future uses of biotechnology for the US Army defines biotechnology as a technology that "uses organisms, or tissues, cells, or molecular components derived from living things, to act on living things" and "[it] acts by intervening in the workings of cells or the molecular components of cells, including their genetic material" (National Research Council 2001, 10). Ongoing developments in biomedicine offer new ways to understand, see, and imagine soldiers and promise to expand and enhance the body's ability to overcome and survive the battlefield and its myriad stressors.

The overall goals of military performance enhancement projects cover a broad suite of desirable traits and abilities for improvement and show an interest in examining and improving all areas of a soldier's biology:

- battlefield endurance and combat capabilities
- trauma-blocking drugs / trauma prophylaxis
- neuroenhancements/neuroimplants
- enhanced metabolism ("Peak Soldier Performance")
- enhanced wound healing
- enhanced pain management
- vaccinations for readiness/deployments
- protection against environmental threats
- concentration and enhanced decision-making
- possible legacy genetic lines

In what follows, I argue that a key component in the creation and training of soldiers is a conception of health that is different from civilian conceptions of health, a conception that harnesses rather than explicitly heals, one that sees biology as something to overcome and manipulate in order to make it useful. Through the mobilization and instrumentalization of health, states manipulate the bodies of soldiers while claiming that this manipulation is to protect the well-being and health of the soldier. This follows from my earlier book, *Fallen Elites: The Military Other in Post-Unification Germany* (2011), where I examined how soldiers are imagined, made, and unmade through policy and ideology. Here, I look at how a different kind of ideology is developed and employed to make and unmake soldiers, an

Table I.1 Selected US Military "Supersoldier" and Performance Enhancement Projects, 1956–Present

Project	Date	Developer/Sponsor	Location
Soldier of the Futurarmy	November 1956	Robert B. Riggs	N/A
Idiophylactic Soldier	May 1962	Marion B. Sulzberger	US Army Medical Research and Materiel Command, Washington, DC
Land Warrior	1994	US Army	US Army Infantry Center, Fort Benning, GA
Objective Force Warrior	1998; unveiled October 1999	US Army	Natick Soldier Support Center / Oak Ridge National Laboratory / US Armor Center, Fort Knox, KY
"Augmented Cognition"	2001	DARPA	Arlington, VA
Future Force Warrior	2001	US Army	Natick Soldier Support Center, Natick, MA / Fort Bliss, TX
Metabolically Dominant Soldier	2002	DARPA	Arlington, VA
Future Combat System	2003–9	US Army	Natick Soldier Support Center, Natick, MA
Inner Armor	2007	DARPA; project manager Michael Callahan	Approved in Arlington, VA
Biological Control	2016	DARPA; project manager Dr. Paul Sheehan	Approved in Arlington, VA

Project	Date	Developer/Sponsor	Location
Living Foundries	2016	DARPA; Project manager Dr. Renee Wegrynz	Approved in Arlington, VA / Workshop in Arlington, VA
Safe Genes	2017	DARPA	Arlington, VA

ideology that is based on biology and that can be literally implanted and modulated in the body of the soldier. Military ideology without an explicit biological underpinning depends upon "will," an almost fanatical belief in one's superiority, one's ability to overcome all odds and adversaries, and a tenacious ability to continue on with the mission, regardless of pain or personal cost. "Will" is a kind of political and psychological training and armor, cultivated to make the soldier believe he is invincible and unstoppable, whatever the odds. Military ideology based on biology is intended to circumvent the slipperiness and uncertainty of "will" and go straight to the source of bodily ability. "Will" is fine, but an enhanced "will" is hopefully even better and more reliable on the battlefield.

In the late 1990s and into the following decade, I conducted fieldwork with former East German Army and Border Guard officers (Bickford 2011). One afternoon, during a discussion about East German, Soviet, and US military technology and tactics, a former Nationale Volksarmee (NVA, National People's Army) lieutenant colonel said to me: "Technology is just an example of American cowardice. We would have used real men to accomplish what you use technology to do." His comment stuck with me long after I left Berlin, prompting me to think about the links between technology, war, masculinity, and cowardice. Of course, the NVA officer was trying to tell me that East German soldiers were simply superior men and soldiers to US soldiers and did not need all the high-tech weaponry and military technology that US soldiers had to use to prop themselves up and keep them going in the field. The East German military would have relied on "real" men with innate mental and physical strength and willpower—"natural" heroes—to fight and win on the battlefield. But he was also onto something bigger, and this has made me look at US military performance enhancement research and biomedical technologies in a new light: on the new and evolving pharmacological battlefields of the twenty-first century, enhancements are seen as antidotes to natural cowardice. This is not a battlefield for the "real," normal, soldier but for the chemical hero.

Pharmaceuticals, Assemblages, and the Soldier System of Systems

Recently anthropologists have turned their attention to the study of pharmaceuticals and chemicals (see, e.g., Dumit 2012; Hardon and Sanabria 2017; Hayden 2007, 2012; Petryna 2003; Petryna, Lakoff, and Kleinman 2006; Shapiro and Kirksey 2017; Sunder Rajan 2006, 2017). While opening up a number of important insights and areas of research, this interest in pharmaceuticals and "chemical cultures" around the world highlights a surprising blind spot: there is little to no work on the connections between the military and pharmacology in anthropology or on the military's interest in pharmaceuticals, synthetic biology, or genomics, despite the military's interest and role as a driver of funding and research.

US military interest in pharmaceuticals for care, curing, and performance enhancement goes back decades, and the use of licit and illicit drugs by soldiers has shaped all US military engagements around the world since World War II. The military's current interest in and use of pharmaceuticals as a way to simultaneously protect and compel soldiers is part of the ongoing "Revolution in Military Affairs" (RMA), the hoped-for paradigm shift in US military research and development, strategy and tactics, and understanding of the world as "threat." This is reminiscent of Orin Starn's (1991) observations about anthropology, fieldwork, and revolution in Peru, but this time with a twist: the RMA is going on all around us, yet we are often strangely blind to it and to the influence it exerts on our research. While there has been a welcomed increase in interest in the military, militarization, and military cultures in anthropology, for the most part anthropology has remained uninterested in these changes and developments, even though most of what contemporary anthropologists study and where they study is impacted by military affairs. This most definitely includes biotechnology and pharmacology.

As Anita Hardon and Emilia Sanabria write, a "broad range of institutional rationalities underpin the management of therapeutic agents" (2017, 121); for the US military, these rationalities include health, protection, enhancement, and offensive and defensive planning for the emergent pharmaceutical battlefield. Rather than thinking about US military performance enhancement projects as a rational, singular, unified whole, we need to think about them as more akin to an assemblage, as constantly changing and emerging, made up of myriad shifting goals, ideas, scientists, security experts, technologies, laboratories, experiments, and drugs (Bell et al. 2018; Bigo 2009; Nail 2017). The military's term for the new vision of the combination of the soldier with new forms of technology and biotechnology—the soldier as a "system of systems"—is a surprisingly good way of describing the multiple and overlapping areas of concern that go into imagining and making the new soldier. Of course, the common goal is the "enhanced soldier," but the field of research and funding is much more open, fluid, and contingent. Chemical infrastructures bring together, though in disjointed ways, experts, disciplinary knowledges, and ways of knowing and assessing such infrastructures (Hardon and Sanabria 2017, 125). Performance enhancement projects form structures, groups, and nodes of researchers at military and non-military research sites that imagine soldiers of the future and future threats and imagine forms of production to make material these ideas of the future through pharmaceuticals and biomedical technologies.

The supersoldier does not necessarily represent a single soldier or individual but a technological community and commonality of effort—a kind of technical-political-economic effort that wraps around the soldier. Of course, the soldier appears to be a unified whole, but from a different angle, the soldier—the system of systems—is composed of a vast array of technologies and medicines designed and created by thousands of researchers and workers, spread across all fifty states. The soldier might not be autochthonous, but the technologies seem to spring from everywhere (see table I.2). For example, the US Army Natick Soldier RD&E Center's "Warfighter Directorate" (WD) "partners with numerous Department of Defense (DoD) agencies, industry, academia and the international community to achieve mission success. The WD operates over 70 laboratories and testing facilities" (NSRDEC 2014). The military is very clear about the fact that it cannot necessarily do this research on its own, and it is not in the position to produce the required and desired drugs and biotechnologies.

One of the key recommendations of a National Academies Press report titled *Opportunities in Biotechnology for Future Army Applications* focuses on the Army's need to work with private industry and develop new forms of partnership agreements.

Table I.2 Selected US Military Research Organizations and Research Sites

Facility	Location
Natick Soldier Research, Development, and Engineering Center (NSRDEC)	Natick, MA
United States Army Research Institute for Environmental Medicine (USARIEM)	Natick, MA
Oak Ridge National Laboratory	Oak Ridge, TN
Defense Advanced Research Projects Agency (DARPA)	Arlington County, VA
Military Operational Medicine Research Program (MOMRP)	Fort Detrick, MD
United States Army Center for Health Promotion and Preventive Medicine (USACHPPM)	Aberdeen Proving Ground, MD

To keep pace with the unprecedented rate of discovery and the anticipated increase in biotechnology developments, the Army will have to establish new, effective partnerships with the emerging biotechnology industry, participate in research, leverage research and developments in the commercial sector, and develop its internal capabilities (organization and personnel) to act on opportunities as they arise. . . . The biotechnology industry is much less dependent on the military for its existence than other industries with which the Army and other services have routinely interacted. Therefore, the Army will have to use different mechanisms for involving industry in meeting Army needs. (National Research Council 2001, 3)

The military must partner with industry and academia to achieve its goals of developing performance enhancement drugs or it must use pre-existing drugs in counterindicated ways to achieve the effects and results it wants (for information on military/industry research and partnerships, see, e.g., Jacobsen 2015 and Weinberger 2017). Kaushik Sunder Rajan (2017) writes that there has been a progressive capture of health by the market; the military long ago captured "health" as an organizing principle and logic, and has long sought to develop and use new forms of biotechnology and pharmacology to protect soldiers and enhance their abilities on the battlefield. Sunder Rajan also analyzes the "state-market nexus" of pharmaceutical research and development (2006; see also Hardon and Sanabria 2017). Military and state security needs for pharmaceuticals and vaccines are part of the bigger picture of pharmaceutical production, whether for the production of new kinds of pharmaceuticals or for the continued production of existing drugs for counterindicated uses by the military. What is important to track is the increasingly close connections and coordination between the military and "big pharma," the "military-pharmacology complex" that continues to grow as the military increases its focus on preparing to dominate the pharmacological battlefield. As the biomedical and pharmacological revolutions move forward and pick up speed, so too will the revolution in biomilitary affairs move apace and find purchase in ever-greater and expanding areas of military and civilian life. The mistake is to think of "supersoldier" projects as fringe science or simply as science fiction; rather, these projects represent a significant moment in the relationship between the military and science and the military and private industry. Military performance enhancement projects represent a distinct way of thinking about combat and trauma and a concern for both the soldier and the future of combat operations. They also represent a significant investment in soldier technologies and soldiering, as they encompass a myriad of subprojects, related research areas, and a wide range of research centers and sites.

The Double-Bind of the Military Biomedical Imagination

A central theme of *Chemical Heroes* is the dream and the double-bind of military biotechnology and pharmacology: military performance enhancing drugs can and do in fact save soldiers' lives, but in so doing enable the military to deploy soldiers in areas and environments previously considered too dangerous or somehow off limits, and deploy them at ever-faster rates between missions and for new types of missions. US military biomedical and pharmacological interventions bind soldiers to a form of medicine that protects, on the one hand, and compels, on the other. This all comes down to the following questions: What do we want from our soldiers, and what are we prepared to do to them in order to make them conform to this desire? Just how far are we willing to go to alter their bodies in order to make them fit the desire or perceived need for supersoldiers as a way to counter perceived threats and insecurities, both before and after conflict?

Rather than focusing strictly on the cultural, legal, and political dimensions of anticipation, preemption, and "potentiality," one of the things I want to do here is analyze what the materiality of military anticipation, preemption, and concerns with "potential" look like, how they are made in practice, and how the military's concerns with these issues are literally productive. As such, I examine what Ian Hacking (2002) refers to as the "historical ontology" of soldiers; Andrew Lakoff (2017) uses Hacking's idea to good effect in his examination of global health emergencies. Hacking's idea of historical ontology traces how things are imagined and come into being through scientific research and language. Lakoff, summarizing Hacking's approach, writes that historical ontology "asks how taken-for-granted objects of existence . . . are brought into being through contingent and often-overlooked historical processes" (2017, 7). Working through a historical ontology of the soldier, I look at how the often-overlooked imagining and making of US soldiers is accomplished through military medicine and biomedical research, with the goal of making new kinds of militarized life, on and off the battlefield.

Following from this, I also engage with what Sheila Jasanoff and Sang-Hyun Kim refer to as the "sociotechnical imaginary," the "collectively imagined forms of social life and social order reflected in the design and fulfillment of nation-specific scientific and/or technological projects" (2015, 120). Jasanoff and Kim further define their arguments around sociotechnical imaginaries to include "collectively held, institutionally stabilized, and publicly performed visions of desirable futures, animated by shared understandings of forms of social life and social order attainable through, and supportive of, advances in science and technology" (2015, 4).

The ways in which we imagine both anticipation and soldiers are directly related to how we imagine soldiers being "used"; they make the links between sociotechnical military imaginaries and practice (Jasanoff and Kim 2015, 323). US supersoldier projects are a sociotechnical imaginary and a vision of a dangerous and uncertain future, a future we can only control by focusing on intensive biomedical research into military performance enhancement technologies in the present. The idea of the supersoldier is embedded in our everyday lives through a concern with "supporting the troops"; this support includes doing everything possible to protect the soldier.

My starting points are the biomedical and biotechnical imagination of warfare and what happens before embodiment and violence; these are primarily questions of anticipation and preemption (V. Adams, Murphy, and Clarke 2009; Lakoff 2015, 2017; Masco 2014; Massumi 2015; Manzocco 2019). While attentive to post-traumatic stress disorder (PTSD), questions of "moral injury" (Finley 2011; Shay 1995; Sherman 2015; Terry 2017; Wool 2015), and current trends in resiliency training (Howell 2015; Jauregui 2015; Picano 2017; Simmons and Yoder 2013), my interest is in the larger question of how the military conceives of solutions for preventing combat trauma through psychopharmacological and biotechnical interventions *before* combat rather than the current solutions or treatments for postcombat trauma. In this sense, I am interested in the discussions of trauma and combat in the military; how military officials, military medical professionals, and other researchers discuss, imagine, and conceive of ways to make "supersoldiers" who can better withstand combat and combat trauma; and how they attempt to make the experience of war trauma a thing of the past. How is military medical policy formulated, for example, and how are soldier enhancements conceived of, designed, implemented, and funded? What kinds of investments is the United States making into these research programs, and what is the scope of these projects? And what might it ultimately mean to be a "medicalized" soldier in the US military?

As anthropologist Catherine Lutz (2007) writes, militarization, while concerned with the material reshaping of society in preparation for war, is also a discursive process, designed to change societal values in order to legitimate the use of force and violence. As I have argued elsewhere (Bickford 2011), militarization is also a statement on the ethical implications of warfare, a comment on the "moral imaginary" of politicians, and the military—and in this case, military doctors and medical researchers—about how soldiers should be and how they should be created, trained, and prepared. Military medicine, psychopharmacology, and biotechnology, and their promises of protection, not only impact soldiers but also help shape the policy, political, and cultural landscapes of military service and military deployment by promising "positive" health interventions for our soldiers. The internal regulation of the soldier becomes the external protection of the state: what might seem like a positive, life-saving measure could also be another way—despite possibly being a positive medical intervention that saves a soldier's life—of making soldiers fight, of ensuring compliance and deployability, and of harnessing a "resource" for national security and policy purposes in a more effective and predictable manner.

A question that often does not come up in discussions of "super-soldiers" or "enhanced" soldiers is: How did we get here? What is the history—or the multiple histories or research trajectories—of the

US soldier-as-supersoldier and the development and emergence of the sociotechnical imaginary of supersoldiers in US military thinking (Taylor 2004)? We can think about the projects, budgets, programs, and ethics of soldier enhancement, but we also need to think about the various iterations of the "American soldier," and how cultural ideals and imaginings of the "good" or "unbeatable" US soldier came into being. The ways in which we imagine soldiers are directly related to ways in which we imagine soldiers being "used."

One reason for the need to think about performance enhancements and trauma blockers is the fact that the US military is an all-volunteer force. A watershed moment occurred in 1973 for the US military, as the Abrams Doctrine brought about the end of the draft and the conscript military in the United States, forcing the military to rely solely on volunteers to fill the ranks. Throughout the mid to late Cold War, this did not necessarily present much of a problem, as economic downturns ensured a steady supply of volunteers entering the military. With the exception of Vietnam (and the Korean War, which lasted from 1950 to 1953), there were no other long-term military engagements during the Cold War, and the US military did not have to confront multiple deployments into combat zones. However, with the beginning of the second Gulf War in 2003, and the ongoing "forever war" (to use Dexter Filkins's [2009] felicitous phrase), the military has had to face the fact that its volunteers routinely face two, three, four, or more combat deployments. In short, there is no longer a steady supply of conscripts to take up the slack as physical and psychiatric casualties mount, and the US military is forced to think about ways to keep volunteer soldiers on the front lines for extended and repeated periods of time. The US military must figure out how to make do with volunteers, all that means, and all that they can be made to be. Uttered in frustration to a group of soldiers confronting him about the military's lack of armor and equipment during the early days of the war in Iraq, Donald Rumsfeld's quip about going to war with the Army you have at the time speaks in many ways to the military's desire to have the Army of the future.

As the US military increasingly sees the entire world as a battlefield, it must anticipate, imagine, and design new ways to protect soldiers in order to make them deployable anywhere in the world. Zeroing in on this trend, I bookend current US military performance enhancement projects with two US military biomedical "armor" projects intended to protect soldiers against the environment and disease. Employing a kind of anticipatory military biomedicine—which forms a central focus of this book—both projects called for the embedding of built-in and unseen biomedical technologies and prophylaxes in the body of the soldier, and view environmental stressors and infectious disease as major factors in soldier breakdown and mission failure: Marion B. Sulzberger's 1962 proposal to create soldiers for the US military who had their own built-in, unseen, biomedical armor— what he termed *Idiophylaxis*—and the Defense Advanced Research Projects Agency's (DARPA) 2007 "Inner Armor" program, designed to create "kill-proof" US soldiers. The arc of Idiophylaxis and Inner Armor graphically displays and covers the modern US military's quest to develop internally armored, "kill-proof" soldiers through advances in military biotechnology and psychopharmacological research. Within this arc we can see the drives and attempts to develop the technologies—both "skin-in" and "skin-out"— that will create the fully protected soldier who provides 100 percent certainty on and off the battlefield. Sulzberger's Idiophylaxis and today's plans for enhanced soldiers equipped with their own inner armor are part of a genealogy of ideas and dreams of the soldier who can resist any and all battlefield and environmental conditions, who will be possibly "kill-proof" and physically and mentally impervious to the horrors of war (Bickford 2018). They are also part of a genealogy of military biomedical research and the increasing importance of biology in military planning, research priorities, and funding. If, as the saying goes, physics was the key military science of the Cold War, biology and various forms of biomedical research will be the key military sciences of the twenty-first century (Hammes 2010, 5) and create possibilities for soldier performance that simply did not exist during the Cold War.

"Spinning and Grinning": Grunts, REMFs, NAAFI, and Enhanced Performance

Between 1984 and 1989, I spent five years on active duty in the US Army. After Basic Training at Fort Leonard Wood, Missouri; intensive language training at the Defense Language Institute in San Francisco and Monterey, California; and signals intelligence intercept and analysis training in Texas, I was assigned to a signals intelligence unit located in Berlin. I spent three years assigned to Field Station Berlin, situated atop Teufelsberg ("Devil's Mountain")—a three-hundred-meter-tall mound of rubble from World War II, built on top of a former *Wehrmacht* training facility—in Berlin's Grünewald Forest. Arriving in 1986 and leaving in 1989, I was stationed there before the fall of the Berlin Wall and the dissolution of the German

Democratic Republic and, subsequently, the Warsaw Pact and the Soviet Union. As a signals intelligence linguist (specifically, an "Electronic Warfare Signals Intelligence Cryptologic Voice Interceptor, German Integrated Systems Specialist"), I sat for eight to ten hours per day (sometimes longer), listening to and translating intercepted communications.

I was perhaps the quintessential late–Cold War "REMF" (Rear-Echelon Motherfucker), a military slang term differentiating REMFs from "Grunts"—the "real" combat troops of the military (the recent designation for a REMF is a "POG": "People other than Grunts"; some soldiers are also known as "Fobbits"—soldiers deployed to a forward operating base but who somehow always remain in the FOB; this might come close to being a REMF, though there is a difference). Despite my supreme REMF-ness (which in hindsight was kind of strange, given that we were all surrounded in Berlin, and which shows that being a REMF did not have as much to do with being near the front lines as it did with one's job), I did have to periodically train and practice for combat. In the event of a war, if we were somehow not at the field station, we would have formed a "provisional rifle company" (e.g., cannon fodder) or driven ammunition trucks (again, cannon fodder). We knew that Field Station Berlin would have been one of the first targets attacked in any conflict with the Warsaw Pact, as we were a giant electronic "ear" sitting in the middle of Soviet and East German forces. The rumor was that the Soviets would attack the field station with chemical weapons in order to kill us but preserve all the sophisticated computer and other technologies located in the field station. The other rumor was that our own artillery would then attack us, to make sure the same sophisticated computer and other technologies did not fall into Soviet or East German hands. We also heard whispers that the Military Police were to shoot any of us who survived the first two attacks; this always struck me as excessive. In any event, we were all fairly certain that our war would have been nasty, brutish, and short.

I have no recollection of any discussions of taking drugs in combat, or any kind of enhancements we would use. But in hindsight, and working through this project, I have asked myself: Would I have taken enhancement drugs? Cogniceuticals—drugs that improve attention span and cognition and help prevent mental exhaustion—are a key focus of military performance enhancement research. Would I have taken a drug that would allow me to forget what I had done in combat? Or something that would at least block my initial fear of going into combat? Or helped me translate better and faster, and stay focused for longer periods of time? I would like to say that I would not have taken any drugs offered, but the honest answer is: I don't know. When Max Weber wrote about "life chances and life choices" (Weber 1978, 926–38) when thinking about how people experience class, he was probably not thinking about military performance enhancement drugs. But what does it mean to be in a position to have to make this choice about such drugs that affect life chances and choices, willingly or not? Who will have to make this choice, and how does the nexus of military biomedicine and class help us understand what military performance enhancement will be and mean in the future? Perhaps these are the questions that this book really revolves around. What if? I don't know. I simply don't know what I would have done, and maybe most soldiers are not really sure either. Maybe you don't have the benefit of choice to make decisions about your future when you know you soon might not have a future. Or maybe the only way you can have a future (regardless of your fears about that future) is to take the drugs the military offers—or orders you to take.

Performance enhancement drugs are potentially useful not only to the combat soldier but for all soldiers. While my job was not physically demanding, it was mentally taxing, as sitting and listening intently for long periods of time with headsets is exhausting, and the static, white noise, atmospheric squeaks, hisses, pops, and bounces take their toll on your ability to concentrate (not to mention causing intense headaches and earaches). Depending on the quality of the signal and the intercept, the sheer amount of static and garbling one had to somehow block out while listening to the message would often exhaust you after even a few minutes. But we had no cogniceuticals. We had coffee, tea, and tobacco; the Noncommissioned Officer (NCO) breakfast—black coffee and cigarettes—is something that many in the Army come to know quite well.

The highlight of the day at the field station was the arrival of the food truck from the British version of the post exchange (PX)—the Navy, Army, Air Force Institutes (NAAFI). The "NAAFI run" was a highly structured and choreographed event that often involved ordering and carrying forty or more cups of hot tea, stacked two or more tiers high, back through the halls to the section and often accompanied by the carriers singing the "Wesley House Song," sung to the tune of "Tequila" (and woe be to the poor sap who spilled or dropped the tea). The super strong, hot, sweet, milky tea sold by the NAAFI was a much-welcomed boost, and I would often drink four or five cups in the space of fifteen to twenty minutes. The jolt provided by the caffeine and sugar would keep me going for hours and help alleviate the stress and exhaustion of sitting with headphones on, "spinning and grinning" (watching the reel-to-reel tapes slowly spin around and around, and sometimes becoming hypnotized by the spinning tapes) and listening to static at volumes that caused hearing loss. Of course, once the tea wore off, it was on to coffee.

Self-medicating to cope with one's job or career is a common occurrence in both licit and illicit economies (Hardon and Sanabria 2017). And of course, the use of drugs by corporations and in factories is a feature of the workplace that weaves its way through the history of capitalism (Haug 1986; Schivelbusch 1992). Caffeine, alcohol, and tobacco have always been used, and newer drugs like Ritalin and antidepressants—as well as opioids—are increasingly prevalent in the workplace and as a result of workplace conditions (Webster 2018). While the military is fine with soldiers having coffee and/or tea, it is increasingly concerned with tobacco use, and soldiers are not supposed to self-medicate to cope with the stress of military service or other issues, be they emotional or physical, but of course they do (though the military does use mandatory drug testing as a way to address this). Self-medicating can render a soldier less than useful in key situations and also means that the soldier's health as a site of intervention and control is not fully under the military's control.

As the cliché goes, war is 90 percent boredom and 10 percent terror. But so too is the everyday experience of military service, the daily labor of the soldier. How then does the military deal with soldiers who are bored 90 percent of the time? Of course, military service is not always boring, but it can be, compelling soldiers to come up with creative ways to deal with hours and hours of soul-crushing monotony. During advanced signals intelligence training in Texas, we were locked in a room for months on end from 11:30 p.m. until 7:30 a.m. for training purposes; given that it was a secure site, we were not allowed any books, writing paper, and so on. One morning around 3:30 a.m., we had finished our work for the day (night, really) but were still locked in the room until 7:30 a.m. With nothing to do, we improvised: we found a large, dead beetle in the room, stripped off part of the faux veneer on the side of a table, and began to play "Bug Ball," taking turns pitching the dead beetle and batting with the veneer strip, running around the room from base to base, laughing maniacally because of the sheer ridiculousness of the situation. We played for about an hour, until our training sergeant came in and caught us. From then on, we were given more training materials to keep us busy throughout the night. The bored soldier is one who can get into trouble; the actual supersoldier might be the soldier who is enhanced to better deal with boredom and the mundane aspects of military life, a soldier for whom even boredom becomes

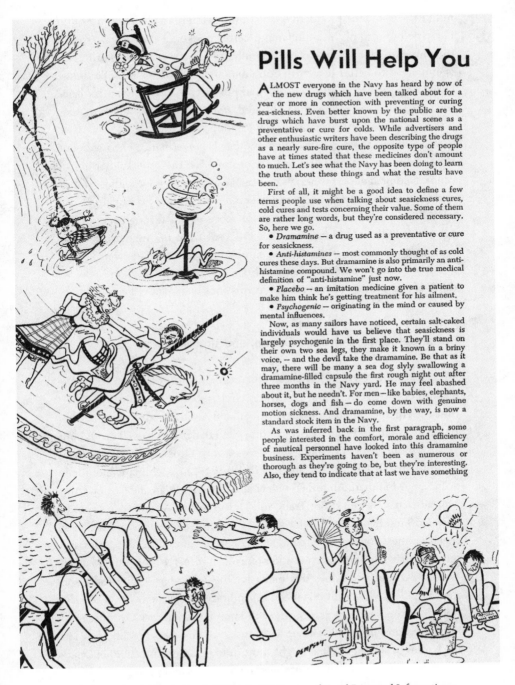

Pills Will Help You

ALMOST everyone in the Navy has heard by now of the new drugs which have been talked about for a year or more in connection with preventing or curing sea-sickness. Even better known by the public are the drugs which have burst upon the national scene as a preventative or cure for colds. While advertisers and other enthusiastic writers have been describing the drugs as a nearly sure-fire cure, the opposite type of people have at times stated that these medicines don't amount to much. Let's see what the Navy has been doing to learn the truth about these things and what the results have been.

First of all, it might be a good idea to define a few terms people use when talking about seasickness cures, cold cures and tests concerning their value. Some of them are rather long words, but they're considered necessary. So, here we go.

- *Dramamine* – a drug used as a preventative or cure for seasickness.
- *Anti-histamines* – most commonly thought of as cold cures these days. But dramamine is also primarily an anti-histamine compound. We won't go into the true medical definition of "anti-histamine" just now.
- *Placebo* – an imitation medicine given a patient to make him think he's getting treatment for his ailment.
- *Psychogenic* – originating in the mind or caused by mental influences.

Now, as many sailors have noticed, certain salt-caked individuals would have us believe that seasickness is largely psychogenic in the first place. They'll stand on their own two sea legs, they make it known in a briny voice, -- and the devil take the dramamine. Be that as it may, there will be many a sea dog slyly swallowing a dramamine-filled capsule the first rough night out after three months in the Navy yard. He may feel abashed about it, but he needn't. For men—like babies, elephants, horses, dogs and fish—do come down with genuine motion sickness. And dramamine, by the way, is now a standard stock item in the Navy.

As was inferred back in the first paragraph, some people interested in the comfort, morale and efficiency of nautical personnel have looked into this dramamine business. Experiments haven't been as numerous or thorough as they're going to be, but they're interesting. Also, they tend to indicate that at last we have something

Figure I.3 "Pills Will Help You." *All Hands: The Bureau of Naval Personnel Information Bulletin,* June 1950.

militarily useful and productive. The future soldier is a term not just of the fantastic but also of the mundane: a better worker, a soldier who can do the mundane training and chores of military service more efficiently, who is enhanced to better deal with boredom, and is a soldier for whom even boredom becomes militarily useful and productive. On a day-to-day basis, the supersoldier might be the nonbored, nonproblematic soldier: the perfect soldier/child—the infant/ry—on Ritalin.

It is not just the combat soldier who needs performance enhancement, which complicates our ideas and notions of what the supersoldier is. You can be a combat supersoldier, or you can be a superlinguist soldier, or a superlogistics soldier, or a superadmin soldier. All military occupations and specialties can be enhanced and made more useful through pharmacology (see figure I.3). This is not that different from the increasing use of cognition-enhancing stimulants on campus or in the business world. What is different is the potential degree of use, the tasks at hand, and how we think of the military as it performs its missions on drugs.

Enhancements, Common Sense, and the Mundane

We can use military performance enhancement projects to consider the debates occurring in military bioethics circles about what constitutes permissible enhancements to soldiers (Annas and Annas 2009; Ashcroft 2008; Beard, Galliott, and Lynch 2016; Braun, von Hlatky, and Nossal 2017; Ford and Glymour 2014; Frisina 2003; Gross 2006; Gross and Carrick 2013; Killion, Bury, de Pontbriand, and Belanich 2009; Lin, Mehlman, and Abney 2013; Lin, Mehlman, Abney, French et al. 2014; Mehlman and Corley 2014; Moreno 2012; Singer 2008; Tracy and Flower 2014). And we can begin to pose working hypotheses about why certain enhancements are chosen at specific times. For example, political, economic, and military rivalries and tensions drive military science and biomedical research; this much is well established. But what does this mean for the soldier or soldier-to-be and their families? What will this mean for military recruitment, and the race, class, and gender issues associated with joining the military? Do these political tensions ultimately end up as "translated" embedded technologies in the bodies of soldiers? What might it mean to be an enhanced, idiophylactic, "kill-proof" soldier? What if the enhancements and protections do not work as promised? Is it ethical for the military to directly shape a soldier's future through biotechnology and other forms of enhancement, even if the soldier volunteers for it? And what happens to the "kill-proof" soldier after war and combat are over and they try to return to civilian life (Beard, Galliott, and Lynch 2016; Lin, Mehlman, and Abney 2013; Singer 2008)? We might be able to biomedically design, engineer, and manufacture "bold" soldiers and chemical heroes, but what then?

Enhancements are not just computer chips implanted in soldiers' brains (but these conceptions make good clickbait): they also constitute the mundane, the everyday, and things that we do not generally consider to be enhancements, as I will discuss later (see also Wong 2013). As I mentioned at the beginning of this chapter, I too was "enhanced" in Basic Training and periodically throughout my time in the Army, through militarily useful vaccinations. Not all of it is completely frightening and straight out of a bad science fiction film (though some proposals do seem like it). However, these aspects of the "mundane" constitute the slippery slopes of military performance enhancement and help keep it potentially out of public view, or at least public critique. Rather than something appearing in a military horror story, like droves of soldiers with brain implants, some of the most important enhancement programs and technologies might be quotidian and mundane but the most militarily important, useful, and cost-effective. A consideration of the "mundane enhancement" does not mean that I dismiss military enhancements as troubling. Far from it: the mundane means that enhancements can slide under the radar and perhaps be seen simply as positive, nonthreatening, or ethically acceptable interventions, when in fact they present all sorts of problems and issues of which we need to be aware. The importance of understanding the mundane, as Les Back (2015) and Jill Ebrey (2016) write, lies in the possibility of linking the "smallest story to the largest social transformation" (Back 2015, 834). The US military's research into soldier performance enhancement is one such social transformation.

The mundane can also be seen as leading into "common sense." Protecting soldiers through any means available is not only an ethical question but one of common sense (Herzfeld 2001). Within the present-day US socio-political-technical context, it might seem like common sense that "anything good" to protect our soldiers is OK. They fight to protect us and preserve our freedoms, so it is only common sense and right that we do everything to protect them. Thinking about performance enhancements in the military through the lens of common sense brings it back into the cultural and the everyday; it is not just something that bioethicists debate. A report produced by the US Army Natick Soldier Research, Development, and Engineering Center (NSRDEC) titled "Future Soldier 2030 Initiative" sums up the desire, need, and possible problems facing the military's drive toward enhanced soldiers and the need to contend with emergent, common-sense ideas of acceptable enhancements: "Consumer demand and scientific exploration will yield an explosion in cognitive and physical enhancers, including nootropic (smart) drugs, neural prosthetics, and permanent physical prosthetics. These could yield dramatic enhancements in Soldier performance and provide a tremendous edge in combat, but will require the Army to grapple with very serious and difficult ethical issues. At the same time, if societal ethics change to embrace such enhancers, the Army will need to decide to use these types of systems" (NSRDEC 2009, 3). The military will have to pay close attention to new pharmaceutical enhancers as they enter development and the market. And it is very aware that it will have to pay close attention to cultural attitudes and perceptions of perfor-mance enhancement drugs. If ideas about performance enhancing drugs change, the military will have an easier time requiring soldiers to take them, and the opportunity to be enhanced could help increase recruitment.

Commonsense notions of soldiering and enhancements might be much more powerful and convincing to the military if it knows that the common-sense consensus on enhancements is that they are fine and to be tolerated, since we should do anything and everything we can to protect our soldiers. In many ways, it comes down to "Is it OK to drug soldiers?" versus "Is it ethical to drug soldiers?" "OK" is the everyday, mundane, folk/common-sense application of morality, ethics, and values. How will people under-stand and feel the "OK" versus the "ethical"? Will parents be OK with their children joining the military and becoming enhanced? How will they feel if they receive a letter like the one Supersoldier Bob sends home? As I will discuss in the coming chapters, projects like Idiophylaxis, the Objective Force Warrior, the Future Force Warrior, and Inner Armor might help a sol-dier survive war, but it is far from clear that these technologies will help a soldier survive peace. In the mythology of the heroic warrior, it is the hero who often finds it difficult or impossible to return home (Campbell 1973; Hautzinger and Scandlyn 2014; Shay 1995; Sherman 2015).

Biological Solutions to National Security Problems

Fundamentally, a military is about fighting and killing. All members of the military are made aware of this from day one of Basic Training, regard-less of their Military Occupational Specialty (MOS in US Army parlance).

Of course, soldiers branch out and perform other kinds of missions, and combat is not the sole activity of the soldier, even if you are in the infantry or Special Operations. But the military needs you to know how to fight, and to be ready and prepared to fight when needed, which could be at any moment.

The need to fight at a moment's notice means that soldiers need to be physically and mentally ready to fight anytime, anywhere; this ability to fight on command underpins national security. We need to examine the biological underpinnings of national security: How do understandings and visions of biology and the ordering of biology influence national security, military policy and action, and how we imagine soldiers? How do we think about and analyze the strategic macrolevel of war and (in)security, and think about how it plays out at the microlevel of the biology of soldiers? I examine these links through military medicine and research efforts designed to enhance the performance of soldiers. While the US is moving ever closer to drones and other autonomous technologies like battlefield robots (Gusterson 2016; Scharre 2018), the soldier is still the linchpin of military success. Until soldiers are replaced with machines, we will try to make soldiers as predictable, reliable, and durable as machines.

Since states started making soldiers, two things have been obvious: soldiers are never up to the task, and the state needs to make them be up to the task. From the state's point of view, the soldier oscillates between cowardice and heroism, compliance and failure. The important thing to understand and consider when examining these projects is not whether these technologies will work—they may or may not—but that the desire to protect results in an unceasing attempt to protect. This goes for the desire to enhance as well—one drug or suite of drugs might not work, but there are always other paths to consider and other pharmacopeias to explore. The soldier may be both the beginning and the end points of enhancement and protection logics and rationales, but she is also the conduit and the enabler for these kinds of interventions. The soldier is both the prompt and the problem.

Lurking below the surface of the soldier's skin is the one battlefield the military cannot afford to ignore, the enemy the military and the soldier must face on a daily basis and which can cause the military to lose before it even begins: the biology of the soldier. The interior of the soldier is the new terrain of combat, the new battlefield, fought against and with anticipation and imagination, against all sorts of enemies, human, environmental, bacterial, and viral, enemies the soldier might not be aware of but which can kill him in an instant, enemies that are faceless, heartless, unfeeling, and uncaring. This militarized interior becomes the ultimate proof of the state's love for the soldier: we love you so much and care about your welfare so much we will change you from the inside out, possibly forever. It is also proof positive that your safety is our number one concern. Skin-in solutions become—paradoxically—the most obvious, visible, and "seen" proof through intervention that the military will do all it can to protect soldiers.

Mark Burchell, a former UK Royal Marine Commando, explains what happens to the soldier on the battlefield, how the soldier's body starts to work against him in combat, and the amount of energy the soldier has to expend to stay alive and remain effective.

> During combat, his disciplined body is conditioned to move, to react, to respond, to overcome. Physiological actions and reactions are fast, and his body is burning an enormous amount of energy, that's why he is lean and muscular, because he subscribes to a life of willful labor. . . . The body will sweat profusely in an attempt to cool down, but every last muscle is being timeworn by a stream of adrenaline gushing through an inner system working ever harder to stay in the fight. . . . As air is heavily sucked into the lungs, blood is oxygenated and the muscles are fed so this war machine can continue to function. . . . The body's energy is being exhausted and absorbed by the same environment that once offered protection. (2014, 216)

All of this happens quickly, so the soldier is soon in danger in running out of energy, no matter how well trained and conditioned he is before combat. US Army recruiting slogans like "Army Strong" and "An Army of One" hint at the desire to have enhanced supersoldiers who are better than unenhanced soldiers and who have the firepower and combat capabilities of entire companies of soldiers. This same "body" could then be used for recruiting/promotional purposes in order to entice people to enlist in the military. Soldier augmentation offers the potential for obviating difficulties in military recruitment that the United States has experienced after the Iraq War that has compelled it to ease standards for enlistment, including lower standards of physical fitness and higher age ceilings (Schachtman 2007).

While vigorously exploring new and improved external protection technologies, the US military has long focused on ways to internally armor the soldier. Much of the vision and portrayal of the enhanced "supersoldier" comes from US military medicine and biotechnology research. US military biomedical and performance enhancement research is intended to anticipate threats (however the military defines "threat" at a given time and place) and manipulate the bodies of soldiers to meet and counter these threats (Bickford 2008, 2018; Clarke et al. 2010, 4–6; Galliot and Lotz 2015; Lin, Mehlman, Abney, and Galliot 2014; Perkins and Steevens 2015; see also Terry 2017). Some of these internal protections might seem farfetched (such as making the soldier immune from nuclear flash burns) or quotidian and mundane (like making the soldier more resistant to bug bites and blisters) (Bickford 2018; Sulzberger 1962a; Wong 2013; see also Biljan, Pavić, and Šitum 2008; Brennan et al. 2012). Regardless, the biological makeup of the soldier is the site of intense research and design, imagination, and planning. Military environmental and performance enhancement research are not only about adapting or reacting at the level of combat systems, tactics, or strategy; they are also about reacting to and anticipating possible battlefields and environments at the level of the biology of the individual soldier.

Enhancements intended to be embedded in the body of the soldier—"skin-in" enhancements—constitute the direct manipulation and militarization of the soldier's own biology for military purposes. The vast array of projects conducted and underway demonstrate the breadth of military performance enhancement research in the US: projects incorporating both skin-in and skin-out technologies like the Land Warrior, Objective Force Warrior, and Future Force Warrior suite of programs; and skin-in projects focused on biomedical enhancements and the "tweaking" of the soldier's biology such as Peak Soldier Performance and Metabolically Dominant Soldier; attention-enhancing drugs like Modafinil, designed to "enhance situational awareness" and prevent the "degradation of decision-making"; trauma-blocking drugs like Propranolol, intended to block traumatic memories and possibly prevent PTSD; attempts to harness the "sleep/wake cycle" and keep soldiers alert and in combat for days on end; "power dreaming" as a way to care for PTSD; specially designed performance enhancing foods; hyperhydration to reduce the logistics stress of carrying water into combat; and projects like Idiophylaxis and Inner Armor, concerned with mitigating environmental and disease threats to the soldier. All of these projects demonstrate the intensity of the military's focus on the interior of the soldier.

"Better Warriors through Chemistry":
Bodies, Labor, and Warfare

Some like to argue that humans are wired for war, that it is in our DNA, and that it goes back to our "evolutionary past." But if we are wired for war—premade for war—why do states have to go to such great measures to get people to fight and kill, and why do humans have to be enhanced to conduct warfare? If warfare is somehow deeply encoded in our DNA, our bodies and DNA are not up to the task of the kind of warfare we have devised and are developing for the future. Our bodies are just not up to the tasks and rigors of combat we have dreamed up and set up for ourselves, so we must change our bodies—and possibly our DNA—to keep up with our imagination. Conceptions of the enhanced military body in many ways completely deny evolution and the physical limits of the body—anything is possible, and the body explodes into a fractal of possibilities and iterations based on military fear and anticipation. The military's concern with developing performance enhancement drugs and harnessing new trends in genetics and neurology is a way of trying to elude the genetic "fate" of weakness, the inherent weakness of the human body on the battlefield (Petryna 2003, 14). Military performance enhancement is concerned with the biomedical protection of soldiers and the risk management and modulation of weakness—and cowardice—for soldiers. It is the development of a new kind of institutional risk management for itself and its goals (Clarke et al. 2010). In a promotional video for its "Exoskeleton Integrated Soldier Protection System," Revision Military, a US military equipment and technology company, used the following tag line about human fragility to advertise its new technologies: "Rely on the human body alone, and you may need to pick between mission and safety. Combine innovation and the human body, and you have an unstoppable capability" (Revision Military 2015).

My concern here is not so much an analysis or theorization of biopower and communities (Esposito 2008, 2011; see also Petryna 2003); rather, I use "biopower" as a way to analyze and detail the history, plans, and ideas behind a suite of biomedical interventions that focus on the direct intervention by the military and the state in the biology of the soldier, and to think about the implications and bioethics of military performance enhancement and military medicine. As iterations of military biopower, US military biomedical research and performance enhancement projects are intended to manipulate and mediate the war/embodiment dialectic, shaping it in "positive" and militarily useful ways (Bickford 2018; Clarke et al. 2010, 4–6; Foucault 1979, 1980; Hogle 2005; Scarry 1985; Terry 2017). As Jennifer Terry describes it, biomedicine in a military setting incorporates the "multiplying branches of modern biological sciences in their convergence with medical research, treatment, and profiteering" (2017, 3). She also adds that "national security, warfare, and biomedical logics form a nexus in which deliberate violence—war—is bound up with far-reaching aspirations about improving life" (27). As concerted methods of improvement and enhancement, US military projects like Idiophylaxis and Inner Armor reflect similar aspirations about life and fortitude; in their overlaps we see abiding values tied to life and its improvement. And yet they also signal something new: the ability to make these visions come to life in the bodies of soldiers themselves. Improving life in the abstract, to extend Terry's argument to these projects, depends on improving the life of war's most critical instrument—the body of the soldier. While biomedical logics are about anticipation, for military performance enhancement projects, they are not only about anticipating the "future as a salve for the present" (Terry 2017, 54). This anticipation is also about a future of military fear, uncertainty, and surprise, of threats unknown and possibly inexorable. Increasingly, the task of this kind of anticipation is to find solutions and embed them inside the bodies of soldiers *before* combat and deployment even take place in order to mitigate future military uncertainty. These attempted antidotes to future fears will literally be embodied in present soldiers.

My interest in this biomilitary dialectic is in how advances in biomedicine offer the military new ways to understand, imagine, and design soldiers, and how these advances promise to expand and enhance the soldier's ability to overcome and survive the battlefield and possibly all enemies and combat stressors. Though attentive to the discourse of improvement, my analysis of military biotechnology and performance enhancement nevertheless diverges from that of Terry in its point on the "arc" of soldiering. I examine military biomedical projects as interventions designed to keep the soldier "whole" and useful before and during combat rather than as interventions designed to help heal the soldier after combat. My focus on military biomedicine and performance enhancement is on how "improvement" and "enhancement" are anticipated, imagined, planned, and designed *before* combat, with a focus here on military pharmaceuticals as "inner armor." Biomedicine, genomics, and synthetic biology might make it possible to take all the images, dreams, and ideals of supersoldiers, all the discussions and ideas and arguments about "willpower" and inner

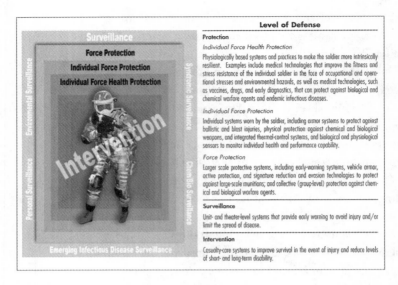

Level of Defense

Protection

Individual Force Health Protection
Physiologically based systems and practices to make the soldier more intrinsically resilient. Examples include medical technologies that improve the fitness and stress resistance of the individual soldier in the face of occupational and operational stresses and environmental hazards, as well as medical technologies, such as vaccines, drugs, and early diagnostics, that can protect against biological and chemical warfare agents and endemic infectious diseases.

Individual Force Protection
Individual systems worn by the soldier, including armor systems to protect against ballistic and blast injuries, physical protection against chemical and biological weapons, and integrated thermal-control systems, and biological and physiological sensors to monitor individual health and performance capability.

Force Protection
Larger scale protective systems, including early-warning systems, vehicle armor, active protection, and signature reduction and evasion technologies to protect against large-scale munitions; and collective (group-level) protection against chemical and biological warfare agents.

Surveillance
Unit- and theater-level systems that provide early warning to avoid injury and/or limit the spread of disease.

Intervention
Casualty-care systems to improve survival in the event of injury and reduce levels of short- and long-term disability.

Figure I.4 "Level of Defense." Lester Martinez-Lopez: "Biotechnology Enablers for the Soldier System of Systems," 2004.

strength, and make them real, "things" that can be synthesized and transplanted into soldiers.

The ultimate goal of military performance enhancement is to create a new type of "supersoldier," a soldier with different expectations of performance, capabilities, and survivability from previous types of American soldiers. As stated in the "Army Medical Science and Technology Initiatives in Advanced Biotechnology Briefing," the problem of certainty of performance in combat is being addressed by "novel neuroprotective drugs" (Romano 2004, 12), and a "recurring finding" is that "biotechnology offers major payoffs to the military in improved soldier health and performance" (3). And according to the former chief of the US Navy's Operational Test and Evaluation Force, Rear Admiral Stephen Baker, "Futurists say that if anything's going to happen in the way of leaps in technology, it'll be in the field of medicine. . . . This 'better warrior through chemistry' field is being looked at very closely" (Knickerbocker 2002).

Unseen and built-in armor are ways of thinking about the connections, entanglements, and relations of power that bind the soldier to the military and remain unseen, and perhaps unfelt, but are nonetheless present in both the body and the medical records of the soldier as proof of protection (see figure I.4). The unseen armor of the soldier is also in some ways the unforeseeable: we cannot necessarily foresee all threats that a soldier will face, but unseen, built-in armor will provide the soldier with ongoing protection. We can think about possible outcomes and the ethics of the permissible, but built-in, "skin-in" armor is the undiscovered country of military research.

By paying close attention to US military performance enhancement plans and directions, we can analyze how the military thinks about the future and the kinds of soldiers it thinks it will need. Imagining the "unknown unknowns" and the world as a system of systems of threats and potential threats and emergent threats provides the military with an unbounded system of fear—and opportunities. And viewing the body of the soldier as an endless system of systems of unknown unknowns, of frailty and weakness, "explodes" the body into a potentially endless system of systems of possibilities for enhancement and protection against the unknown unknowns.

New forms of pharmaceuticals and new ways of engineering human biology present the military with new ways of harnessing the biology and labor power of the soldier. *Chemical Heroes* is the juxtaposition of an intentional process—biomedical enhancement research—with that which is contingent and unpredictable. If capitalism is about anything—and particularly the convergence of capitalism and the military—it is about attempted predictability, standardization, immediacy, and regulation. Predictable, controllable heroism is just another component of human resource management and military Taylorism.

Performance enhancement is about the creation and extraction of evermore reliable and dependable military labor, but labor made to seem heroic and glamorous through the use of advanced technology to make the soldier seem and feel like a fearless mythological warrior. Today, the US soldier represents a capital investment, with each soldier often costing upward of $1 million per year to train, maintain, equip, deploy, and care for, according to a recent figure (Shaughnessy 2012, as cited in Lin, Mehlman, Abney, and Galliot 2014). Gone are the days of the soldier as cannon fodder; rather than thinking of the soldier as totally expendable, the politics of soldiers and soldiering now entail a concern with protection, of ensuring the survivability of the soldier. The politics of military protection in the US today dictate and drive a massive research and development regime designed to prevent US soldiers from suffering any casualties or injury—at least in theory. In an era of increasingly lethal weapons, we are to somehow believe that our soldiers will not suffer trauma or die in combat.

Part I

Thematic Framings

ONE

"Innovate at the Speed of Change"

War, Anticipation, Imagination

Vision: To create the ultimate battlefield advantage for our
Warfighters that ensures them the decisive edge now and
in the future.

» **United States Army Natick Soldier RD&E Center,**
  "Warfighter Directorate"

Soldiers do not simply emerge sui generis; they are first imagined, designed, and made into a specific form at specific times and in political, cultural, military, and technological contexts (Bickford 2011, 2018). They are the vectors and products of a wide array of policies, research programs, images, imagination work, technologies, and desired outcomes. One form of power that binds a soldier to the military is not what is normally understood as military discipline or coercion but forms of anticipatory and proactive/prophylactic military medicine, and the reshaping and remaking of the enlistee's body to fit military needs. These conceptions of health and medical practice are intended to protect and improve the soldier while compelling the soldier to perform and fight, all in the name of "readiness." Of course, these interventions might save the soldier in combat, but they also make it easier to deploy the soldier and sustain operations.

Soldiers represent the state in myriad ways, and we can learn much about how state actors think about themselves, the state, the military, war, combat, killing and wounding, and moral/ethical questions about killing and death by examining soldiers and how the military, military researchers, and politicians imagine the kinds of soldiers they want. The "idea" of the soldier also offers us an insight into how a state thinks about life, death, war, and ethics. US military projects focused on the development of "supersoldiers" represent more than advances in combat protection and enhancement; they are also commentaries on weakness, anxiety, vulnerability, and security, as played out on, in, and through the bodies of soldiers.

———

In 2000 the US Army began a new recruitment campaign titled "An Army of One." Replacing the "Be All That You Can Be" slogan of the 1980s (which DARPA later revised to "Be All That You Can Be, and a Lot More" (Singer 2008) and which soldiers in the 1980s and 1990s changed to "Be All That You Never Wanted To Be" as a form of protest), the Army of One campaign stressed the individuality of the soldier within the military as a mass, unified organization, emphasizing that the soldier, while part of a team with a common goal, was still an individual. Complete with slick videos and the release of an online game—"America's Army"—designed to take prospective recruits through basic training and beyond, the new recruitment campaign was designed to make the Army hip and exciting, a fun adventure. What the Army of One campaign hinted at but did not detail is the development of supersoldier projects and technologies that hope to really make the individual soldier into an "Army of One."

Starting in the late 1980s, the US military began funding soldier-enhancement research programs and "system of systems" programs like Land Warrior, Objective Force Warrior, Future Force Warrior, and the Future Combat System, as well as the Ground Warrior system and the Nett Warrior program. All of these programs represented intensive technological development efforts designed to increase the fighting capability, firepower, and survivability of the individual soldier while simultaneously integrating him into a suite of weapons platforms, intelligence systems, and sensor systems to expand operational capabilities and situational awareness, for both the soldier and all leaders up the command ladder (Beidel 2010; Bonsignore 2009; Douglas et al. 2001; Erwin 2007; Feickert 2005, 2008, 2009; Gourley 2012, 2013a, 2013b; *Military Technology* 2006; Niruthan 2018; Pernin et al. 2012; *Soldiers* 2006; Tolzmann 2012). With the Objective Force Warrior program, for example, the US military hoped for an exponential increase in the lethality of the individual soldier and the ability of an individual soldier to cover and control more ground than earlier US soldiers. In theory, this would allow for a smaller, deadlier military; as the conceptual designs for the Objective Force Warrior state, the Objective Force Warrior would be

Figure 1.1 "Army Strong" recruiting poster, early 2000s.

twenty times more lethal than those in the Land Warrior program, and the later Future Force Warrior would be even more lethal and effective on the battlefield. In this sense, the Army of One and Army Strong media campaigns could also be seen as a way of preparing the public for a time when enhanced soldiers really might be armies of one, with the firepower and combat effectiveness of entire companies of soldiers (see Figure 1.1).

Joseph Masco sees national security affect as "an atmosphere that can become a deeply felt emotional structure when directed by mass media or official declarations into a collective event" (2014, 17). "Support the Troops" is a version of this emotional structure built around the care and protection of soldiers. Unlike the widespread fear propaganda around nuclear war that Masco details (2006, 2014; see also Gusterson 1996), which presented direct and specific instances of threat, the soldier becomes the lens through which the military focuses and modulates ideas around defense and national security threats. The "soldier" becomes the focal point of concentration and concern for threats and, focusing on the care, protection, and well-being of the soldier, US civilians are brought into the fold to think about broader security threats. It is easier to focus fear around soldiers than it is to think about pharmacological battlefields or the military's concern with climate change. By personalizing these threats as specific—or open-ended—threats to the soldier, by creating an emotional connection to soldiers through "support the troops" campaigns, the US defense establishment can make us all feel fear and concern for these diffuse future threats.

Battles are first waged and fought in between memory and imagination—in the space of anticipation where anything is possible, you have to be hyperaware and constantly on guard and on watch, and the guiding principle is always "what if?" (Masco 2014). It is in this space that soldiers are imagined and designed: What will we need and what do we want from our soldiers? What will they face, and where will they face it? What will the battlefield conditions be? What will their soldiers be able to do? Will their soldiers be able to resist trauma and violence better than ours? Will their "will" to fight and survive be stronger than ours? Or will the specter of cowardice—always present, always looming and lowering and glowering—sweep through our ranks? Guarding against all of this are forms of anticipation, preemption, and imagination.

One of the ways in which citizens are made into soldiers—and soldiers are always citizens first—is through the imaginative work of military biomedical research and design. Protection is in many ways analogous to imagination, anticipation, and preemption: it is the imagining of fear and threats, the thought of danger and "what if?" (Masco 2014), and the scramble to anticipate and preempt these threats from ever happening in the first place. If you want to protect life, you have to first imagine the threats that put it in danger and imagine the myriad ways death, wounding, and mission failure can come. To protect is to imagine something from which someone needs to be protected and imagine ways in which the person can in fact be protected from the imagined threat. The military constantly thinks about and plans for all sorts of threats, and all sorts of political and military scenarios are anticipated, "war-gamed," and considered. An enhancement is the biotechnical and physical manifestation of a feeling of threat: the feeling is turned into an object and embedded in the body of the soldier. This process constitutes the "what if?" or "what might they do?" of military planning, and from these processes of anticipation and preemption, biomedical enhancements and "skin-in" and "skin-out" solutions are developed for the soldier of the imagined and anticipated future.

For Karl Marx, one of the defining aspects of capitalism was that "all that is solid melts into air." This "melting vision" was Marx's observation and analysis that under capitalism, all "fixed and frozen" relationships were pulled asunder, "melted" by the new demands and logics of the organization of labor and life under the new economic system (Berman 1975). This applies to new forms of warfare and our ideas of "the soldier" as well: all fixed and frozen ideas and images of war and the soldier are rapidly melting away as new forms of biomedical technologies make new kinds of soldiers possible. As our ideas melt away, the space created allows for a new vision of the future, new visions of military potential. But this "melting vision" also applies to how the military sees war and combat and how it envisions the supersoldier. War and combat "melt" the soldier, wound and destroy (and sometimes literally melt) the soldier physically and mentally; enhancements are a vision of a nonmelting future of soldiering, of soldiers who do not come apart in combat, who remain whole and intact during and after combat. Enhancements will put out the sparks that cause the soldier to melt and dissipate; the Army Futures Command motto, "Innovate at the Speed of Change," is a vision of preventing the melting of things, of staying ahead of change and making sure things are whole. It is a vision of completeness, of keeping things together. Brian Massumi comes close to this idea of the military's vision for supersoldiers: "Preemption is pro-action: action on the conditions of action, prior to its actually taking shape. The second way to act totally and intangibly on a situation is to act on perception. It is perception which prepares a body for action and reaction" (2015, 70). A statement in the United States Army Natick Soldier Research, Development, and Engineering Center's "Future Soldier Initiative" makes this clear: "The future is always uncertain. However, by applying logic and imagination to current situations and technologies, the Future Soldier concept was developed to identify capabilities a Soldier might carry into battle. . . . Our intent is to stir imaginations, and start a dialogue about how best to equip the Soldier" (NSRDEC 2009).

The army's "vision" is a vision of the future and a vision of its attempts to shape and change our vision of and into the future. It is a way to make us look at things the ways it would like us to see, to see its vision of its world, of how it sees the world and makes the future world. We are to see its vision of its world and the future world of combat and combat stressors it imagines. The army's vision is also about shaping how we see and imagine—and how it sees and imagines—the enhanced supersoldier. It is a response to the dilemma of representing and visualizing internal, unseen enhancements, and the development of metaphors to visualize these enhancements embedded in the body of the soldier.

"Shock and Awe": Technology and Vision

The US military initiated the attack on Iraq in 2003 with what it called "Shock and Awe." The initial attack was to be so profoundly violent, destabilizing, and awe-inspiring that the Iraqi military would surrender, and the world would witness the overwhelming military might of the modern

US military. "Shock and Awe" is a visual practice, but not just simply about bombs and explosions; it is also a new practice and aesthetic of portraying new kinds of soldiers. It is a shaping of the visual and affective fields of supersoldiers as "shock and awe" soldiers; we can think of them and "feel" that they might actually be able to act as superheroes. Supersoldier research is not necessarily secret; information about soldier protection and the fantastic biomedical projects underway is useful for making people support this research. Secret research obviously exists, but the proliferation and publicity around biomedical enhancements is a sign of state care for soldiers and their well-being. The "openness" around these issues becomes a kind of affective fact of care and concern.

The military is also keen on publicizing certain aspects of the kinds of research it undertakes, as the "public secret" (G. Jones 2014) of military performance enhancement research acts as its own kind of shock and awe weapon. The image and portrayal of new, potentially unbeatable US soldiers can act as a deterrent in their own right, or at least make others think twice about challenging US military might. The proliferation of information can also be seen as a way to both control and shape how we think about soldiers, and how the "enemy" might imagine US soldiers; as Massumi writes, propaganda becomes a kind of rumor production (2015, 79; see also Masco's 2014 argument about secrecy).

We can think about how ideas and notions of "anticipation," "preemption," "potential," and "vision" are designed and created for political or military systems, and we can think about how they infiltrate and permeate everyday life and thought (Adams, Murphy, and Clarke 2009; Masco 2014; Massumi 2015; Radin 2017; Taussig, Hoeyer, and Helmreich 2013). But how are these notions operationalized by the military and made "real" in the bodies of soldiers? How do you take a "vision" and change how a soldier is made? What are the technologies that actually make "anticipation" work through soldiers? As Vincanne Adams, Michelle Murphy, and Adele Clarke write, "Anticipation pervades the ways we think about, feel, and address our contemporary problems" (2009, 248). Performance enhancement is a way to temporalize anticipated and imagined future problems in the present and assuage military/political uncertainty about the soldier and the mission.

Uncertainty and anxiety around preparation and protection require military planners to think about how soldiers will have to be in order to be effective and survive combat. We know war destroys bodies and psyches, and we know that militaries try to come to terms afterward with the fragmentation and destruction of lives. But how do they imagine and plan for preventing the fragmentation and destruction of soldiers' bodies and minds? The task is to imagine ways of not having to put the soldier back together again after combat but instead constructing him or her in such a way before combat that the thin, wisp-shell of the body and the psyche do not dissipate in the face of it all.

War, Waiting, and the Space in Between

If militarization is concerned with the ways people and societies prepare for war and violence (Bickford 2011, 2015; Gillis 1989; Kohn 2009; Lutz 2009; Price 2013), part of this preparation is imagining the forms these preparations should take, how they should be organized, and imagining and preparing soldiers and militaries for the next war, or wars to come. In that sense, unlike for veterans and civilians, there really is no "afterwar" (Sherman 2015; Terry 2017; Wool 2015) or even postwar for military planners and researchers: there is only constant preparedness, constant innovation and imagination, and constant worry and fear about what comes next (Masco 2014; Massumi 2015; see also Lakoff 2015, 2017). Perhaps more important than "afterwar," at least in terms of military research and planning, is "waiting": "Being in the thick of war has been watered down and drawn out into an endless waiting, both sides poised for action. The baseline state is now this always-on of low-boil poising for action. One is always in the thin of it. . . . The relation between action and waiting has been inverted. Waiting no longer stretches between actions. Action breaks into waiting" (Massumi 2015, 69). It is in this space of waiting and "nonbattle" (Virilio 1975) that anticipation, imagination, and preemption shape new ways of making and designing soldiers. An enhancement is anticipatory and preemptive: you are enhancing against something you both know and do not know. In this sense, militarization—perhaps best understood as anticipation, preemption, and "waiting"—is frightening in that it never stops: the "new" drives fear, and fear drives preparation and funding. This waiting is productive: it is the calm before the inevitable storm, the time to prepare and get ready, and the time to actively shape how the next eruption of violence will take form (or not). The military and military theorists are simply waiting, planning for, and designing new kinds of weapons and armor to deal with the anticipated and imagined threats and foes that the "eruption" of violence and action will demand (Massumi 2015; Virilio 1975).

Joanna Radin's work on the development of cold storage for blood offers insights for thinking about military-biological anticipation and how the military thinks about the future. These kinds of forays into anticipating and predicting military-biomedical futures are a kind of "salvage biology," as Radin phrases it in her discussion of the uses of cold blood during the Cold War (2017, 6). She uses the "discourse of salvage" as a way to think about anticipation and the creation of a new blood-based infrastructure for managing future risks to population health (6). As a way of thinking about the military, enhancements, and future risk, salvage biology is a good way to imagine how soldiers would be imagined, made, and "salvaged" from the ravages of war before they even entered it, and perhaps again after they have left it. Radin discusses the idea of salvage biology as a kind of extraction from the bodies of native peoples (6); this idea of salvage also applies to the military extraction of biological potential and labor from soldiers.

Since the military can never be quite sure about what to expect, designs and plans are perforce inherently contingent. The experiments it conducts are in many ways an estimation or a guess; some will be pretty close to what is needed, while some might be totally off the mark. Radin also discusses the work of historian Hans-Jörg Rheinberger, who describes laboratory experiments as "systems of manipulation designed to give unknown answers to questions that the experimenters themselves are not yet able to clearly ask" (Radin 2017, 81; see also Rheinberger 2017). We can think of military performance enhancement research much like Rheinberger describes experiments: military scientists can imagine and anticipate what the soldier might encounter as ways of contending with a presumably violent future and design technologies to attend to and preempt these imagined futures, even if the solutions imagined and designed are not necessarily on the mark. Indeed, as Karl Friedl, former commander of the United States Army Research Institute for Environmental Medicine (USARIEM), notes of military performance enhancement research, "attempts to improve human biology may solve the wrong problem by trying to improve inherent human capabilities to fit inappropriate demands of tactics, tasks, and equipment matched to humans" (2015, S72). Referencing the work of François Jacob, Radin argues that these "set ups" are, as Jacob put it, "machines for making the future" (Radin 2017, 81). The military, military theorists, and military researchers are constantly imagining and anticipating new threats and new countermeasures and developing unknown questions with possibly unknown results in an endless game of militarized cat and militarized mouse.

Part of preparing for uncertain and dangerous futures is the design and production of "supersoldiers," the human embodiment of Jacob's "machines for making the future."

Between Vision and Preemption: Imagining the Soldier of the Future

The work of military performance enhancement research is the work of anticipation, imagination, and design, or what the military frequently refers to as "vision," that is, how soldiers will be, how they will fight efficiently and effectively, how the military will do more with less, how soldiers will control vast amounts of space, how they will dominate the battlefield, how the future will be ours through our advanced and cutting-edge technology, and how soldiers will never die. Like the fictional Dr. Evil from the *Austin Powers* films, who demands "sharks with laser beams attached to their heads" (but who must settle for mutated, ill-tempered sea bass when told that sharks were put on the endangered species list and clearing up the red tape would take months), military researchers can imagine all sorts of interventions, enhancements, and improvements, and are often tasked with doing exactly this. From soldiers who will not need to sleep, who can eat grass when necessary, or mimic the ability of animals, military-enhancement researchers imagine and dream of turning soldiers into superhumans. To read military performance enhancement plans is to read the work of serious play and imagination; sharks with laser beams are actually not that farfetched, even if the researchers themselves are nothing like Dr. Evil.

We can use the idea of "vision" to think about the making of supersoldiers. Ongoing developments in biomedicine offer new ways to understand, see, and imagine soldiers and promise to expand and enhance the body's ability to overcome and survive the battlefield and its multiple and mutating stressors. Soldiers must first be imagined before they are made, and future battlefields, diseases, combat conditions, weapons, and systems must be imagined, analyzed, and processed as the moving goalposts of "enhancement." Friedl notes that US Army concepts for soldier enhancement in the 1970s focused on creating a series of "simply pharmacological solutions" to battlefield performance, with the goal of creating "brave pills," "smart pills," and "endurance pills" (2015, S71). Bravery, intelligence, endurance: these three areas continue to form a triad in US military performance enhancement research, but each of these attributes is subjective and open to interpretation. What exactly constitutes "bravery," "smartness," and "endurance"? How would you go about synthesizing these attributes into a pill that all soldiers could take to make them perform as supersoldiers on the battlefield?

Idiophylaxis, DARPA's Inner Armor, and other projects like the Objective Force Warrior and the Future Force Warrior highlight how the soldier is suspended between the "lessons learned" from the last war and the imagined horrors of the next. This suspension also means that imagination, fantasy, and a kind of playfulness—albeit a serious sort of playfulness—are necessary for imagining and making soldiers. To think of supersoldiers as superheroes or comic book action heroes is to engage in a kind of imaginative play around war and heroism, bravery and knights in shining armor, of humans who are much more than human. A report titled "Future Soldier 2030 Initiative: Future Soldiers Need to Own the Fight!" from the US Army Natick Soldier RD&E Center details aspects of the "Future Soldier 2030" ensemble of technologies and efforts underway in "Human Performance and Training," "Soldier Protection," "Lethality," "Mobility and Logistics," "Soldier Network," "Soldier Sensors," and "Soldier Power and Energy." As the report makes clear, however, "Our intent is to stir imaginations, and start a dialogue about how best to equip the Soldier" (2009, 2). And as the 2001 Oak Ridge Laboratory Objective Force Warrior report makes clear, researchers were tasked during brainstorming sessions to think about enhancements using the prompt "Wouldn't it be cool, if . . ." to explore and exploit the "art of the possible" (National Security Directorate, Oak Ridge National Laboratory 2001). Richard Stouder states that the "art of the possible" will develop soldiers who "aided by technology . . . will remain persuasive in peace and invincible in war" (2002, 4). The "possible" here is anything and everything that could give US soldiers an advantage on and off the battlefield, now and in the future. In many ways, thinking about imagination and play is the entrée point to thinking about the links between biomedicine, technology, the military, and policy, the human, the superhuman, the posthuman, ethics, labor, and military service. Achilles, Superman, Captain America, Iron Man: all are examples of the serious play of supersoldiers and men of steel. But Achilles is both the template and cautionary tale: this is what we imagine an almost kill-proof soldier can do, and this time, we will leave no part of the body unprotected.

Ontopower and the Soldier

"Vision" implies a gaze into the future, an attempt to predict what soldiers will face and how soldiers will need to be modified in order to face whatever threats and dangers will confront them. Military "vision" hinges on forms of preemption, and this involves what Massumi calls *ontopower*: "a power through which being becomes" (2015, 71). Massumi also sees "ontopower" as the process of preempting "incipient tendencies towards unknown but certain future threats" to life (Massumi 2015, 9–12; see also Büscher 2018). Ontopower, according to Massumi, is a new kind of power that has emerged since the 1990s, a form of power focused on preemption as a new kind of weapon. For Massumi, ontopower is primarily about US military attempts to develop preemptive perceptual systems designed to counter national security threats. Massumi looks at how US military systems are moving toward increasingly rapid reaction times as a form of preemption, forms based on "nonconscious perceptual processes" and "priming" (2015, 66) to allow the US military to react in the "fraction of a second prior to conscious decision making" (Chaput 2017, 2237).

Since the 1990s, as Massumi argues, the US military has operated on preemption, concentrating on "the modulation of the readiness potential, the productive power to influence what comes next" (2015, 97; see also Chaput 2017, 2237; Masco 2014). For Massumi and his reading of US military strategic planning, as well as speeches by George W. Bush, ontopower is focused on national security threats posed by terrorism and a shift toward preemption and the ability to control future conflict and engagements through increasingly offensive—and autonomous—means. But security is not simply a disembodied process of intelligence analysis; it is also the safety, reliability, and combat effectiveness of the lowest-ranking soldier on the battlefield. A focus on systems of surveillance can lead to neglecting the fact that all these systems and systems of systems are made up of people, even if they appear autonomous. In the case of infantry combat, it is still the soldier on the ground who does most of the fighting, killing, and dying.

Much of Massumi's discussion of ontopower and bodies looks at how the military—through DARPA's "Augmented Cognition" program, designed to speed up a soldier's thought and decision-making process, for example— is attempting to develop forms of almost immediate, unreflected action in soldiers as a way to counter fatigue and the degradation of decision-making in soldiers (2015, 66–67; see also Ford and Glymour 2014; Lin, Mehlman, and Abney 2013; Moreno 2012; Wong 2013). While DARPA and other military research units are focusing on cognition as a form of preemption—almost a kind of mind reading of the future—preemption and performance enhancement are not necessarily about unreflected action on the part of enhanced soldiers. While response times are critical, unreflected responses, or responses that are not linked into a system of planned action, firing protocols, or rules of engagement, for example, will only lead back to a kind of detrimental berserker-like response. Preemption does not necessarily rely solely on unreflection; rather, preemption, as linked to MPE projects, is about reflection and awareness, a keenness of vision and forethought about what is to come and what might come. While Massumi is correct in his contention that the US military has increased its focus on preemption, a focus on US military biomedical enhancement research and supersoldier research shows that this has long been a staple of US military intentions. While the current focus might be on security and intelligence systems and the development of a kind of machinelike response rate, preemption has long been centered around the body of the soldier. Massumi nods to this in his discussion of "bare activity" and the desire to transform the body into a kind of prelinguistic decision-making machine (Chaput 2017, 2237). Again, Massumi is correct in this assertion but misses US military research focused on the body not just as a decision-making machine but as a form of self-armor. Of course, some of the performance enhancement projects currently underway are focused on cognition enhancement and reshaping the neurology of soldiers to make them more efficient on the battlefield; this has been an ongoing effort since before the 1990s (even if it becomes more clear or obvious in the 1990s). We can read US military performance enhancement programs as concerned with preemption well before the 1990s, with attempts to fix responses in the body of the soldier. If the soldier can be enhanced to withstand the unknown unknowns, she can shape the battlefield ("shape the battlefield" is a US military strategic planning term). Preemption has not always been about terrorism; it was also a key part of US Cold War planning and research (Masco 2014), at least in terms of developing new kinds of soldiers. The way the military imagines and envisions soldiers is a look into the future, a look not just at the technology but into an imagined and hoped-for future of domination and the "decisive edge" on the battlefield. Changing a soldier's biological makeup to respond to fears of imagined future threats transforms the soldier into a living, breathing manifestation of military preemption and anticipation.

Military researchers examine what soldiers have faced in the past and then predict, anticipate, and imagine what they will face in the future. In that sense, military performance enhancement research revolves around reconciling two different times and events in the body of the soldier: wars past and future. Based on analyses of past conflicts and stressors, as well as ongoing research into new and emerging weapons systems, nuclear/biological/chemical threats, emerging illness and disease vectors, and environmental threats, MPE researchers work through attempts to develop preemptive modes of biomedical interventions and armor into being and, as such, bring new types of soldiers into being based on preemption to counter any and all threats to national security. In other words, vision and preemption are to find their anchor and expression in the body of the enhanced soldier, and help bring such a soldier into being. This is a soldier who is ready at all times, against all threats, and is always ready for action (Massumi 2015). Linking ontopower and performance enhancements, the general formula seems to be: preemption drives protection, protection creates forms of biomedical armor, and armor equals action and the ability to act. But this linkage will never be a completed, final project, as the "unknown unknown" threats lingering out there now, and in the future, will always necessitate interventions in the soldier's body to counter the threats to come.

Armor—whether internal or external—acts as a kind of material form of anticipation and preemption, either through body armor or making the body its own anticipatory and preemptive kind of biomedical armor. Body armor works against kinetic and ballistic threats, but it is not permanent. Body armor anticipates and preempts kinetic threats from small arms fire, heavy machine-gun fire, grenades, shrapnel, and (possibly) mortar and artillery rounds (though body armor will not necessarily protect a soldier from the blast wave or overpressure generated by these munitions, and it is often the blast/shockwave and overpressure that kill soldiers rather than shrapnel; indeed, the US military's GBU-43/B Massive Ordnance Air Bomb (MOAB—sometimes referred to as the "Mother of All Bombs") is designed to kill by generating a massive amount of overpressure). Body armor can save a soldier, but it does not protect all of the soldier, or all of the time. You need to turn the body of the soldier into a form of biological preemption to armor and protect itself. There are a variety of threats and ideas about threats that need to be anticipated and preempted: mosquito bites, blisters, illness, disease, environmental threats, dehydration problems, metabolic threats, nuclear flash burns—

all need to be thought of as forms of preemption and anticipation. And of course, there are new ideas for weapons, weapons that have yet to be developed but which still pose a threat through the very idea of them. In the world of military weapon design and performance enhancement design, you need to convince soldiers that their bodies are a kind of "total" armor, devoid of weakness, impervious to physical and emotional threat: our armor, ourselves.

In *Seeing Like a State*, James C. Scott (1998) writes about how states make things and people "legible" through different kinds of discourses, policies, and practices. In the case of the United States, the supersoldier is the state's attempt to make visible and legible its fears of the future through biomedicine; the enhancements it imagines, designs, and develops for the internal armoring of soldiers are the biomedical manifestations of anticipation and the possible preemption of imagined future threats, and through this imagining and embedding in the soldier, it brings into a virtual, ideal being these very same imagined threats in the body of the soldier. Supersoldiers are the state's attempts to cure its blindness of the future, its "unknown unknowns"; visioning the future makes the supersoldier and the imagined threats of the future visible and present in the present.

Potential, Preemption, Optimization, and the Future Soldier in the Present

Linked to anticipation and preemption is the increasing interest in anthropology and the social sciences in "potentiality," drawing from Gilles Deleuze's (1966) early interest in virtuality and potential (see also Povinelli 2011; Taussig, Hoeyer, and Helmreich 2013). For Deleuze, the virtual is the "ideal" that is also simultaneously "real." We can think of supersoldiers as both ideal and real in the sense that they represent a kind of "ideal" soldier, and while perhaps not quite as real as the military would like them to be, they are nonetheless real in the sense that the military is working on and, in some cases, deploying the biotechnologies and pharmaceuticals needed to make supersoldiers. This "ideal" also represents what the military sees as the potential of the soldier's body and power. As Karen-Sue Taussig, Klaus Hoeyer, and Stefan Helmreich write, since the beginning of the Human Genome Project, there has been a "reconfiguration" of expectations about the potentials of knowledge in biology and biomedicine (2013, S3; see also Rabinow 1996 and Rabinow and Bennett 2009 for his work on genomics and "biosociality"). The military has followed this reconfiguration very closely and is actively pursuing a reconfiguration of the soldier in order to extract and realize the "full" potential of the soldier on the battlefield. In the new configuration of biomedicine and biotechnology, potentiality "is articulated—either by explicit naming or implicit framing or both—as a hopeful idiom through which to imagine benefits of new medical interventions"; however, these new potentials can also be negative and dystopian (Taussig, Hoeyer, and Helmreich 2013, S4). For the military, this is both positive and negative: new medical technologies will have potentially positive impacts for soldiers in terms of performance enhancement, wound healing, new prosthetics, and new forms of protection. But they will also have potentially negative impacts in the forms of new "pharmaceutical" warfare and other biosecurity threats (Chen and Sharp 2014; Lakoff and Collier 2008). We also have to think about the perspectival aspects of potentiality: what might be seen as a potentially positive biomedical advance in the military—like military performance enhancement technologies—might be seen by civilians as potentially troubling and disturbing.

The idea of a military-biological-environmental future imminently becoming a threat drives the need to make the supersoldier in the present—we need to make and imagine the supersoldier in the present to counter the idea or at least think we are ready for the rapidly emergent threats of the future. Ultimately, the military's interest in "potentiality" is about ensuring that the future is not virtual or "open" but closed: it is about biomedical research in the present meant to lock down and foreclose possible security threats in the future. It is to make sure that the future belongs to the US through the manipulation of the biology of the soldier in the present. While there is the potential for the dual use of pharmaceuticals, and the potential of the dual use of enhancement technologies somewhere down the line, the primary users—the targets of enhancement—are US soldiers. Rather than representing an open idea of technology or of sociotechnological futures, for the US military, it is one of a closed future, a walling-off of potentiality for others; only by creating firewalls around biotechnology can the US military optimize its potential and weaponize them and use them as force multipliers.

Military performance enhancement posits the world as one of anticipated warfare against a mix of anticipated and unanticipated potential threats. The future soldier will have to contend with the known threats, the anticipated threats, and the unanticipated but somehow expected threats of the logic of preemption (Massumi 2015). The future soldier as the target of unknown threats becomes a kind of blank slate for the military; the soldier is the object of unknown and unclear threats, but protection is also uncertain. If threats include the "known unknowns" and the "unknown unknowns," then protection lies somewhere in a zone of indeterminacy. That is, the military has to regulate the known areas of the body that it needs to enhance and protect and diagnose the unknown areas of the body that it needs to enhance to meet unknown—but somehow known to be out there—threats. The unknown unknowns of preemptive warfare meet the unknown unknowns of the recesses of the soldier.

The threats of the future are "felt into reality" in the bodies of soldiers by military planners and researchers (Massumi 2015). Ontopower resides in the process of becoming—that is, citizens become soldiers and then become enhanced soldiers. Enhancing soldiers compels soldiers to become a kind of human whose body has been made to modulate anticipation—it can react to any and all unknown threats. The body is made to respond not to a specific threat but to an undefined suite of threats, a new environment of threats that lurk out there in nature but are unknown. It is the emergence of a new conception of militarized life predicated on preventing death, a kind of necropolitical actor enhanced to survive the dangers of the battlefield and ensure the death of the enemy (Mbembe 2003).

The body of the soldier is not unified as such; it is a system of systems designed to provide flexible responses to flexible threats, with each biological subsystem considered for enhancement according to specific performance requirements and in response to anticipated threats on the battlefield. Enhancements are to make the body perform in ways that in a sense are unknown but imagined as necessary to confront imagined unknown threats. Threats are imagined and felt, and through this feeling of insecurity, supersoldiers are brought into being as an imagined response to anticipated threats. Enhancements are a form of preemption, preemption designed to give the impression in the present that imagined future threats can and will be countered. As Massumi writes, preemption is designed to "put out the smoke of future fires" (2015, 202); the supersoldier, as the personification of preemption, is the one who will extinguish the future fires (even if the supersoldier might also be the one starting them).

"There's Strong. Then There's Army Strong":
Narratives of Strength and the Superhuman

In many ways, the idea of the "supersoldier" works as a kind of performative in J. L. Austin's sense: the words in some ways make it so, bringing something into being that was not there to begin with (Austin 1975). "Supersoldiers" become a kind of performative "affective fact" (Hacking 2002; Massumi 2015) that we in some ways feel and imagine more than know. "Supersoldiers" are made in our imaginations through discussions and articles about them and the kinds of research going on to enhance soldier performance, like the *Wired* and *Vox* clickbait about "supersoldiers" and brain implants, for example; their "ideal potential" becomes seemingly real and actual, and we begin to think and feel that our soldiers are "really" capable of performing the fantastic. As we read about and imagine enhanced soldiers, we bring them into being in a kind of spectral sense, lurking just outside what we think is real and possible, moral and ethical, with some wishing that they were real, right now. When thinking about our soldiers as "supersoldiers," we also imagine adversaries as already being in some manner supersoldiers, adversaries who possess abilities and qualities that present existential threats to our soldiers and our state, which means we have to safeguard against this and further enhance our soldiers: a biomedical arms race in the present to assuage our fears of a frightening military-biological future.

Each iteration of the soldier is one of strength and prowess, and as the US Army has changed over the years, so too have the representations of its soldiers. Not only do US military supersoldier plans trade in images of strength and the superhuman, they also weave narratives about soldiers as superheroes. We can read US military performance enhancement documents and plans as the creation of a new mythology, the miraculous biomedical birth of the new supersoldier, the once-and-future invulnerable warrior. The switch from "soldier" to "warrior" was a conscious public relations strategy on the part of the US military; "soldier" makes us think of the faceless mass of conscription and is a fairly bland moniker, whereas "warrior" conjures up images and feelings of the superior individual fighter who stands and fights alone, one who has a "calling" for the military (and this "calling" for the military is an important but overlooked aspect of the US military as all-volunteer force: you have to be "called" to it to volunteer).

In a vein similar to Paul Fussell's (1975) discussion of the use of heroic language in World War I, the US military uses a specific vocabulary that helps shape how we think of "supersoldiers" when talking about and imagining performance enhancement technologies. Fussell examined the language used by the British press to describe war and soldiers at the beginning of World War I. The message was one of honor and glory, unwavering bravery and strength, steely resolve in the face of the godless enemy and murderous fire; it was language used to mask and promote war to the masses who would do the fighting and dying and send their loved ones off to the slaughter.

We can see the same logic at work in discussions and descriptions of supersoldiers in the United States. While directly related to new forms of warfare and new conceptions of the soldier, terms and phrases help distance and mask what is to come; it is the use of a cold, precise, biomedical language to indicate the emergence of new kinds of soldiers and a new kind of hyperrational glory on the battlefield. Some of the common narrative themes and terms found in US military soldier-enhancement plans and reports include discussions and portrayals of the following:

- strength
- weakness
- environment
- climate
- stressors
- invincibility
- dominance
- wound/killing mitigation
- enhancements
- bodies
- psychopharmacology
- breakdown/repair
- command
- control
- systems
- sensors
- warfighter
- warrior
- vision
- overmatch
- system of systems
- 20x effects
- metabolic dominance
- kill-proofing
- pharmacological battlefield
- force multiplier
- resiliency
- skin-in/skin-out

While Fussell points out the links between this kind of glory language, Christianity, and medieval romances, the language of the supersoldier is devoid of religion and romance (George Mosse [1990] makes a similar argument about the creation of national armies in Germany and France). Instead, it stresses a kind of cold, technocratic heroism and engagement with the world and draws from science fiction and superhero stories (Gray 1994); it increasingly takes on the language and audit and algorithm culture (Besteman and Gusterson 2019; Graeber 2016). Unclassified military performance enhancement plans provide the structure of an ongoing story of technological desire, imagination, and creation, and give us an entrée point into how US military researchers dream of the kill-proof, invincible soldier. It is an updated version of a millennia-old story that continues to find purchase in the bodies of those we decide to sacrifice or exchange for gain and dominance, power, terrain, and treasure.

The military does not use the term *supersoldier*; rather, it uses terms like *warfighter* or *enhanced warfighter*. For civilians—and new soldiers inculcated in "Hollywood" conceptions of the supersoldier—these visions of US soldiers are of invincible, movie-like soldiers who cannot be harmed and who can perform the seemingly impossible. Peter Singer (2008) looks at how the military wants to draw from superhero comic books and science fiction to design and make supersoldiers, and Chris Hables Gray (1989, 1994) tracked this trend in the 1980s. These new soldiers never give up; they do not bleed, they kill with ruthless efficiency for a just and moral cause, and they suffer no consequences for their actions (see also Johanna Bourke's [1999] discussion of soldiers and war and Hollywood). The supersoldier is in many ways the imagined human equivalent of a drone. With a kind of all-seeing technology, the supersoldier-as-drone anticipates and preempts all threats. Each promises a vision of warfare that is safe and sanitized, with little risk or danger for either the human drone operator or the enhanced soldier (Gusterson 2016).

The body of the supersoldier is a blank slate of constant enhancement, improvement, and upgrades, a modular "system of systems" that can be reordered and configured for any and all contingencies on an "as needed" basis. As the site of anticipation and preemption, the body of the supersoldier becomes both the locus and the rationale of protection and production. It becomes the sign, and the space, and the instrument of national defense and offense in the name of protection. The supersoldier allows us to think that we can control the future through the control of the body of the soldier in the present. And it lets us think that we can put out the smoke of future fires while simultaneously being the ones who set the fires we think we need. As the personification of anticipation and preemption, they vouchsafe a future we think is ours. The way we imagine and envision soldiers is a look into the future—not just of the technology, but a look into an imagined and hoped-for future of domination. The image of the enhanced soldier is not necessarily simply one of survivability but one of control—control before, during, and after combat. It is an image of certainty and predictability, and, perhaps most importantly, an image of warfare devoid of trauma, blood, wounding, pain, and death.

TWO

The Superman Solution

The New Man, Superheroes, and the Supersoldier

A generation that had gone to school on a horse-drawn
streetcar now stood under the open sky in a countryside in
which nothing remained unchanged but the clouds, and
beneath these clouds, in a force field of destructive torrents
and explosions, was the tiny, fragile human body.

» **Walter Benjamin**, *The Storyteller*

While the projects I examine later in the book, like Robert Rigg's Soldier of
the Futurarmy, Marion Sulzberger's Idiophylactic Soldier, and subsequent
US military projects like the Objective Force Warrior, the Future Force
Warrior, and the Future Combat System, as well as DARPA's Inner Armor
program, are very much a part of the Cold War legacy and contemporary
concerns with the US military's global engagements, these projects and
visions are also part of the larger twentieth-century trends, concerns, and
imaginations of a "machine-like" body and a "New Man" and superhero
resistant to stress and trauma, able to provide substantial amounts of labor
on the battlefield or in the factory. Imagining the New Man as an inorganic
machine is a method of imagining ways to counter the innate frailty of the
organic body.

Industrialization and industrial warfare provided the pressures and rationales for the development of a New Man as both internally armored
laborer and internally armored warrior. The carnage of the factory and the

carnage of the battlefield called for the development of a "man-machine" that could withstand the new stresses of modernity and the modern battlefield. The devastation wrought by new weapons systems and military technologies on bodies and psyches during World War I prompted the rethinking of the soldier from the inside out. The rethinking of the soldier, though, took part mainly on the far right and was seen as an opportunity to conceive of a New Man who not only could withstand war but also loved war and violence, and who could do more on the battlefield than "normal" soldiers. While contemporary images and designs for US supersoldiers might seem "new" in the sense of advances and leaps forward in military biomedical research, genomics, synthetic biology, and other forms of biotechnology, the goals of internally armoring and modulating the US supersoldier are firmly planted in twentieth-century fascist and communist dreams and desires of "men of steel," even if they are not overtly or directly linked to fascism or communism.

What follows is cautionary: my point here is to expand our ideas of what the "supersoldier" is, its history, and the possible social, cultural, and political legacies and ramifications of military performance enhancement research based on an analysis of the history and often-hidden subtexts and connections of these projects. US military medical personnel or researchers are not all patently fascists—or communists, for that matter—but US biomedical research seems at times to skirt fascist and communist militarism's conceptions of the heroic New Man and approach to the suppression of weakness and emotions, and the cultivation of ways of engaging and experiencing the world, but now developed and cultivated through biomedical and pharmacological means. US military biomedical performance enhancement research is concerned with the creation of "supersoldiers" as antidotes to perceptions of national and individual weakness on and off the battlefield. That is, soldiers have to be made strong enough to survive multiple deployments, and so ensure the strength and superiority of US foreign and military policies. They also need to be made strong enough to survive leaving the military and returning to civilian life. But the best of intentions around protection and safety can quickly outrun the desires and goals of the scientists and researchers charged with developing new forms of biomedical armor for soldiers if there is not an awareness of how military biomedicine is situated in cultural, political, and historical contexts. Military performance enhancement research does not happen in a sterile, laboratory-like vacuum detached from social worlds, and images and ideas that might seem new and novel can often be traced back to earlier troubling cultural and historical precedents.

Ideas of the New Man—at least in military terms—were most pronounced in fascist thought and imagery, though the New Man of communism was an important trope in early Soviet military thought and propaganda. The New Soviet Man was more focused on labor and overcoming the natural world than war and combat. Pre–World War I industrialists and those in charge of factories faced the same kinds of questions that the military increasingly faced in the age of industrialized warfare: How do you extract more labor from the worker in increasingly adverse and arduous conditions? How can you make the worker—the soldier—work longer, faster, and more efficiently on a consistent basis under increasingly dangerous conditions, and make him resilient to the damaging effects of his labor, his equipment, and his work environment? As Maurizia Boscagli writes about the diminution of physical strength by the machine between the turn of the century and World War I, "Masculine corporality had been structured to signify strength and energy in the very period when these qualities were being appropriated by machines—hence the modernist desire to signify the body as a mechanical apparatus, to not simply emulate and challenge technology but instead to identify with it" (1996, 129).

The solution to the erosion of masculinity and strength brought about by mechanization is to somehow make soldiers and workers seem more like the machines they use, mimicking the durability and unquestioning and unflagging performance of inanimate technologies. But how do you in turn address the body as a machine, with all the questions and concerns about breakdown and repair that you would have to deal with if dealing with a machine, when it is really still made of flesh and blood? Metaphors do not bleed and suffer.

———

The New Man of early twentieth-century fascism, communism—and to some extent capitalism—represented both an ideal human and the man of a utopian future (Berman 1975; Skradol 2009, 41). The man-machine was part of a much wider cultural and aesthetic trend in Europe during the late nineteenth and early twentieth centuries that focused on the mechanization of the body, the body-as-machine, and the body transformed by modernity and industrialization (Ben-Ghiat 2004; Biro 1994; Boscagli 1996; Braudy 2003; Cheng 2009; Eksteins 2000; Jarvis 2004; Mosse 1990, 1996a; Rabin-bach 1992). The ideal of the internally armored body—a body incorporating a mechanized, machinelike disposition, functionality, and certainty of performance, and one immune to pain and suffering—was central to the man-machine and the New Man of both fascism and communism (McCallum 2018; Mosse 1990, 1996a, 1996b; Spotts 2004). Emerging at a time when industrialization and mechanization came to dominate everyday life, the New Man of fascism and communism can be seen as an attempt to incorporate Taylorist notions of orderability, functionality, and regularity into the military and into soldiers' and workers' bodies (Boscagli 1996, 146).

The Soviet New Man as a "man of steel" was a much more positive, utopian version of the New Man, with a focus on labor as a way to bring about an ideal society and ideal future through the transformative effects of his labor and industrial production; indeed, "Stalin" means "steel," as he was to be the literal embodiment of the Soviet man of steel and "Hero of Labor" (Haynes 2003; Kelly 2016; McCallum 2018; Soboleva 2017; Vujošević 2017). The focus on the New Man and labor is important, however, as similar concerns and desires around the extraction of more labor and combat power arise around US military performance enhancement technologies. There were portrayals of the Soviet soldier as a hero before World War II, and a kind of "cult of war" arose around soldiers after World War II (Haynes 2003; McCallum 2018). Soviet portrayals of the New Man as a soldier—particularly after 1945—focused more on nuanced understandings of war and trauma and comradeship, in contradistinction to earlier fascist portrayals and conceptions of the New Man/soldier as all-conquering hero (McCallum 2018).

In contrast, with its explicit embrace of war and violence, fascism celebrated the armored body of the steely soldier as a way of conquering "inferior" humans and overcoming undesirable traits like weakness, "softness," and laziness (Ben-Ghiat 2004, 173). The supersoldier of fascism was a soldier imagined to have a metallized and steeled body, a body made hyperstrong and hyperviolent through the cultivation of a political/ideological "will." This was a body that felt little or no pain, had no remorse or memory, and was focused solely on orders and the task at hand; it was the soldier as a kind of nonhuman, compliant machine (Gray 1989, 1994).

The New Man as soldier was an image of the soldier as overlord, of future combat devoid of trauma, emotion, and possibly death for the soldier; it was a (proto)fascist dystopian fantasy of unchecked, joyful violence and domination. Protofascist conceptions of the New Man drew on many sources; in its militarized forms, it had roots in the prewar German *Wandervogel* (Rovers), a youth movement that took on an increasingly nationalist and militarist character prior to World War I (Mann 2004, 150–51; Waite 1952), and the direct experiences of German storm troopers during World War I, who were armed with the latest in destructive technology and trained to infiltrate enemy trench systems. The Italian Futurists played a key role in popularizing protofascist images and conceptions of the "man-machine" and warfare during and after World War I (Braudy 2003, 402–3). In *War, the World's Only Hygiene* (1911–15), the Italian Futurist author Filippo Tommaso Marinetti (see figure 2.1) describes a New Man based on the machine, "multiplied by the motor," without memory, and composed of both reason and "the lust for danger and daily heroism" (Marinetti 1971, as quoted in Boscagli 1996, 137). Indeed, Boscagli argues that the "Futurist man-machine is the model of a new technological-military body devoid of individuality. By virtue of his mechanical qualities he is capable of accomplishing more incredible and heroic deeds than a normal human being" (132). As Berman notes of the Italian Futurists and their celebration of new technologies to remake the world, this reimagining and remaking meant that some important human emotions would have to die: "We look for the creation of a nonhuman type in whom moral suffering, goodness of heart, affection, and love, those corrosive poisons of vital energy, interrupters of our powerful bodily electricity, will be abolished" (1975, 25). But, as Berman notes, the Italian Futurists threw themselves into World War I ("war, the world's only hygiene"), and within the span of two years, the leaders of Futurism were dead, killed in battle "by the machines they loved" (26).

The internally armored soldier of World War I was the offspring—in Marinetti's sense—of a symbiotic relationship between warfare and technology: with the increased lethality of weapons came a response aimed toward an increased internal mechanization and anesthetization of the body to offset the fear of these new technologies. The war experiences of these soldiers were the experiences of "Nietzschean bare-chested men . . . against the full force of the weaponry of a technological age" (Jay Baird, quoted in Fritz 1996, 687). To use the language of military cybernetics, "a self-fulfilling positive feedback loop" (DeLanda 1991, 49) was created in order to both employ and cope with the effects of these weapons: an increase in the destructive power of weaponry calls for an increase in defensive technology and an ever-increasingly hardened body, which prompts a further increase in destructive power to overcome these countermeasures, and so forth.

Where German and Italian fascism and Soviet communism envisioned a hardened supersoldier/worker created through propaganda and the

Figure 2.1 Filippo Tommaso Marinetti, 1917.

cultivation of "willpower" as a kind of inner armor and inner strength, the US now imagines hard, resilient soldiers produced methodically, carefully, and predictably through pharmacology and internally embedded bio-technologies. Technological integration and transformation and the development of inner strength and "inner armor" are also the central concern of current biomedical research programs in the US military. The New Man represented both an ideal human and the man of a utopian future (Berman 1975; Skradol 2009, 41). The New Man as supersoldier is an image of a future form of combat without fear and feeling, and death deferred for the soldier; it was a kind of military utopian fantasy of violence unfettered and unleashed. Consider the following observations by Ernst Jünger, World War I German storm trooper, postwar far right-wing *Freikorps* paramilitary member, and influential author and war theorist (see figure 2.2), describing the emergence of the New Man in World War I.

> I am overcome with recognition: this is the new man, the storm pioneer, the elite of Central Europe. A whole new race, smart, strong, and filled with will. What reveals itself here as a vision will tomorrow be the axis around which life revolves still faster and faster. . . . The glowing twilight of a declining age is at once a dawn in which one arms oneself for new, for harder battles. Far behind, the gigantic cities, the hosts of machines, the empires, whose inner bonds have been rent in the storm,

Figure 2.2 Ernst Jünger (*left*), 73rd Hanoverian Fusilier Regiment, preparing for a trench raid, 1917.

await the new men, the cunning, battle-tested men who are ruthless toward themselves and others. This war is not the end but the prelude to violence. ([1922] 1994, 19)

Yet Jünger was also painfully aware of the emotional impact of this new kind of war on soldiers, writing in his memoir of World War I combat, *In Stahlgewittern* (*Storm of Steel*), "the state, which relieves us of our responsibility, cannot take away our remorse; we must exercise it. Sorrow, regret, pursued me deep into my dreams" ([1920] 2003).

Almost seventy years later, as the US military was beginning to intensify efforts to design its version of the New Man based on the biomedical transformation of the soldier, Col. Frederick W. Timmerman Jr. of the US Army's Center for Army Leadership wrote: "In a physiological sense, when needed, soldiers may actually appear to be three miles tall and twenty miles wide. Of course, in a true physical sense nothing will have changed. Rather, by transforming the way technology is applied, by looking at the problem from a biological perspective—focusing on transforming and extending the soldier's physiological capabilities . . . the problem from this perspective then becomes—how do you employ technology to extend the soldier's natural biological capabilities (the superman solution)?" (1987, 51; see also Gray 1997, 210). Timmerman's statement evokes the dystopian vision of the New Man/soldier of Jünger's prose. And both passages make clear that the "normal" human body—the body without specific improvement or modification—is not up to the task of combat success, much less survival, and that a new vision of the soldier, and a new kind of anticipatory intervention in the lives and bodies of soldiers, is what will allow them to survive and win on the battlefield. Jünger and Timmerman point to the need to manipulate the soldier's biology, either to make him "merciless to himself and to others" or by "transforming and extending the soldier's physiological capabilities." The new human that Jünger dreamed of was also the new soldier of the future and future warfare, as he was quick to realize. The Futurists' dream of the new "nonhuman" type has an eerie similarity to Jünger's New Man, who is "merciless to himself" and who must "excise" his own suffering, and to the possibilities of new biomedical and pharmacological possibilities of suppressing emotion and memory in soldiers (see chapter 7). According to Klaus Theweleit and his psychoanalysis of the fascist male, for the fascist man-machine, "instinctual life" is controlled and transformed into a "dynamic of regularized functions . . . devoid of feeling, powerful" (1987–89, 189; see also Gray 1997). The fascist body is a body with a "mechanized physique, with the psyche eliminated" (Theweleit 1987–89, 162). As Susan Buck-Morss describes it, the fascist body is a body that can be "measured against the norm," a "calculated and orderable" body constructed to withstand the stresses of modernity—or modern combat (1992, 33).

Jünger states that war requires an entirely new race, while Timmerman declares that the goal is to achieve a superman solution, and that this change will be achieved through a change and transformation of the biology of the soldier. For Jünger, the New Man represented the internally armored warrior male at the pinnacle of an emergent new ontological order, the New Man as overlord (Huyssen 1995, 8). Indeed, as Andreas Huyssen writes, "The new nationalist vision . . . was built around the metaphysically coded gestalt of the warrior-worker with the warrior's body constructed as the ultimate fighting machine. Jünger's description of the blood of youth confronting deadly matter on the battlefield and the fantasy of their interpenetration in 'streams of liquid metal' thus provides us with a genealogy of the T 1000 from *Terminator II*: the big white killer male, invincible and beyond organic death" (8). Jünger provides not only the genealogy for the T 1000 but, by implication, the genealogy for some of the visions and imaginations of US supersoldier projects: the internally armored, machinelike body of the implicitly white, male supersoldier, who, if a project like DARPA's Inner Armor ever came to fruition, could actually be "kill-proof" (see also McElya 2016 for a discussion of the Unknown Soldier at Arlington National Cemetery as implicitly white and male).

As Huyssen observes, Jünger's writing and fantasies of the New Man offered a way to cope with and protect against the traumatic memories of war, and were marked by the "attempt to forget that tiny, fragile human body, or rather, to equip it with an impenetrable armor protecting it against the memory of the traumatic experience of the trenches" (1993, 12). Jünger was overwhelmed by the destructive forces of modernity on the battlefield, resulting in a repudiation of his own body as organic and vulnerable (13). Military enhancement projects and plans to use pharmaceuticals to block out and modulate traumatic memories from the battlefield can be seen as a continuation of Jünger's attempts to forget the tiny, fragile human body, equip it with impenetrable armor, and provide a recognition and renunciation of the fragility of the organic body.

Imaginations and desired potentials of the US supersoldier lie somewhere between the fascist New Man and the Soviet New Man—or rather, the US supersoldier is a kind of amalgamation of the two: merciless toward himself in combat and in terms of the suppression of weakness but also the good "hero of labor," providing ever-increasing amounts of combat power and labor on and off the battlefield. While the US military's biomedical body problem is about labor, it is also about political representation and the optics of supersoldier research. Wittingly or not, the authoritarian/fascist body often becomes the spectral template of a kind of military medicine and medical ideology that mimics aspects of fascism in its desire to produce hardened, kill-proof, unfeeling soldiers. The need to repress fear, pain, and memory in the face of increasingly deadly military technologies drives the soldier more closely to desiring to be just like the machines trying to kill him. This is not just about the body but about memory and design and medicine and production, with the end point being a body that can perform the horrible labor and work of war without the physical, emotional, or moral costs. Military performance enhancements can preempt fascist ideas and ideological constructions of the body and ideas of "will" by preloading the body and premaking the body through biotechnology. It might mimic the armored body of fascism, but it could become a kind of fascism through technology that is not dependent on overt politics, experience, or will, but has the essence of distilled experience implanted in it. While Jünger and Marinetti are not the intellectual grandfathers of US military performance enhancement research, their concerns with combat and violence and the fragility of the tiny, organic human on the battlefield are predecessors of similar US concerns. The problem is that Jünger and Marinetti's solutions to these concerns led to a vision of a hypermilitarized society ruled by new men, birthed by the battlefield. The potential is that US "skin-in" solutions could easily become a kind of biopolitical "Triumph of the Pill"—without perhaps the explicit political horrors of fascism but nonetheless troubling and problematic. New forms of psychopharmacology and biotechnology might be able to approximate earlier ideas of the armored body of the New Man and the modulation and suppression of pain and experience for political goals, or rather, these goals could be met through these drugs if there are not strict guidelines and ethics surrounding their deployment and usage. Timmerman's "superman solution" could easily become a dystopian biopolitical solution.

Captain America, Iron Man, and the Soldier as Superhero

As Jamon Halvaksz observes, superheroes are a form of modern mythology, or "supermythology," as he calls it, and play a vital role in how we think about ourselves, the future, and our lived experiences: "Superheroes are really a modern mythology, or *supermythology*, offering moral and sociological instruction and instilling a sense of awe in their target demographic. Through story, artistry, and imagination, comic books bring to life alternative visions of our past, present, and future. They reflect our lived experience, even as they offer guidance into alternative assemblages of reality" (2016).

Like earlier conceptions of the New Man of fascism and communism, US military supersoldier projects act as a supermythology, often resembling and reading like a story about superheroes in a comic book or action movie. We can imagine ourselves as the military superheroes, defeating the enemy with ease and protecting our families and homeland from all threats, both human and nonhuman. Military enhancement projects both draw from and reinforce ideas about superheroes and in so doing shape how we see potential supersoldiers and their capabilities. For H. Christian Breede, Captain America and Iron Man are examples of the problems and potentials of "skin-in" and "skin-out" technologies: "The differences between two of Marvel comics' most popular superheroes—Captain America

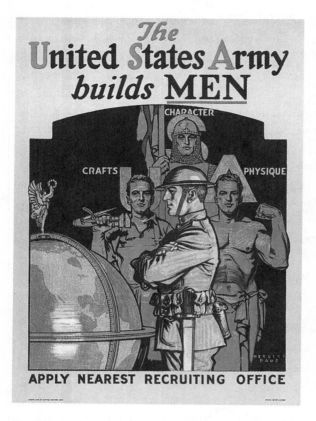

Figure 2.3 Herbert Andrew Paus, "The United States Army Builds Men." US Army recruiting poster, 1917.

and Iron Man—capture the primary dichotomy facing research into improving the survivability and effectiveness of soldiers today. Where Iron Man puts on a suit of armor—essentially an exo-skeleton, Captain America has been enhanced in ways that go beyond simply donning and doffing equipment. Which way is better suited to maintaining the connection between soldier and society?" (2017, 8).

We can play out the plot of the war story in our mind, write the heroic narrative, and imagine that we are part of the "good guys" fighting the global peril of the "bad guys" (the current US military is very fond of calling the enemy "the bad guys"). And we can imagine the glory and fame heaped upon us after we are victorious. As Timmerman writes, the primary role of the soldier is to "create images of strength"; the soldier-as-superhero becomes the "psychological reference point" for a society to resist the disin-

Figure 2.4 "In the Face of Obstacles—Courage." US Army poster, World War II.

tegration of its will (1987, 50). These images and reports/stories are not just make-believe, "just so" stories: they impact—and will impact—the lives of soldiers, their families, their community, and their enemies, and have political-economic ramifications far beyond the impact of "mere" warrior myths. They might shape and be shaped by notions of military masculinity, but the effects of these projects go far beyond identity politics: they inform and shape military strategy and politics and shape how the US government decides to intervene around the world.

Early propaganda images of the US soldier from World War I and World War II focused on the strong and virile soldier and included men with bulging muscles and hardened bodies, images that were very much in keeping with modernist notions of the New Man and the man-as-machine (see figure 2.3). Christina Jarvis (2004) discusses the use of muscular imagery to produce and promote a kind of resolute, and ultimately victorious, US soldier. These bodies were enhanced not so much by technology as by ideology, and the strong, muscular bodies of the soldier were the stand-ins for the strong, muscular state. Pumped by ideology and will, the soldier was the message and the promise of dominance and victory (see figure 2.4).

While these posters and images promoted the idea of the muscular and undefeatable US soldier, they were also personalized. The GI might have been standardized and "government issue," but in an effort to make them seem like the "everyman" citizen-soldier, they were made human. But as US soldiers have become more and more identified with technology, this personalization has disappeared. In keeping with current security protocols, soldiers—like police—are portrayed as anonymous entities, often with their faces covered and identifiers removed.

The superhero represents the ability to overcome and defeat current and imagined/future foes, threats, and adversaries; the superhero is often the might of the state, condensed and congealed into human (or humanoid) form. The most obvious portrayal of the superhero dream of the supersoldier in the US context is Captain America (see figure 2.5). Appearing in 1941, Captain America was a metaphor for the weak man and weak state going into overdrive to rise up and defeat an existential threat and combat an extremely toxic militarized masculinity in the form of Nazism. Captain America is also a kind of high-modernist response to the armored body of fascism—the body pumped up on ideology and "will"—and the quintessential American response and belief in (bio)technology to save the day. Superman might have been the man of steel, but he was still an "alien"; Steve Rogers is a "real" American, the autochthonous hero rising up to save the nation-state, the weak made strong through American military medical science.

Postwar US comic books embraced the tough, cynical, battle-weary GI in the form of SGT Rock and The Losers. Unlike superheroes or imaginary supersoldiers, SGT Rock and The Losers followed US soldiers through World War II and at least tried to show some of the misery, horror, and trauma of war rather than a clean, sanitized, and propaganda-driven image of the US soldier. These soldiers were still exemplary soldiers, however, drawing on almost superhuman reserves of strength and fortitude, not to mention superior intelligence and cunning, to survive combat.

Previous incarnations of the strong, virile US soldier included men with bulging muscles and hardened bodies. While technology was clearly present in early portrayals of US soldiers, it was more of a presentation of the body on display, the strong body of the soldier as the strong body of

Figure 2.5 Captain America movie poster, 2011.

the state. It was a "drilled" and hardened body of the soldier that all could see—not the technology—that was important (Jarvis 2004). In contrast, modern US soldiers are portrayed as technological marvels: you do not see the actual physical body of the soldier; you see technology and equipment that replaces the body, and you read/hear about drugs that make the weak body strong and the fragile body armored. How then do you portray an "enhanced" body if the body is not enhanced by political/economic ideology and an overt ideological sign, as is the case for most portrayals of the armored, "steeled" male body from World Wars I and II and the early to mid-twentieth century? In other words, if the enhancement is seen as "biomedical" and not ideological—internal versus explicitly external and on display—how do we go about portraying or imagining this type of soldier? In many ways, the technologies "fill in" for the soldier, and the soldier as "system of systems" is then just a platform for the display of new technologies. For enhanced US soldiers, "biomedicine" becomes a kind of unquestionable and unmarked ideology and sign of care and protection.

While "skin-in" solutions will constitute the ultimate soldier enhancement, they are part of a great suite of technologies and plans to create supersoldiers. Enhancing the body of the soldier allows for the maximum utility of "skin-out" solutions: anyone can put on external technologies, but only enhanced soldiers will be able to fully maximize and use these technologies. Portraying "men of steel" means portraying and imagining both skin-in and skin-out forms of the metalized/armored body. Contemporary Hollywood films and characters like Captain America, Iron Man, Robocop, the Terminator, and others that trade in portrayals of enhanced supersoldiers, cyborgs, and superheroes all fuel our imagination and perception of what an enhanced soldier might be capable of, what they might look like, and what they might mean for us (Bourke 1999; Gray 1994; Singer 2008; Zehr 2018). But we also need to look at the military's plans for enhanced soldiers, how they view biotechnology and the body, battlefield stressors, future war and combat, and the actual needs of soldiers in terms of what it is like to be in combat, on the battlefield, and afterward. With project names like Land Warrior, Objective Force Warrior, and Future Force Warrior, the military taps into the imaginative semantic world of the superhero, allowing potential soldiers—future warriors—to imagine themselves as the stars and heroes of their own high-tech military epic. It might be fun to watch the movies and read the comic books, but we need to look at the military's plans, needs, and desires before we can start making sense of the vast array of performance enhancement projects currently underway. Some of this might mimic or draw from science fiction and Hollywood blockbusters, but much of it might be very different. Video games might be good for recruiting or creating interest in the military (Maradin 2013; Stahl 2006; Mike Thompson [2008] 2019), but they are not necessarily an accurate portrayal of military reality. You can also see how artists and others imagine supersoldiers and often confuse the images from those of "superheroes" to how the military actually imagines and designs soldiers.

The importance of projecting images of strength and invincibility is not lost on the US military. As Timmerman wrote,

> A primary role for soldiers should be to create images of strength and sustain the psychological reference points needed by society to resist an opponent's efforts to disintegrate its will. In this way, soldiers become a psychological as well as a physical barrier between the society and its enemies. . . . Concerning the psychological role, what soldiers do or whom they can kill have never been as important as whom their potential enemy thinks they can kill, and the positive regard and support their own society has for them. War has always been a matter of images.

That is what makes its psychological character so compelling. Soldiers who are provided the technology, skill and support to mold their image as needed for a given situation or threat will then have a definite advantage. In the mind of their enemy, they will possess the capability to make the enemy's worst nightmare come true. Arrayed behind the soldier, technology can then be used to degrade a potential opponent's ability to sort out what is real or imaginary in the environment. (1987, 50)

While the use of biomedicine in performance enhancement research is a scientific problem, subject to political critique, it is also one of aesthetics. Susan Buck-Morss highlights the importance of understanding "aesthetics"—*aisthetikos*—in the original definition of the term: that is, as concerned with the body's sensory capabilities and the reception of the world through tactility, emotion, and experience (Buck-Morss 1992, 18; see also Bickford 2010, 2011; Feldman 1994; MacLeish 2012). In "The Ideology of the Aesthetic," Eagleton writes that the central focus of aesthetics is the "manipulation of the body through 'manners'": "What matters in aesthetics is not art, but this whole project in reconstructing the human subject from the inside, informing its subtlest affections and bodily responses with this law which is not a law" (1989, 78). It is the "art of the possible."

Perhaps another way to think about this is that we can imagine very different kinds of politics and representations of the armored body around performance enhancement, but the effects might be the same. As Benjamin (1968) made clear, there is a tendency toward fascism when you aestheticize violence. States use both art—in the sense of imagining, designing, and portraying soldiers, and causing soldiers and civilians to imagine themselves as (potential) supersoldiers—and medicine as forms of aesthetics and anesthetics to create, manipulate, and control the body of the soldier, to make manipulation and discipline and biomedical enhancement seem natural, as the law that is not a law. Both medicine and manners affect the actions and behavior of the individual by causing her to feel a sense of protection: from either physical harm or social approbation. In a military setting, manners can be considered analogous to drill and ceremony, intensive training, and learning how to act and react tactically on the battlefield; that is, how the soldier learns to act and hold his body in an unthinking, naturalized way and learns to accept himself as a part of the "mass." As such, both art and medicine are a form of "armor" for the individual, particularly for the soldier. Aesthetics—in the sense discussed by Buck-Morss and Eagleton—is an instrument of power directed at the body in order to create the military body: it is the use of ritual as a form of power, as a form of coercion and control designed to create internally armored soldiers, to instill an anesthetic—a sense of "will"—to overcome hardship, fear, and terror. Aesthetics are used to bring about both the portrayal and the shaping of the militarily desirable body, and the somatization of internal, psychological "armor." The development of aestheticized and anesthetized soldiers occurs within specific regimes of power, politics, and history; it is an intentional project on the part of the state. The internally armored soldier can be seen as a metonym of the armored state, perhaps as the end result of the state's statement on how it sees its own (in)security, as played out in the bodies of its soldiers. This entails a sort of "double" armoring: the soldier is armored to such a degree that she does not feel pain or register emotion, and civilians are to be protected from the realities of war and conflict in order to continue sending soldiers to the military.

As a rhetorical device or metaphor, the "supersoldier" excites and terrifies because it represents superiority, mastery, and deathlessness without remorse or sanction; the internally and externally armored body creates the soldier that potentially transcends norms, both physical and moral, and is allowed and sanctioned by the state to transcend these norms. And perhaps most disturbingly, the supersoldier can represent an impossible desire and fantasy to kill and destroy without harm or cost to the soldier or society.

Supersoldiers represent both the ideal of citizenship and the ideal of technology: the best and most selfless citizens rising up to defend the nation-state, protected—and willing to volunteer their bodies for enhancement and protection—by the best technology the state can produce because it is through this production and the bodies and lives of soldiers that the state protects and perpetuates itself. They represent a kind of militarized biological citizenship based on the willingness of the civilian to allow himself to be enhanced for military purposes (Heath, Rapp, and Taussig 2007; Kahn 2014; Petryna 2003; Rabinow 1996; Rabinow and Bennett 2009; Rose 2007; Rose and Novas 2005).

We can read and understand US supersoldier projects as a kind of national narrative and sociotechnical imaginary of strength and invincibility, as a story about the invulnerable soldier who will always be a hero and never a coward. It is a vision of an already armored and protected future, a future made secure by advances in the present. We can look at the narrative thread of the "supersoldier" over time and place it within various socioeconomic, cultural, and security eras and epistemes (Foucault 2003). The stories are about the strong soldier, about ethics, about transformation and the shaping of the soldier's body to fit national security needs. The stories tell us how US military researchers and officials imagine the supersoldier, what she is to be and become: "There's Strong. Then there's Army Strong." Anodyne reports on biomedical progress in environmental protection for the soldier, hyperhydration, vaccinations, and metabolic dominance mark the fantasies of protection, heroism, perfection, invulnerability, invincibility, deathlessness, control, predictability, bloodlessness, and victory. Now, and perhaps literally through DNA manipulation, genomics, synthetic biology, neuro-implants, and performance enhancement drugs, the US military is moving into position to produce the kinds of men—and women—it wants through biotechnology, and not just through ideology, training, and the cultivation of "will" (Braun, von Hlatky, and Nossal 2017; Cavanagh 2018; Kamieński 2016a, 2016b; Moreno 2012).

The supersoldier is intended as a "shock and awe" iteration of the soldier and an image of deterrence personified: we are to view them and immediately know and understand that they have been enhanced to such a degree as to make them invincible—to fight them would be folly and certain death; as Jünger imagined, cities and people would be "torn asunder" by the New Man. Descriptions like "overmatch," "dominance," "20x effects," "force multiplier," and "kill-proof" conjure an idea of the invincible US soldier, built and supported by superior biomedical and military technology. We design weapons systems to produce shocking and awe-inspiring effects, and this carries over to the individual soldier as well. We are to be shocked by them in terms of their capabilities, and in awe of what they are, what they represent, and what they can do. We can marvel at what they are capable of, what they can endure, and at the violence they wield and deploy. And we can feel confident and safe and protected because they are on watch and they are our superheroes. We no longer talk about GIs: we talk about warriors.

Supersoldiers also provide another vision of the future and hold another kind of fascination for us. They are examples of what might be possible for humans to become, a stand-in for ourselves and what we could possibly be and do. Who does not want to run as fast as a cheetah, jump 12 feet vertically, or see in the dark? Or be able to think more quickly and efficiently, to have a brain that acts like a "computer"? We see ourselves and our future possible selves in the enhanced soldier, initially focusing on the positive, "wouldn't it be cool if . . ." aspects of human enhancement technologies. Underneath the coolness factor, however, is an undercurrent of dread or foreboding of these possibilities. I would like to have these capabilities, but do I want others to have them? Can I live with others having capabilities that I do not have, capabilities that might give them advantages over me that they would not normally have? Enhancement might be well and good on the battlefield, but they pose an array of ethical, cultural, and political issues off the battlefield. As David Malet writes, even seemingly simple questions, such as the responsibilities of states to retired augmented soldiers, or in the case of irreversible enhancements, questions of proprietary law and ownership, will require new doctrines (2016, 163).

We want our soldiers to be human, and survive as humans, albeit as some kind of superhuman that is still just like us, or at least conforms to a kind of sentimental notion of the everyman. Perhaps this is why Superman posed as the milquetoast Clark Kent, boring suit and nerdy glasses as signifiers of unenhancement. Performance enhancements, such as robotic implants, computer chips, and so on, fuel a fantasy of the posthuman, or nonhuman, or a soldier beyond the pale. We might be enraptured by the science fiction nature of such a soldier, but we are also frightened by the Frankenstein-like quality of the soldier who defies neat categories of the human and the nonhuman.

As past images and imaginations of the armored New Man show, we are not in completely new terrain: maybe the brand phrase "Shock and Awe," perhaps, or the project names, such as Future Force Warrior, but not the sentiment or the intention. To frighten your enemy into submission is the surest way to victory, a kind of counting coup that trumps pure violence. The image and the rhetoric of the supersoldier are the power and violence of the mythic soldier: this is a militarized aesthetic that both enhances and numbs, heightens and frightens, hopefully ensuring submission and victory at the mere thought or sight of the soldier. "Shock and Awe" is the aesthetic and anesthetic of not just smart bombs and drones but the post–Cold War era of the supersoldier as well. The portrayal and language are a kind of drug, perhaps an irresistible drug: the message is intended to be as narcotic and addictive as the projects, interventions, and promises themselves. These images and visions are to both numb us to the horrors of war and excite us about the possibilities of war as an ever-finer, more excellent game that we can anticipate, control, and win.

THREE

Government (T)Issue

Military Medicine, Performance Enhancement, and the Biology of the Soldier

Soldiers having no physical, physiological, or cognitive limitations will be key to survival and operational dominance in the future.

» **Michael Goldblatt**, former director, US Defense
Sciences Office

When we think about military medicine, we generally think about how it can save soldiers (and civilians), or rather, how it intervenes after the fact, after injury and trauma, to care for wounded soldiers (see Finley 2011; Messinger 2010; Terry 2017; Wool 2015; see also Geroulanos and Meyers 2018 on military medicine, science, and fragmentation in World War I). We usually do not pay attention to the ways in which military medicine and design come together to make soldiers beforehand. Military medicine—in the sense of a directed application of medicine and not a specific intervention as a moment of healing—also becomes a way of "reading" military anxiety, anticipation, and intentions, a way of reading concerns about soldier's health and deployability, and a way of reading how technology might be applied to solve certain military problems or allow the military to cope with problems it imagines it will have in the near future.

Military medicine is a vast system of care, a system providing health and security to US soldiers (as well as to their families, and those who qualify for access to US military medical facilities). When we think of the military as a care setting (Hardon and Sanabria 2017, 124), we usually think of it in terms of the care of wounded soldiers and veterans (Messinger 2010; Terry 2017; Wool 2015) or in the everyday care of soldiers as they go about their missions and daily duty (every day, soldiers report for "sick call" to be seen for a variety of ailments and injuries). But the military is also a care setting in the sense of developing and deploying "care" as an operative logic, as something that can be used to be protective, productive, and compelling. Military medicine is predicated on the development of prophylactic care measures to ensure that soldiers are ready—and through knowing they are cared for, willing—to go into combat and successfully carry out their mission. Care is also about caring for them after combat, but care is a key principle in the precombat making of soldiers and the process of turning a civilian into a soldier. As an avenue of intervention, care provides the rationale that opens up and permits the military's redesign and manipulation of the soldier's body. Of course, not all military care is malign, but care presents opportunities for medical interventions that are perhaps more neutral than completely benign. Care for the soldier helps drive issues of preemption: to fully care for the soldier is to fully imagine and preempt every and all threat to the soldier's health and well-being. In this sense, care is productive: it is the justification for biomedical interventions in the body of the soldier, the precursor for the development of radical technologies of biomedical protection and security in the form of performance enhancements.

In this chapter, I examine how the US military imagines and links questions of care, anticipation, and preemption to military medicine and the ways it imagines biomedical enhancements as a way to identify organic weakness and transform it into something akin to inorganic strength. Military care and the development of biomedical forms of protection and enhancement entail a concern with risk, not just for the soldier but for the state as well. Anthony Giddens describes modernity as a "culture of risk" (1991, 3–5). In this sense, "care" is about mitigating and modulating a culture of risk, be it industrial or martial. Military performance enhancements are indicative of the military's concern for risk and attempts to develop "cures" for risky environments and actions. But enhancements are productive: new enhancements will fuel and create new forms of risk, creating a feedback loop. Performance enhancements are a kind of antidote to the stresses of (post)modernity, a way to imagine how the soldier can extract more success from risk while making risk almost riskless. Performance enhancement technologies are a way of commodifying and regulating risk through biomedicine, of fitting risk into military planning and action in a way that is at least, in theory, not disruptive.

Readiness: Deployability, Action, and the Work of War

Many people enlist in the US military as a way to move up a rung on the class ladder and access health care and other benefits they might not enjoy, for both themselves and their families (Bailey 2013; Christensen 2016; Perez 2006). When you join the US military, you sign a contract that binds you to the military, signing away fundamental rights to your body and health to military priorities and contingencies, all in the name of military "readiness" and deployability. But signing a contract to access opportunities gives the military the opportunity to access the interior of the soon-to-be soldier's body.

Soldiers, drawn from what is seen by the military as the weak and frail material of the civilian world, enter the military and are immediately subjected to a period of transformation designed to make them compliant, strong, resilient, and useful. Basic Training, and later Advanced Individual Training (AIT), mold the person into the soldier, breaking them down and building them back up again. But that is not enough: they must also be changed internally to meet the demands of combat and the myriad stressors and threats they will encounter. Once a soldier enters Basic Training, the military immediately asserts this right to the control of an enlistee's health through a series of vaccinations; these are to both protect the soldier and make the soldier deployable and useful. These vaccinations also dramatically make the point to the new recruit that the military will change their bodies to fit the needs of the military for combat. As such, the contract binds you to an agreement to allow the military to "protect" your health as it sees fit in order to protect and maintain national security. None of this is done on the fly or in a slapdash manner: all steps are planned out, and each step has a certain number of goals and criteria to be met to ensure civilians are becoming "proper" or useful soldiers.

The ability to fight-on-demand hinges on "readiness." Readiness is a US military term that encompasses a wide range of conditions and demands on the soldier. Fundamentally, it is the command concern with having a unit that is combat-ready and combat-capable at all times (Committee on Armed Services 2008). This means that the personnel in the unit must be ready to be deployed at a moment's notice or must be ready to conduct combat operations on demand. It also means that they must be physically fit and healthy enough to fight on demand. Unlike civilian medicine, US military medicine is highly instrumental, primarily concerned with maximizing the usefulness and deployability—the readiness—of soldiers. According to Dan, a US military doctor: "You want to make soldiers into lean, green, fighting machines. And you want to turn them into work horses." Jerry, another medical officer, told me: "There are a lot of things that are important in the military—equipment, logistics, you name it. But the most important thing? Readiness. Everything else is measured from that."

Military performance enhancements are focused on imagining how to make the body useful at all times for the military and mitigating possible future negative influences and stressors on performance. Marion Sulzberger, the dermatologist and military researcher who developed the "Idiophylactic Soldier" (1962b) in the early 1960s (see chapter 5), was very clear that enhancements were not just about protection but also about labor and extracting as much work from soldiers as possible.

The drive behind modifying or enhancing a soldier is to preclude certain kinds of actions and responses in the future; enhancements are intended to prevent a degradation of combat/labor ability or functioning, based on anticipated events, stimuli, stressors, and biological/cognitive autonomic responses. If the soldier is the weakest part of the system, then the entire system is at risk. This is not to say that all enhancements are predicated on a negative, but to say that enhancements are about overcoming "normal" responses to things that would inhibit the unenhanced soldier from operating or carrying out the mission. The goal of military performance enhancement is not necessarily to protect soldiers as human beings but to protect them as "military humans," increase their dependability during a mission, protect the state's investment in the combat and labor power of the soldier, and increase their utility and durability on and off the battlefield.

These sorts of medical interventions create a kind of double-bind: they may in fact save soldiers' lives but in so doing will enable the military to continue to deploy soldiers, and so continue to expose them to harm. While touted as "performance enhancement" measures for soldiers, a possible problem with these measures is that they might in fact force and compel soldiers to perform, and perform, and perform again; they could ultimately be not so much technologies of "performance enhancement" as "performance compulsion." What may seem like a positive, life-saving measure might in fact simply be another way—though perhaps also a positive medical intervention—of making soldiers fight, of ensuring compliance and deployability, and of harnessing a "resource" for national security and policy purposes. "Protection" is a way to bind the soldier to the military; "we will protect you" is in many ways just another way of saying "we will compel you."

Military Medicine: Prevention to Performance Enhancement

The recent and ongoing wars in Iraq and Afghanistan, and the War on Terrorism that sends US soldiers around the globe, continue to highlight the mental and physical frailty of soldiers and the devastating consequences of combat on soldiers who survive multiple deployments (Finley 2011; Hautzinger and Scandlyn 2014; Jauregui 2015; A. Jones 2013; Messinger 2010; Terry 2017; Wool 2015). While recent wars have highlighted the remarkable advances of military medicine and military combat training, they have also revealed major flaws in the post-1973 Abrams Doctrine US military, which ended conscription and inaugurated the "all-volunteer force": How exactly do you keep a volunteer military that was designed for a short, devastating, and incredibly violent war with the Warsaw Pact in combat for well over a decade? How do you keep soldiers mentally and physically fit and healthy after multiple combat deployments? Fundamentally, how do you keep an entire military force from medically breaking down? Situations "in the moment"—for example, the Cold War, or the wars in Iraq and Afghanistan—present certain kinds of military medical problems and demand certain kinds of responses and solutions. If contingencies require responses, how are bodies (re)configured and soldiers designed and (re)made to shape a response? How are preemption and anticipation linked to military performance enhancement? Contingencies compel the military to think about what a body can do, what a body can be made to do, and how technology will be employed to make soldiers do and survive the previously unimaginable. Masco writes that "a war of shock locates national security within the human nervous system itself" (2014, 19). Military performance enhancement attempts the same move, but this time, it is not just the nervous system but all biological systems of the soldier that are the targets. The "nervous system" is no longer simply a national security metaphor: the military means to literally transplant biomedical forms of anticipation and preemption into the nervous system and the body of the soldier.

There are long and ongoing debates around what constitutes an "enhancement," with debates focusing on the distinctions between enhancements and therapy, for example. Many of the definitions of military performance enhancement come from bioethicists or philosophers (see, e.g., Annas and Annas 2009; Braun, von Hlatky, and Nossal 2017; Caron 2018; Gross 2006; Gross and Carrick 2013; Mehlman 2004; Mehlman, Lin, and Abney 2013; Moreno 2012; Robbins 2013; Wolfendale 2008).

A focus on preemption and anticipation helps expand discussions of what constitutes a "legitimate" performance enhancement. While these debates are obviously important, they can sometimes obscure the political-cultural aspects of human performance enhancement. Viewed from these angles, military performance enhancement encompasses a much broader set of interventions, in that they are all in one way or another focused on "shaping the battlefield" and influencing future action. They also help us understand the rationale for soldier performance enhancement research in the present (see figure 3.1).

When thinking about military performance enhancement, US Army colonel Karl Friedl states that the key question is, "What aspect of human performance is so important that this one component should be enhanced beyond natural human capabilities, possibly compromising other components of performance?" (2015, S71). Patrick Lin, Maxwell Mehlman, and Keith Abney draw from bioethicist Eric Juengst's (1998) definition of "human enhancement" in their analysis of military performance enhancement: "an enhancement is a medical or biological intervention to the body designed to improve performance, appearance, or capability besides what is necessary to achieve, sustain, or restore health" (2013, 17). Interestingly, Lin, Mehlman, and Abney argue that vaccinations are not enhancements but a form of prevention (2013, 15). However, as I argue later, when looking at Sulzberger's Idiophylactic Soldier and DARPA's Inner Armor program, vaccinations are a form of enhancement, in that they enable and enhance the soldier's ability to be deployed around the world, resist disease, fight effectively, and remain on the battlefield. Soldiers must be enhanced through vaccines in order to be deployable and able to resist the infectious disease stressors of the battlefield; an unvaccinated soldier is fundamentally an unusable soldier.

While the US military has long enhanced its soldiers' performance via drug use—especially the use of amphetamines during World War II,

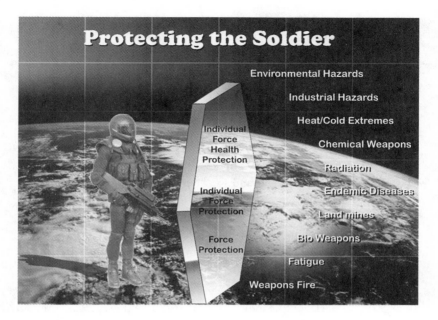

Figure 3.1 "Protecting the Soldier." Claude M. Bolton Jr., "ASA (ALT) Perspective: Military Medicine: Ready and Relevant," 2004.

Korea, Vietnam, and the Gulf Wars (Bergen-Cico 2012; Friedl 2015; Gray 1997; Kamieński 2016a, 2016b; Kan 2009; Mehlman 2014)—today's US military is keenly interested in a variety of new forms of human performance enhancement areas. The military's interest in biotechnology and performance enhancement is part and parcel of the recent "Revolution in Military Affairs" (RMA), the military's attempt to embrace new technologies to ensure dominance well into the twenty-first century. Some of the areas that the military and private contractors and universities are focusing on, all with the goal of making US soldiers more lethal, effective, and durable on the battlefield, include biotechnology, neurobiology and neuroenhancement, genomics, and synthetic biology, along with cognitive performance, improved physical capabilities like strength and endurance, new and improved immunizations and vaccines, personalized medicine, metabolic enhancements, microbiome manipulation, sleep/wake-cycle interventions, attention, memory, planning, learning, language, communication, sight, smell, hearing, touch, taste, stress, environmental conditions, toxins and radiation, and drug delivery systems (Annas and Annas 2009; Giordano 2014; Lin, Mehlman, and Abney 2013,

22–26; Perkins and Steevens 2015; Scharre and Fish 2018; Wurzman and Giordano 2014).

Advances in military technology call for not just a response in terms of better weapons and tactics but ways to strengthen and improve soldiers as well. The *longue durée* of the US Civil War, World War I, and World War II and the advent of "modern" warfare demonstrated just how devastating industrial war could be (DeBruyne and Leland 2015). Protracted wars, coupled with increasingly deadly weapons and new tactics designed to exploit the maximum killing potential of the new weapons systems, were able to exploit human frailty and weakness in ways previously unimaginable to military theorists.

This dynamic both promoted the expansion of military medicine and created new challenges and roles for military physicians. Modern militaries also began to take very seriously the impact of illness and disease on soldiers and readiness, and modern warfare helped drive advances in medicine in general, and military immunology and epidemiology in particular (Sidel and Levy 2014b). Albert E. Cowdrey, in his history of US military medicine, provides a succinct description of the goals of military medicine up to and during World War II, and the military's concern with disease prevention (which, as discussed later, is a major focus of military performance enhancement research): "Military medicine had wider, more impersonal aims. Its ultimate purpose was to conserve the fighting strength of the armed forces. Such a goal demanded a kind of medicine that practiced most of the specialties found in the civilian profession, plus public health, plus a system for extracting, treating, and moving the injured under fire that had no precise equivalent anywhere else. Military medicine meant curing disease and, since wars are won by physically and mentally functioning people, preventing disease as well" (1994, 3). Cowdrey's description of military medicine during World War II remains apt today, but with the addition of "enhancing" soldiers as a key and crucial mission. Each war brings about advances in military medicine: as medical technology and procedures evolve, so too does the ability to save soldiers on the battlefield and ensure that soldiers can enter the battlefield in the first place. Each successive war learns from the last, and this includes the lessons of military medicine. The lessons from World War II, Korea, and Vietnam were clear: US soldiers were vulnerable to a myriad of stressors on and off the battlefield. How then to make them "better," more reliable, and more capable on the battlefield?

Military doctors and biomedical researchers are not tasked simply with the maintenance of health and well-being; rather, their task is to produce, monitor, and intervene, to incorporate technology *in* soldiers. It is ultimately not simply a question of palliative care (which of course is part of the relationship) but of production, and control of the soldier through the "needs" of military health (Howe 2013; Messelken and Baer 2013). A statement from Edmund G. Howe of the Uniformed Services University concerning the goals of military medicine explains the relationship between the military doctor and the military: "The military physician . . . accepts the obligation to place military interests over his own interests and those he might otherwise have as a civilian doctor when he becomes a military officer; he is, in this sense, primarily a soldier with special technical expertise. Thus, when during combat, the soldier comes to the military physician with an injury, both the soldiers and the physician have agreed to prioritize the needs of the military" (1986, 803; see also Howe 2013; Sidel and Levy 2004).

In this sense, there is nothing necessarily new about the intentions and concerns of military medicine to save a soldier's life. What is new is the speed of developments, the scale, and the rapidity with which a soldier can be medevacked from the battlefield to an aid station, and then on to a military hospital. But these advances do not function simply on the battlefield. They also extend into research on performance enhancement technologies and other forms of preventive, prophylactic military medicine designed to protect and enhance the soldier medically before they enter the battlefield or combat, and in a sense negate the need for battlefield care by making them less prone to wounding and injury (see Terry 2017, 57–58, for a similar argument). Fundamentally, it is a shift from conservation and preservation to enhancement and extraction.

Military medicine—in the sense of a directed application of biotechnology to achieve desired effects—is a key component in the design and making of modern soldiers. A definition of "military preventive medicine" contained in the US Department of Defense Instruction Number 6490.3, "Implementation and Application of Joint Medical Surveillance for Deployments," gives the parameters and purview of military medicine concerns: "Military Preventive Medicine—Encompasses the anticipation, prediction, identification, prevention, and control of preventable diseases, illnesses and injuries caused by exposure to biological, chemical, physical or psychological threats or stressors found at home stations and during deployments" (Department of Defense, August 7, 1997, 16).

As this description of military medicine clearly states, first and foremost are the tasks of anticipation and prediction. The "Force Health Protection Concept of Operations for Information Management" from the USACHPPM states that "Force Health Protection" is a "unified strategy that protects service members from all health and environmental hazards associated with military service" (1998, 41) and the "DoD Medical Readiness Vision" emphasizes that "the military medical departments exist to support their combat forces in war and peacetime, to maintain and sustain the well-being of the fighting forces in preparation for war. The military medical departments must be prepared to respond effectively and rapidly to the entire spectrum of potential military operations—from major regional conflicts to Military Operations Other than War (MOOTW)" (1).

The Military Operational Medicine Research Program (MOMRP) is one of the main sites of US military biomedical research and testing. In a 2004 informational paper, one of the tasks of MOMRP is to "provide "skin-in" solutions that protect Soldiers and enhance their performance in operational and training environments that include multiple internal and external stressors" (USAMRMC n.d.). The current MOMRP "Program Overview" states that its mission is "to develop effective biomedical countermeasures against operational stressors and to prevent physical and psychological injuries during training and operations in order to maximize the health, readiness and performance of Service members and their Families, in support of the Army Human Performance Optimization and Enhancement (HPOE), Human Dimension (HD), Multi-Domain Battle (MDB), Army Big 6 Modernization Priorities, and the DoD Total Force Fitness (TFF) concepts. Its continuing mission is to protect the whole Service member—head-to-toe, inside and out, across the operational spectrum. Science to Service member is our focus" (USAMRMC n.d.). Additionally, MOMRP is committed to supporting the "Army Force 2025 and Beyond" (F2025B) program (USAMRMC n.d.), which is the Army's "comprehensive strategy to change and deliver land-power capabilities as a strategic instrument of the future Joint Force" (Stand-To! 2015).

If the US military is going to implant and embed "solutions" to our fears and fantasies around the anticipation of future threats, combat, and potential battlefields—which is what we are doing with military performance enhancement research, biomedical countermeasures, and "skin-in solutions"—we should first think about and understand how the military conceptualizes and defines "enhancement."

Normal versus Enhanced: Better, Stronger, Faster, Longer

We can think of military performance enhancement as having two "sites": inside the body and outside the body of the soldier. As the MOMRP describes it, "skin-out solutions" are those technological applications that improve or protect soldiers, such as new kinds of body armor, helmets, sensors, and so forth. "Skin-in solutions" are those applications that are targeted inside the body of the soldier and are designed to "improve" the biological functioning of the soldier. A MOMRP "Info Paper" from October 21, 2004, states:

> The Military Operational Medicine Research Program (MOMRP) provides biomedical "skin-in" solutions that protect Soldiers and enhance their performance in operational and training environments that include multiple internal and external stressors. . . . It is a unique biomedical research program with relevant core capabilities, a problem-solving orientation, and a human physiology research focus. MOM (military operational medicine) represents unique expertise in both health and performance effects of multiple interacting operational hazards and stressors. The focus is on multistressor interactions involving human tolerances, metabolic physiology, and brain functioning. . . . Examples of MOMRP biomedical research products include physiological response models and tools for mission planning, equipment design specifications and guidelines based on human tolerances, physiologically based nutritional guidelines for ration developers, strategies to enhance psychological resilience, and injury prediction tools for health hazard and Soldier survivability assessors. These products ultimately protect Soldiers, enhance their performance, and provide the "best available" answers for immediate application. (USAMRMC, 2004)

Despite the US military's development of new forms of autonomous weapons systems and its embrace of artificial intelligence (Scharre 2018), in the near-term, at least, the military will still require bodies from which to extract labor and hold and occupy territory captured during combat; drones might be good at killing, but they cannot hold territory or win hearts and minds. As Wilson W. S. Wong writes, military biotechnology "reinforces the primacy of people at the core of military affairs" (2013, 142; Wong also briefly discusses the mundane aspects of military biotechnology but with a different focus). Of course, people are still at the core of the US military, though Wong's point is important in the sense that civilians will be made into high-tech soldiers, and soldiers will continue to remain important for the military, despite the advent of drones and other autonomous weapons systems.

Fundamentally, military performance enhancement is about getting soldiers to do more, do it better, do it longer, and recover from combat trauma and injury more quickly. In 2004 Colonel James Romano, the deputy commander of the US Army Medical Research and Material Command at Fort Detrick, Maryland, stated that the purpose of biomedical research directed toward MPE is to "Increase sustainability of human performance; Protect against more disease and environmental threats; Continuously monitor health for all soldiers; Increase survival after wounding and dramatically increase medical mobility" (Romano 2004, 2).

A useful baseline for thinking about military performance enhancement is to examine athletes and performance enhancements in sports (Annas and Annas 2009; Besnier and Brownell 2012; Friedl 2015; Murray 2008). Special Forces soldiers, for example, are often referred to as "Olympic athletes" in the military. While obviously different (athletes have a choice in taking or accepting an enhancement, for example), there are key overlaps between the two, overlaps that give us some insight into how we can think about enhancements and how the military thinks about soldiers as athletes and what it wants and expects from soldiers.

As Simon Outram (2013) points out, "performance enhancement" in sports is often synonymous with drugs (see also Besnier and Brownell 2012; Courtwright 2014, 543; Friedl 2015; Schneider 2004), but this conflation—at least in the realm of sports—misses the varied roles of performance enhancement technologies. The military delineates this distinction through the "skin-in/skin-out" designation when discussing performance enhancement. Performance enhancement is also often thought of in terms of sports as "doping": athletes trying to gain an unfair advantage over their opponents through different kinds of drugs (Murray 2008). There is great concern around the "fairness" of athletes using performance enhancing drugs yet seemingly little concern in the broader public around military performance enhancement research; an "unfair advantage" on the battlefield, regardless of the impact on the soldier, might be seen as permissible and desirable. Soldiers are in some ways like elite athletes, but in many ways, they are not. They might on average be more fit than civilians, but not all soldiers function at the level of Olympic athletes. As Kenneth Ford and Clark Glymour discuss, however, in the future, military performance enhancements might be able to make all soldiers mimic elite Olympic athletes (2014, 43; see also Moreno 2012). Friedl (2015) makes the important observation that the US military has long been interested in many of the drugs and enhancement technologies that have been banned in the Olympics and other sports; as Joe Bielitzki, the program manager for DARPA's Metabolically Dominant Soldier program commented, his measure of success would be that all the drugs and enhancements he is interested in for US soldiers would be immediately banned by the International Olympic Committee (Singer 2008).

Inherent in all discussions and designs in imagining supersoldiers are the following questions: How exactly will you measure the "enhanced" against the "normal"? Who will count as the "normal" soldier? Will it be based on one's job in the military or on a performance/fitness test? Or perhaps another way to frame the questions would be: How will the military measure the utility or usefulness of an enhancement? The National Research Council Committee on Opportunities in Biotechnology for Future Army Applications report describes the promises and ethical requirements of "performance enhancement" for the military:

> Physicians distinguish between therapy (restoring a function to normal) and enhancement (boosting a function above the norm) and have traditionally been uneasy with the ethics of enhancement. . . . For the military, therapy, enhancement, and augmentation may all be desirable. As long as social norms of acceptable drug use are observed, the Army should welcome drugs that could ease the adjustment to another time zone or to longer periods without food or sleep; the Air Force should welcome a drug that could increase the G-force a pilot can endure before blacking out; and the Navy should welcome a drug that could ease motion sickness. To be acceptable, the drug technologies must be both safe and reversible. Guaranteeing soldiers that they will be able to return to their original physiological profile (excluding normal wear and tear) will be very important. (National Research Council 2001, 64)

Military performance enhancement can be thought of as the ways in which biomedical technologies are applied to make soldiers stronger and more resilient before, during, and after combat and more resistant to the stressors they encounter on the battlefield, be they physical, environmental, medical, or psychological. While this is a fairly broad definition, as we will see, the US military is using a very wide brush to address these issues, and it is really only a question of imagination to consider what might make a soldier more effective on the battlefield or what threats might negatively affect a soldier's battlefield performance.

"Enhancing the Fighting Force"

"The Protection of Health" is a trope used by the US military to intervene medically in order to make soldiers deployable and usable. The connection between health and readiness is one of deployability and not necessarily a definition or conception of health concerned solely with the well-being of the soldier; rather, "health" is understood as the "health" of the military as a fighting force. Military health revolves around the protection of the individual-as-soldier through technological and biomedical means, such as cybernetic research, body armor, improved weaponry, intelligence systems, vaccines, performance enhancing drugs, and mood/emotion-suppression drugs in order to make the soldier—as part of a greater whole—healthy and in top shape to fight. Ultimately, the "health" of the military-as-institution, as a fighting force, is more important than the short- or long-term health of the individual. Military medicine is about "preserving the fighting strength" of the military as a whole and enhancing the combat and survival abilities of soldiers, on and off the battlefield. "Preserving the Force" and "Soldier Health: World Health" are just a few of the mottoes of US military medicine departments and sum up the goals and intentions of these groups.

A key component of the military's plans to modernize and reach the goals of the high-tech "Army 2050" plan is human performance enhancement. The "soldier"—as a frail and underperforming civilian, and the "component" that always breaks down (Sulzberger 1962b)—is the focal point of military modernization, the linchpin to the military as a "system of systems." As stated in the "Human Engineering" section of the US Army Training and Doctrine Command's TRADOC Pamphlet 525-66, "Military Operations: Force Operating Capabilities," whose purpose was to "provide focus to the Army's Science and Technology Master Plan" and warfighting experimentation:

> The Soldier is the single most important aspect of the combat power of the Future Force. The Future Force Soldier is a combat Soldier first and foremost. Despite the expected proliferation of unmanned systems, the role Soldiers will have in the future battlespace demands they remain

the cornerstone for force design and employment. Soldiers, not equipment, accomplish missions and win wars. In order to achieve revolutionary effectiveness across the full spectrum of conflict, human engineering capabilities will enable the Future Force to:

- Decrease task complexity and execution times to improve performance while minimizing sensory, cognitive, and physically [sic] demands on the Soldier.
- Systems that have been engineered to improve Soldier trainability. (TRADOC 2005)

Robert H. Latiff, a former US Air Force general who has written on performance enhancement (from the military's standpoint), states: "Information technology, synthetic biology, and neuroscience all contribute to the broad area of enhancements. The same technologies that might restore an individual's ability to a specific norm could also be used to bring someone above that norm. For the military, that implies enhanced soldiers. . . . Internal enhancements might include pharmaceuticals, genetic modification, biological or metabolic changes, or the surgical implantation of computer chips into the brain" (2017, 40). Latiff brings up the comparison of US "supersoldier" research and science fiction and stresses that the US Department of Defense has been looking into biotechnologies and enhancements for well over a decade.

> Super soldiers have long been the stuff of science fiction. Television shows like *The Six Million Dollar Man* and movies like *Iron Man* and *RoboCop* allow us to imagine what would happen if humans could be augmented with superhuman capabilities. While much of what these depict remains the stuff of science fiction or even scientific impossibility (antigravity suits, for example), a substantial percentage has become reality or is being reached. The Defense Department has been working on these technologies for decades. Past projects such as the "Metabolically Dominant Soldier" and "Soldier Peak Performance" studied biological, genetic, and metabolic ways to improve battlefield performance. The technologies would allow for rapid tissue regeneration, faster healing, greater muscle strength, cognitive enhancement, the ability to operate without sleep for many days without performance degradation, higher metabolic energy, and immunity to pain. (2017, 40–41)

Peter W. Singer, in "How to Be All That You Can Be," outlines the steps the US military is following to mimic the technological and biomedical/biological superpowers of science fiction and comic book characters in soldiers: remake the soldier as a weapons system, build an exoskeleton, use chemical enhancements, use these technologies to deploy smaller teams of soldiers who nonetheless have vast amounts of firepower at their disposal, and finally, weigh the consequences of all these technological and biomedical enhancements and how all this will impact and contradict traditional notions of soldiers (Singer 2008). As Singer writes, "The use of technology enhancers to get ahead of human weakness just doesn't seem to settle well with the self-concept of soldiers, who work so hard to hone their bodies and skills, and see conflict as the ultimate test. If technology becomes a simple substitute, how can they show their excellence?" (2008, 14).

And in their discussion of medical research on US soldiers, Catherine L. Annas and George J. Annas quote DARPA scientist Michael Goldblatt and his idea of the future US supersoldier. For Goldblatt, all "normal" aspects, capabilities, and reactions of the soldier are to be transcended: "Soldiers having no physical, psychological, or cognitive limitations will be key to survival and operational dominance in the future. . . . Indeed, imagine if soldiers could communicate by thought alone. . . . Imagine the threat of a biological attack being inconsequential. And contemplate, for a moment, a world in which learning is as easy as eating, and the replacement of damaged body parts as convenient as a fast-food drive through. . . . These visions are the everyday work of the Defense Services Office [of DARPA]" (2009, 286).

Annas and Annas also discuss the DARPA "Persistence in Combat" project, designed to create soldiers who will be "unstoppable" in combat because pain, wounds, and bleeding will be kept under control and managed through a "pain vaccine" that will stop pain within ten seconds, accelerate wound healing, and contain a chemical cocktail designed to rapidly speed up coagulation (2009, 286). And Victor W. Sidel and Barry S. Levy, in their discussion of the military's interest in biotechnology and enhancements, analyze efforts to develop what Singer (2008) described as "drugs that will boost muscles and energy by a factor of 10, akin to steroids . . . on steroids" (2014a, 3176).

The "Army Research Laboratory Technical Strategy 2015–2035" explains the advantages (and implied necessity) of "Soldier Performance Augmentation," which is focused on "substantial enhancements to warfighter physical, cognitive, and perceptual performance," and which will "greatly shorten the time required to grow leaders, accelerate knowledge, judgement, and experience transfer to empower junior leaders, (and) enable over-match through increased cognitive capacity that turns data into decisions faster" (United States Army Research Laboratory 2014, 3). The research purview of the Army Research Laboratory (ARL) also includes its "Extramural Basic Research Campaign," which includes "Life Sciences": "Life Science is focused on basic research to discover, understand, and exploit biological systems that are expected to create revolutionary capabilities for the Army of 2030 and beyond. Discoveries in this area are expected to lead to capabilities in materials and Soldier performance augmentation, well beyond the limits facing today's Army" (2014, 7).

And, as part of its "Human Sciences Campaign," the Army Research Laboratory has the following goals:

> Innovations developed as part of the Human Sciences Campaign are expected to enhance warfighter physical capabilities by balancing load, improving protection, and enhancing performance. Further, aided and augmented sensory systems matched to individual capabilities and tuned to the operational environment are expected to significantly impact warfighter situational awareness. In addition, knowledge gained in this campaign is expected to facilitate the efficient management of warfighter cognitive load to ensure high proficiency in Army-relevant environments. Warfighter interactions with intelligent systems will be guided by principles derived from brain and behavior fundamental research—a cornerstone of the Human Sciences Campaign. More, applications of these technologies and methodologies in the full range of social and cultural environments—*based on an understanding of networked communications, relationships, and dynamics across diverse social structures*—are expected to be important in poising the Army of 2030 to quickly shape its operational environment. (Army Research Laboratory 2014, 18)

One of the major military research centers for military performance enhancement is the United States Army Research Institute for Environmental Medicine (USARIEM). An article written by US Army colonel Karl E. Friedl, the former commander of USARIEM, and Jeffrey H. Allan, the chief of staff of USARIEM, states unequivocally that the aim of USARIEM "is to conduct biomedical research to protect the health and performance of Soldiers in training and operational environments. This largely involves enhancement of the Soldier capabilities by preventing the degradation of health and performance in the face of external stressors that may include the natural environment or manmade exposures, including our own material systems" (2004, 33).

Table 3.1 USARIEM Scientists, Military Performance Division

physiologists	pharmacologists
systems	statisticians
environmental	biomedical engineers
cellular	biophysicists (modelers)
biochemists	nutritionists
endocrinologists	immunologists
molecular biologists	MDS (clinical research)
cell signaling	
epidemiologists	

Source: USARIEM 2005.

Friedl and Allen also write that "the USARIEM vision is to transition biomedical research findings that are timely and practical to forces deployed anywhere in the world. The primary reason for the Army to have this intramural science capability with both uniformed and civilian scientists is to have experts dedicated to eliciting, conducting, harvesting, and translating relevant science that expands options for Army policymakers and combat and matériel developers" (2004, 34). The types of scientists and researchers working at USARIEM demonstrate again the breadth of interest in all areas of the soldier's biology as sites for enhancement and modification (see table 3.1 and figure 3.2).

Friedl gives a succinct description of what he calls the "product line" for creating healthy US soldiers.

> In this "product line" of optimizing the physiology of the healthy Soldier, the translation of research discoveries into practical applications for the US Army has generally occurred through three different categories of research customers: materiel developers, combat developers, and preventive medicine experts. . . . Recommendations that will enhance personal equipment such as rations or clothing are transitioned to the Research Development and Engineering Command (RDECOM), specifically the Natick Soldier Center (co-located with USARIEM). Application of training methods and stressor countermea-

USARIEM

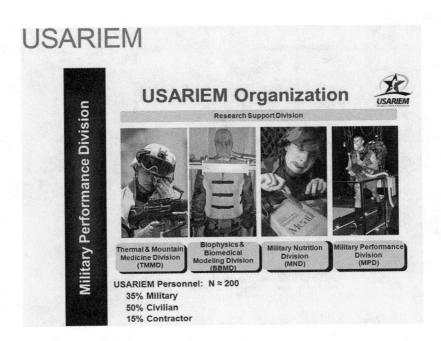

Figure 3.2 USARIEM organizational structure, n.d.

sures are developed by the Training and Doctrine Command (TRA-DOC), often with field testing and transition of research concepts by the Infantry Center (Fort Benning, Georgia). Preventive medicine specialists develop policy and guidance at the Army Medical Department Center and School (AMEDD C&S, Fort Sam Houston, San Antonio, Texas) and disseminate the information to the Army through the Center for Health Promotion and Preventive Medicine (CHPPM, Aberdeen, Maryland). The products of this biomedical performance research are not restricted to medics but, in fact, usually go into the hands of every Soldier with the intention of keeping Soldiers healthy and out of medical channels. (2005, 4)

Many of the descriptions and definitions that the military uses to talk about performance enhancement are prefaced by descriptions of the operational environments and threats that soldiers face on the battlefield (see figure 3.3). In many ways, these descriptions are both accurate and imagined, as they detail the real conditions of combat as well as the imagined and anticipated conditions of future combat. Major-General Lester Martinez-Lopez, former commanding general of the US Army

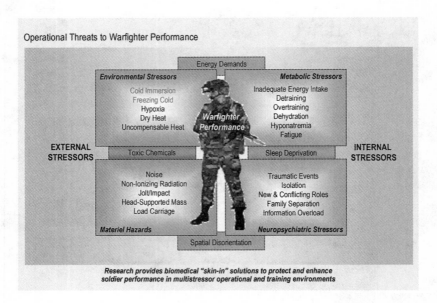

Operational Threats to Warfighter Performance

	Energy Demands	
Environmental Stressors		**Metabolic Stressors**
Cold Immersion		Inadequate Energy Intake
Freezing Cold		Detraining
Hypoxia	*Warfighter Performance*	Overtraining
Dry Heat		Dehydration
Uncompensable Heat		Hyponatremia
		Fatigue
EXTERNAL STRESSORS	Toxic Chemicals — Sleep Deprivation	**INTERNAL STRESSORS**
Noise		Traumatic Events
Non-Ionizing Radiation		Isolation
Jolt/Impact		New & Conflicting Roles
Head-Supported Mass		Family Separation
Load Carriage		Information Overload
Materiel Hazards		**Neuropsychiatric Stressors**
	Spatial Disorientation	

Research provides biomedical "skin-in" solutions to protect and enhance soldier performance in multistressor operational and training environments

Figure 3.3 "Skin-In Solutions." Karl E. Friedl, "What Does Military Biomedical Research Contribute to Sustaining Soldier Performance in Cold Environments?" 2005, 3.

Medical Research and Material Command (usamrmc), sums up the stressors that modern US soldiers face.

> The soldier's occupational environment is extremely stressful, both physically and mentally. Work is conducted outdoors in all types of weather and at all altitudes. The workload continues around the clock and is subject to sudden, rapid changes in intensity. Soldiers are required to remain attentive and vigilant and process increasing amounts of information very quickly. In the future, even greater demands will be made upon soldiers. Future operational concepts call for highly mobile forces enabled by increasingly sophisticated weapons systems. . . . The soldier of the future must be physically ready to deploy on a moment's notice; upon arrival, he or she must be ready to fight, anywhere in the world. . . . These requirements will make substantial cognitive, perceptual, and emotional demands on soldiers. Highly mobile operations will also increase the dispersion and isolation of small units and individual soldiers, changing the way support services, such as medical support, are delivered and making it imperative that soldiers remain fit and healthy. Future soldiers will have to

be capable of going without sleep or resupply for extended periods of time. (Martinez-Lopez 2004, 18)

This broad description of the "occupational environment"—warfare—nonetheless sums up the areas of concern that the military hopes to address through performance enhancement. Taking these concerns into account, the US military is not simply focusing on protection in a defensive sense; military medicine and biotechnology are increasingly predicated on protection and enhancing the offensive capabilities of a soldier. As Guo writes, "the military application of biotechnology will make military medicine a fighting power in addition to a tool of maintaining and strengthening the fighting power of the army . . . the goal of medicine is transforming from "saving oneself and killing the enemy" to "strengthening oneself and controlling the enemy" (2006, 1153; see also Malet 2016, 66).

Soldiers are always threatened and at risk: this is the nature of being a soldier, and through the development of new weapons—be they ballistic, biological, chemical, or nuclear—modern warfare seems to be on an unending upward track toward ever-increasing danger and lethality. In contemporary warfare, there is no front line, and even if the soldier is not directly engaged in combat, he is still in a risky environment that encompasses exposure to new diseases and illnesses, heat and/or cold extremes, rigorous work schedules, dangerous equipment, and realistic training exercises designed to mimic combat, to name just a few. The present, and the future, are predicated on continuous, unceasing risk.

"Secure the Present and Ensure the Future": Biotechnology and Future Threats

If the future of war is unpredictable, and if the military and military thinkers spend a lot of time trying to predict and anticipate the nature of future war, then biologically enhanced and engineered soldiers might allow for a certain flexibility in response: the soldier and the body will be tailored to the conflict. While this may or may not work, it provides a certain reassurance—or image of reassurance—that the future can to some measure be controlled and confronted.

In a promotional video for the US Army's Future Combat System (FCS) titled "Future Combat System: Assault on Normandy," (n.d.), United States Army Brigadier General Charles Cartwright (the FCS "Program Manager

Unit of Action") states, "[That] is the commitment of the FCS: to secure the present and ensure the future." The hope is that increased technology in and on the soldier today will ensure a stable future and minimize risk, both for the soldier and the state (for analyses of the Future Combat System, see Erwin 2007; Feickert 2005, 2008, 2009).

The military works with a variety of definitions and ideas of what biotechnology is, what it can do, and what it can hopefully accomplish. A report on the future uses of biotechnology for the US Army defines biotechnology as a technology that "uses organisms, or tissues, cells, or molecular components derived from living things, to act on living things," and "[it] acts by intervening in the workings of cells or the molecular components of cells, including their genetic material" (National Research Council 2001, 10). Edward J. Perkins and Jeffrey A. Steevens, in their *Small Wars Journal* article, define biotechnology as "the manipulation (as through genetic engineering) of living organisms or their components to produce useful products (as pest resistant crops, new bacterial strains, or novel pharmaceuticals). . . . Here we also include technologies based on DNA sequencing, use of biological molecules, and biomaterials, and include biochemistry, biosynthesis, cellular biology, physiology, biochemical engineering, and understanding the interface between biological and engineered systems" (2015).

Section Q of the 1998 *Army Science and Technology Master Plan* (ASTMP) provides the underlying objectives and goals of ongoing US military biomedical research, goals that still obtain today, and which make explicit the military's focus on the interior of the soldier: "Military Medical and Biomedical Science and Technology programs are a unique national resource focused to yield superior capabilities for medical support and services to US armed forces. Unlike other national and international medical and biomedical S&T investments, military research is concerned with preserving the combatant's health and optimizing mission capabilities despite extraordinary battle, nonbattle, and disease threats. It is also unlike most of the more widely visible Army modernization programs because its technology is incorporated *in* service men and women rather than into the systems they use" (United States Army 1998, Q1, emphasis added).

In a 2014 presentation at the NDIA Science Engineering and Technology Conference, Jeffrey D. Singleton, director for Basic Research, Office of the Deputy Assistant Secretary of the Army for Research and Development, discussed the "Basic Research Major Efforts" for "Human Science/Cybernetics": "Goal: Manage Soldier emotion and fatigue states, cognitive performance, and examine leading edge methodologies to improve the classification of neural state and behavior in operationally relevant environment. Use cybernetics to [*sic*] human system integration" (2014 9). Perkins and Steevens, again in their *Small Wars Journal* article, discuss the variety of uses biotechnology will have for soldier performance enhancement (it is worth quoting them at length).

> On demand biomanufacturing integrated into temporary tattoos or band-aids will provide unique capabilities to augment soldier sensing, medication, and identification. Sensing threats might include chemicals (TICS/TIMS [toxic industrial chemicals / toxic industrial materials]), CBRN [chemical, biological, radiological, and nuclear], temperature and humidity. Sensors will be wearable, integrated into clothing or even temporary tattoos using nanosilver ink. . . .
>
> These tattoos will be imprinted on soldiers prior to deployment and include physiological sensors that do not require blood to monitor metabolic products (to determine energy levels), hydration level, cortisol level to determine stress and fatigue, and use as feedback to determine emergency medical states. For example a soldier might be experiencing a high level of stress or exhaustion. Sensors will detect and process the event, then synthetic biology created microbes will respond with the correct treatment by producing and releasing biomolecules such as endorphins to alleviate the stress. If a soldier is exhausted, the sensors detect a metabolic signal and initiate, through a synthetic protein (to avoid false initiation events), a genetically modified microbe in the Soldier's gastrointestinal system to release a biomolecule such as a steroid or other stimulating agent. If a soldier is exposed to a chemical agent, the same cascade could release a pharmaceutical agent directly to the blood system or produce it through genetically modified microbes. (Perkins and Steevens 2015)

Malet, who examines the intersections of military biotechnology and international security, discusses DARPA's 2010 project "Feedback Regulated Automatic Molecular Release" (FRAMR), which focused on the development of biodegradable, self-regulating drug-delivery systems that would deliver precise therapeutic or performance enhancing pharmaceuticals in combat (Malet 2016, 75). FRAMR was intended to enable "feedback-regulated release in response to biomarkers correlated with drug efficacy and/or toxicity" (DARPA 2008, 36–37). Commenting on DARPA's interest in stress and the soldier, Malet also writes: "DARPA, in noting the 'negative impact that stress has on the cognitive, emotional, and physical well-being of warfight-ers is irrefutable,' proposes 'novel molecular biological techniques, coupled with in-vivo measurement biotechnologies, can allow for the management of the stress pathways and behavioral analysis in real time'" (2016, 75, quot-ing DARPA 2010).

As warfare evolves and advances, the interior of the soldier, in all its myriad layers, functions, and systems, is the last frontier of militarization. If anticipation and preemption are to work on the battlefield, they have to first work in the bodies of soldiers. The body of the soldier is not only the "inscribed surface" of events (Foucault 1979, 1980) but also—through mili-tary biomedical research—the inscribed and regulated *interior* of events. This interior regulation is crucial to external politics and warfare. Just as Ernst Jünger described the "encoding of the (male) body" as "total mobili-zation down to the innermost core" (Huyssen 1995, 134), vaccinations and psycho-pharmaceuticals, are, in this instance, power inscribed not only *on* the body but *in* it, down to the molecular level.

Fragmentation and Freedom

After World War I, Ernst Jünger wrote of "war as inner experience" (*Der Kampf als inneres Erlebnis* ([1922] 2012), that is, as something experienced with extreme emotional intensity by the soldier, an intensity that would change the soldier forever. Jonathan D. Moreno (2012) discusses an as-pect of performance enhancement research that hints at a similar process as described by Jünger—the need for "skin-in" enhancements to come to terms with war as an "inner experience": "In a sense, all warfare ultimately happens between our ears. . . . If targeted interventions are made possible by the greatly enhanced knowledge of the brain and nervous system now being generated at a feverish pace in our top neuroscience labs, comple-mented by ingenious new engineering and pharmaceutical products, the battle of the brain will have truly begun. The powers that can claim the advantage and establish a 'neurotechnology gap' . . . will establish both tactical and strategic advantages that can render them dominant in the twenty-first century" (2012, 30). While Moreno's focus is on neurotechnology, the point is the same: it is the internal development, enhancement, and retooling of the soldier that will provide militaries with the advantage on the battlefield—wherever and whatever it might be—in the coming de-cades. Warfare is a biological concern of the state occurring "between the ears" of the soldier, as it were. But as Kamieński remarks, "The murderous pace of an increasingly impulsive war requires military personnel to function not only on the verge of psychological capacity of the human body but also well beyond it" (2016b, 264). The trick is getting soldiers to exceed those boundaries physically, mentally, and emotionally without falling apart.

Poets and scholars have long focused on the disintegration of (male) bodies in combat, both physically and mentally, and much of the rhetoric and imagery around armored bodies in the twentieth century focused on fantasies of wholeness. The great promise of military performance enhancement is that it will hopefully keep the body whole and intact and keep it from fragmenting. And by keeping the body whole, strategy, tactics, and objectives will remain whole—or at least not as fragmented as before.

Hans-Georg Gadamer, in his "Apologia for the Art of Healing," claims that the task of medicine "ultimately consists in withdrawing itself and helping to set the other person free" (1996, 43). When linked to military medicine and performance enhancements, Gadamer's statement on science, technology, and medicine takes on a particular significance: "The concept of technology which is connected with the idea of science in the modern era thus takes on specifically intensified and increased possibilities in the field of medicine and its healing procedures. The capacity to produce desired effects makes itself independent, represents the application of a theoretical body of knowledge. As such, however, it is not a matter of healing, but rather of effecting something and so of producing something" (35).

Military health—and civilian health as well—operates on a sense of "freedom"; that is, one is to be free of worry about certain types of wounding or injury. Military performance enhancement projects are all concerned with a kind of freedom from injury and death and a strategic-level freedom from operational worry.

Performance enhancements are not just about producing effects; they also produce—or hopefully produce—a form of military freedom. That is, the military can be free to trust soldiers in combat, trust that they will not break down, and be free of worry about mission failure. Enhancement in this sense is not just about enhancing the soldier; it is also about enhancing certainty of the future, of mitigating the stress and disorientation of anticipation, of making sure preemption actually preempts. "Performance enhancement" is in many ways a discussion about trust, or rather a failure to trust: the soldier will not be good enough, strong enough, fast enough, tough enough, brave enough, resilient enough, durable enough, willing to shoot and kill.

Hugh Gusterson, following Foucault (1979), Elaine Scarry (1985), and Talal Asad (1983), remarks that "mutilated bodies are points of exchange between power and knowledge" (1996, 103). The crucial link between power and knowledge, in terms of military performance enhancement research and biotechnology, is not the mutilated, but the researchers, planners, and designers: warfare must be anticipated and bodies must be planned, designed, and manipulated in certain ways to then produce bodies predicated on "freedom." But it is exactly this deployment of "freedom" that binds and constricts the soldier in a regime of health and turns him into a delegate of national security and power projection; military health must ensure that the soldier is constantly made "free" of weakness through application of new technologies, pharmaceuticals, and equipment. It is not a conception of health that necessarily seeks to "restore" the health of the patient; rather, it is the techne of the soldier, which, Gadamer argues, is "that knowledge which constitutes a specific and tried ability in the context of producing things" (1996, 32). It is the military's use of "health" to produce something new: a soldier-delegate potentially immune to wounding and—possibly, fantastically—to death.

While seemingly defensive in nature, "built-in armor" would also allow the soldier to take part in offensive operations in hostile environments and on "exotic" and "primitive" battlefields that previously either hindered or prohibited engagements. In a world anticipated and seen as one of perpetual struggle and war, in the imagination of military researchers and in accordance with the needs of military planners, soldiers must be armored, physically and emotionally, internally and externally—but most importantly, internally—to make them useful to the military and the state. The techne of the soldier is the internal regulation of the soldier for the protection of the state: what might seem like positive, life-saving measures for the soldier could also be another way of making soldiers fight, ensuring deployability, and of harnessing a "delegate" or "tool" for national security purposes in a more effective and predictable manner. Moreno, in his overview and analysis of military neuroenhancement research, makes the important connection between performance enhancement and the soldier: "the first state or nonstate actor to build a better soldier will have taken an enormous leap in the arms race" (2012, 114). Military performance enhancement is very much an ever-intensifying arms race, a race to enhance and mobilize and operationalize every aspect of the soldier: physical, mental, emotional, genomic, systemic. It is a race to develop new and potentially unbeatable foreign policy tools.

Part II

Early Imaginaries of the US Supersoldier

FOUR

"Science Will Modernize Him"

The Soldier of the Futurarmy

When one man is lost the burden is greater on the remaining men. As casualties go up, the chances for survival for the remainder of the men go down.

» **Lieutenant Colonel Robert B. Rigg,**
   "Soldier of the Futurarmy"

World War II brought about extraordinary advances in military technology; a war that began with horses, biplanes, and bolt-action rifles ended with jets, new forms of mechanization, assault rifles, ballistic missiles, and nuclear weapons. Despite these advances, the US military was still, at least in terms of the basic combat soldier, a fairly traditional force, designed to fight against massed land forces and increasingly planning for the use of nuclear weapons on the battlefield. As advances in warfare quickened, the US military was forced to at least think about and imagine new kinds of soldiers. New external technologies—or at least imagined technologies—would keep the soldier alive and active in combat.

The standard kit for US soldiers at the end of the war consisted of cloth uniforms, canvas ammunition belts and backpacks, the M1 "Steel Pot" helmet, a canteen, an entrenching tool, a knife, and possibly a side arm if you were an officer or other soldier who needed one. Standard-issue weapons were the M1 Garand Rifle, M1 Carbine, the Browning Automatic Rifle (BAR), the Thompson Submachine Gun, and the M3 "Grease Gun." Fundamentally, the only real change from the beginning of the war was the new helmet; gone was the British-designed M1917A1 helmet of World War I fame. This basic configuration of the soldier continued on through the Korean War (and later into the Vietnam War), though US soldiers did receive new rifles in the form of the M14 (and the M16 in Vietnam). Fundamentally, US soldiers entered combat with very little protection; other than their helmets, their bodies were unprotected and exposed, and as always, they remained the target.

The nuclear attacks on Hiroshima and Nagasaki ushered in a new age of warfare—not just of strategic warfare but increasingly the possibility of tactical nuclear war. The advent of this new age demanded a rethinking and reimagining of the US soldier. The lessons learned from the first and second world wars and the new battlefield conditions and possibilities of the Cold War necessitated the imagining of new kinds of soldiers— soldiers who could cope, excel, and survive in the new tactical environment and who could exploit the weaknesses of enemy soldiers who were not equipped or trained to deal with these conditions. The new soldier would be part and parcel of the new "jet age" and the burgeoning "computer age" of warfare.

US Army designs for supersoldiers can be traced back to at least the mid-1950s. Writing in the November 1956 issue of *Army* magazine (the official magazine of the Association of the United States Army), Lieutenant Colonel Robert B. Rigg presented a vision of the future of soldiers and warfare in the nuclear age: the "Soldier of the Futurarmy." The Futurarmy was Rigg's imagining of the soldier of the 1970s, equipped with all sorts of advanced weapons and protective devices (see figure 4.1). Conceived of in 1956, the soldier of the Futurarmy was a soldier who would fight the existential threat of communism and survive all that the "Reds" could throw at him, be it conventional or nuclear or chemical weapons (Rigg had been a US Army observer with the Red Army during World War II, and then an observer with Chinese Nationalist forces in the later stages of the Chinese Revolution). Rigg also wrote a novel about future warfare, *War—1974* (1958), in which he expanded on his ideas of the soldier of the Futurarmy and the coming hypertechnical forms of warfare that would allow the United States to be victorious against communist forces around the world.

Rigg's Futurarmy soldier would wear an advanced uniform made of plastic armor; this would protect against all ballistic threats and be lightweight and comfortable to wear. The Futurarmy soldier would wear a helmet equipped with the latest in communication technology and allow the new soldier to speak to hundreds of other soldiers (the embedded communication helmet reappears in the later Objective Force Warrior, Future

Force Warrior, and Future Combat Systems projects). As Rigg wrote of the (imagined) 1970s Futurarmy soldier:

> Anything but Sad Sack in appearance, this air-age trooper will look as if meant for war. His helmet, unlike the crude pots of the past, will be a scientific masterpiece laden with miniature electronic devices combining communications, comfort, and protection in a degree unanticipated today. Other equipment and clothing will be so compact and light that this future soldier will be much more efficient than today's. He will have greater chances of survival on the battlefield than any soldier up to this date. Furthermore, this American soldier of the 1970s will be a formidable fighter because he will have full confidence in his plastic body armor and apply greater combat skill by virtue of new weapons, modernized communications, and ultra-miniaturized equipment. (1956, 25–26)

Rigg notes that the miniaturization of equipment for the soldier will help reduce the overall weight of equipment the soldier must carry into combat. As he writes, the average weight of equipment that the US soldier carries with him "has hardly varied in weight and bulk since Napoleon's legions fought at Waterloo" (1956, 30). This point is essential, as overloaded soldiers are at a severe disadvantage in combat; this is a recurrent problem for today's US military as well, as it tries to resolve the problem of the "overweight infantryman" who often carries more than one hundred pounds of equipment into combat (King 2017). Lessening the weight of equipment carried into combat means the soldier has more energy and stamina left for combat and will not tire as quickly or easily. Miniaturization is one of the keys to extracting more military labor from soldiers, as Rigg recognized.

The soldier of the Futurarmy would wear a combat uniform that acts as a kind of full-body armor, and he would also wear a helmet that not only protects him but allows him to communicate, hear, and see in ways heretofore unimaginable on the battlefield. While not an internal enhancement, Rigg envisioned infrared technology embedded in soldier's helmets that would allow them to "change darkness into day by one flick of the wrist"; as he imagines, the "push button" soldier that is the soldier of the Futurarmy will be able to operate around the clock.

> As darkness falls the Futurarmy soldier will emerge into the night with seeing eyes because this scientific helmet will place infrared lenses before his eyes. This will be the death knell for Communist guerrillas in the

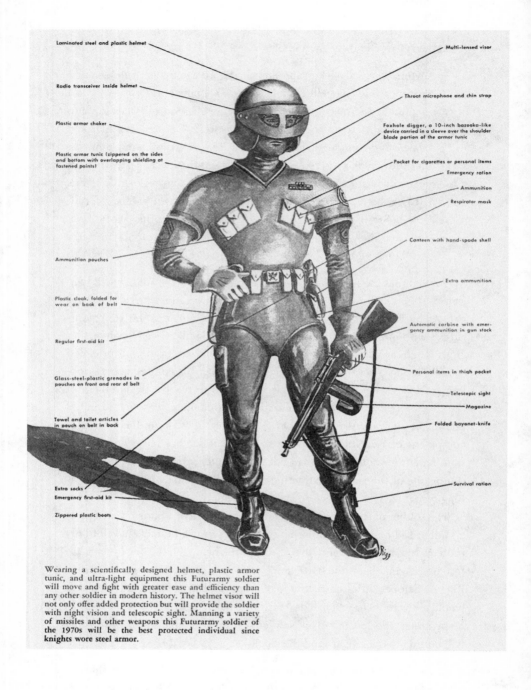

Laminated steel and plastic helmet

Multi-lensed visor

Radio transceiver inside helmet

Throat microphone and chin strap

Plastic armor choker

Foxhole digger, a 10-inch bazooka-like device carried in a sleeve over the shoulder blade portion of the armor tunic

Plastic armor tunic (zippered on the sides and bottom with overlapping shielding at fastened points)

Pocket for cigarettes or personal items

Emergency ration

Ammunition

Respirator mask

Canteen with hand-spade shell

Ammunition pouches

Extra ammunition

Plastic cloak, folded for wear on back of belt

Automatic carbine with emergency ammunition in gun stock

Regular first-aid kit

Personal items in thigh pocket

Glass-steel-plastic grenades in pouches on front and rear of belt

Telescopic sight

Magazine

Towel and toilet articles in pouch on belt in back

Folded bayonet-knife

Extra socks

Survival ration

Emergency first-aid kit

Zippered plastic boots

Wearing a scientifically designed helmet, plastic armor tunic, and ultra-light equipment this Futurarmy soldier will move and fight with greater ease and efficiency than any other soldier in modern history. The helmet visor will not only offer added protection but will provide the soldier with night vision and telescopic sight. Manning a variety of missiles and other weapons this Futurarmy soldier of the 1970s will be the best protected individual since knights wore steel armor.

Figure 4.1 Robert B. Rigg, "Soldier of the Futurarmy," 1956.

jungle. But elsewhere on land where men fight amid missiles in more formal combat, divisions of seeing Americans can arise to advance and converge on enemy soldiers blinded by darkness. Penetrating darkness in such a fashion will be tantamount to making the soldier a relative superman in combat. Only the nation maintaining technological superiority will attain this military advantage. (1956, 27)

The patriotic and vaguely religious tones of Rigg's writing notwithstanding, Rigg was onto a basic idea of soldier enhancement: the desire to extend, outdo, and exceed the physical capabilities of the enemy. "Seeing" US soldiers will outfight both the communists in the jungle and the communists in formal combat; weapons are important but senses are better. Given the speed and protection of the new soldier, war in the era of the Futurarmy will be, according to Rigg, fairly bloodless and boundless: "There will be no bloody beach assaults when Futurarmy soldiers take off from scattered Navy carriers to converge on hostile forces. Enemy shore defenses, even inland ones, will be as obsolete as Chinese Walls in this warfare of no boundaries or barriers" (1956, 34). While Rigg imagined a bloodless form of warfare, he did write about the need to internally armor soldiers and focus medical technologies on soldiers' survival. In his novel *War—1974*, Rigg detailed the actual medical research the US military was conducting in the 1950s to help soldiers overcome the "wound shock" that they often experience in battle.

> Army medical research is today seeking a method of "conditioning" soldiers against the potentially fatal "wound shock" that accompanies severe combat injuries. A possible lead toward this end has been discovered. In laboratory tests, rats have been made so shock-resistant that only 25 percent of those tested succumbed to injuries which would normally be fatal to 75 percent. The rats were conditioned by giving them a series of electrical shocks, similar to those given patients in psychiatric hospitals. As a test of resistance to violent injury the animals have been subjected to tumbling in special whirling drums that were whirled 500 times with each turn. However, Army scientists stress that "experiments are still not at the stage where applications to humans is possible. . . . Army researchers are seeking less drastic means than electric shock of possibly producing the same effect." (1958, 241–42)

Anticipating and envisioning ideas of warfare to come (and anticipating that the communists might soon be on the doorstep of the United States),

Rigg imagined the entire world as the battlefield, with little in the way of environmental or manmade barriers getting in the way of the new US soldier. Warfare in all directions, at all times, in all places, was called "3D" warfare. The speed and 3D nature of warfare in the 1970s, as Rigg saw it, would also require new kinds of officers: "Commanders who cannot think in jet-pilot terms will not last long. The fighting will be on the ground—a series of short battles taking place in different areas, as the lightning force moves and swirls across country like a tornado" (1956, 34; Rigg's imagery here is reminiscent of Jünger's imagery of the New Man). The need to think like a "jet-pilot" prefigures the current US military interest in cognition and decision-making enhancement for soldiers as a way to outthink the enemy and keep up with the new technologies imagined for future conflict.

Much of Rigg's design for the Futurarmy soldier focused on new kinds of equipment, uniforms, and weapons. For example, soldiers would have "glass grenades" and "automatic foxhole diggers" and wear "comfortable" uniforms that provided them some degree of ballistic protection. Tucked away in pockets on the side of their boots would be small self-medical-aid kits for individual use (and all soldiers would be trained to perform basic first aid to one another in emergencies). Survival rations, or, as Rigg described them, "small, hard flakes the size of a penny," would be wedged into the soles of soldier's boots, and small vials of vitamins would be sewn into the back of soldiers' gloves (1956, 28). Soldiers would also carry a poncho that was saturated with antichemical and antinuclear materials; in the event of a chemical or nuclear attack, soldiers could shelter under their ponchos until the all-clear signal was given. The ponchos would also be connected to batteries in the soldier's utility belt; this would provide a degree of heat and comfort during cold nights, but not too much, as Rigg was afraid that "the moment that the soldier is insulated in a complete cocoon of comfort, he will simply be a regimented creature in uniform" (32). Science was there to make warfare easier, but there were "practical limits to which we can safely insulate the soldier to his ordeal and mission of fighting" (32). The goal of applying science to the soldier in this case was clear: "Science can, and will, modernize the military man by miniaturizing everything from the equipment he carries to the toilet articles he uses. Only by saving ounces and fractions of ounces in all items can the total soldier load be perceptibly lightened to give him more freedom of action, endurance, and less fatigue" (30).

Rather than marching or driving into combat, Rigg imagined and designed nuclear-powered transport aircraft that would carry "Centaurs" (flying artillery) and "flying platforms" that would carry "land-spacemen" to attack enemy missiles and other targets (1956, 28). Soldiers would also use "Mata-Hari" spy sensors called "Owls"—dropped and deployed behind enemy lines—to spy on enemy troop movements and other activities. As Rigg mused of the protection and projection of the Futurarmy soldier:

> The Futurarmy soldier will be better protected and projected in combat than any soldier in history because science will modernize him and his environment. He will live, move and fight amid amazing machines—nuclear-powered helicopters, flying tanks, flying platforms, flying artillery, missiles, drone devices, and even mechanical spies. Where the missile can only be destructive, the Futurarmy soldier can be both destructive and possessive. Projected into battle zones by three-dimensional transport devices, this future soldier will be able to arrive and surprise his enemy with a force and suddenness never before known. His will be "doorstep warfare." (1956, 33)

The key phrase here is "science will modernize him." To "modernize" is a way of seeing the future, to understand potential, to design new kinds of armor and weapons for the soldier, to discover and extract the potential combat power of the soldier. "Modernization" is also an attempt to seize, possess, or control the future in the present. This might be a good way to sum up Rigg's work and all subsequent US military soldier-enhancement programs. Rigg saw the march of warfare and war of the future as highly technological, and one filled with all sorts of potential opportunities for the US, if it embraced new technologies. But Rigg's imagination and vision only went so far—or as far as his experience as an Army tank corps officer and military observer allowed him. Rigg's design for the soldier, while predating Sulzberger's Idiophylactic Soldier, is still a fairly conventional design; the soldier himself has not been changed but merely given new and futuristic equipment and weapons. The Futurarmy soldier was equipped with "skin-out" technologies to allow him to fight and survive on the imagined battlefields of the future; there is no real discussion of performance enhancement drugs or technologies that would improve the Futurarmy soldier's abilities. Rigg's design and imagination for the outward armor and appearance of the new soldier would later appear in US Army soldier system designs, and his work led to a US military competition to imagine future warfare and future soldier technologies (see chapter 9). But for all his fantastic pronouncements about equipment and weapons, and the application of science to the soldier, Rigg missed a key component to making the soldier of the Futurarmy truly formidable on the battlefield: biomedical science. It would be up to Dr. Marion B. Sulzberger and his concept of the Idiophylactic Soldier to imagine the next steps in making the US soldier truly super and pharmacological.

FIVE

"A Biological Armor for the Soldier"

Idiophylaxis and the Self-Armoring Soldier

"Unseen Armor to Guard Troops against Nature."

» *Army Stars and Stripes* **headline,**
   November 3, 1962

In this chapter, I trace the development, rationale, and legacy of one attempt to deal with human frailty and the "body problem" in the military, a kind of military futurism devised at the peak of the Cold War: US military researcher and dermatologist Dr. Marion B. Sulzberger's vision of creating soldiers for the US military who had their own kind of special, internally embedded biological armor—what he termed *Idiophylaxis*. In 1962 Sulzberger presented a paper at the Army Science Conference at West Point, under the auspices of the Office of the Chief of Research and Development of the United States Army (Department of the Army 1962). Titled "Progress and Prospects in Idiophylaxis (Built-in Individual Self-Protection of the Combat Soldier)," Sulzberger's call was for a radical rethinking of the combat soldier and the ways in which soldiers were imagined, designed, and developed. Sulzberger's "Idiophylactic Soldier" (1962b) would be a

---

Some of the ideas and discussions in chapter 5 appeared in Andrew Bickford, "From Idiophylaxis to Inner Armor: Imagining the Self-Armoring Soldier in the United States Military from the 1960s to Today," *Comparative Studies in Society and History* 60, no. 4 (October 2018): 810–38.

biomedically enhanced soldier, internally and psychologically "armored" through new forms of biotechnology.

Sulzberger's Idiophylaxis represents an important but little-known milestone in US military biomedical research and interest in soldier performance enhancement and marks the emergence of a synthesis of technologies designed to protect and improve the soldier. Sulzberger's work helps historicize and trace how the US military imagines melding biomedical advances and military necessity, and the political, military, and technological conditions that drive the impetus to make the internally enhanced soldier. Sulzberger's work on the Idiophylactic Soldier anticipates and hints at much of the current US military research on biomedicine, psychopharmacology, psychological preparation, and resiliency training (see, e.g., Gray 1989, 1997; Howell 2014; Jauregui 2015; Lin, Mehlman, and Abney 2013; Moreno 2012; Robson 2014; Sinclair and Britt 2013; Singer 2008). The importance and continued salience of Sulzberger's work can be seen in DARPA's 2007 Inner Armor program, which is the intellectual and conceptual grandchild of Idiophylaxis. Inner Armor bears a remarkable—but strangely unremarked and uncited—resemblance to Sulzberger's conception of Idiophylaxis and seems to draw direct inspiration from and resurrect Sulzberger's dream of the self-armoring soldier (as will be discussed in chapter 8). Much of what Sulzberger outlined in Idiophylaxis in 1962—such as advanced immunizations and embedded protections against disease; "built-in" resistance to heat, cold, and altitude; and the transformation of the soldier's body into its own armor—was taken up and expanded upon in the Inner Armor program, with the goal of creating "kill-proof" idiophylactic soldiers. These concerns with soldier health and frailty and the synthesis of biotechnology and military necessity—similar to Sulzberger's vision—continued on as well in later projects such as the Objective Force Warrior, the Future Force Warrior, and the Future Combat System, and in concepts like "skin-in solutions."

Sulzberger's conception of Idiophylaxis and "built-in armor" is somewhat ambiguous, fuzzy, and playful, as it encompasses a crossover between performance enhancement, immunizations, and biotechnology in ways that we do not generally think of now, and it revolves around notions of preemption. But the fuzziness and ambiguity of his concept are also its strength, because they show the range of things Sulzberger imagined necessary to keep soldiers alive and functioning on the battlefield. His approach signaled a complete rethinking of the soldier from the inside out and helps us understand and problematize later military performance enhancement projects, immunizations, and how we conceptualize "supersoldiers." This kind of serious play and imagination is part and parcel of all military performance enhancement projects and preemption: if synthetic biology is about merging biology with engineering, military performance enhancement research is just as much about merging imaginative play and musings about a "New Man" with biology. Sulzberger's work in the 1960s serves as an entry point to better understand the US military's ongoing quest to design ever-better soldiers and think about the contemporary fantasy and intention to create resilient, self-armoring, "kill-proof" warriors. While many of his ideas were ambiguous, fantastic, and fanciful—and perhaps medically impossible—they continue to resonate and influence military medicine and performance enhancement projects. Sulzberger's Idiophylaxis allows us to think about current US military soldier-enhancement projects in a new light and pose new questions and avenues of inquiry into how states imagine and "make" soldiers through biotechnology and the ordering of the soldier's biology.

Sulzberger envisioned applied military biomedical programs that would anticipate and preempt all infectious disease and environmental threats to the soldier and use cutting-edge biotechnologies to develop soldiers who, through Idiophylaxis, would be both internally armored and continually self-armoring, and thus prevent and mitigate the effects of disease, environmental stressors, and combat trauma. Crucially, Idiophylaxis would implant an auto-anticipation capability—a kind of built-in "virus scanner" akin to what we now find on computers—in the soldier's body. Embedded and unseen, biotechnology anchored in the soldier would make the soldier her own armor and biomonitor, constantly on guard and on the lookout for threats and pathogens presented by both the battlefield and the enemy. Four decades later, plans for providing built-in armor against the environment and diseases around the world, and the importance of medical anticipation and imagination in protecting US soldiers, would be broached again, but this time with the added promise of an "unfair advantage."

Idiophylaxis and the New Biology of War

In a talk given in 1942 titled "War: A Problem for Biology," W. K. Butts, a professor of biology at the University of Chattanooga, tapped into the growing awareness that the war with Nazi Germany and the Japanese empire was a new kind of war, a war that required and demanded both an appreciation for and new developments in biology in order for the war to be won (and an awareness that both Germany and Japan were working on weaponizing biology). Butts talked about the role and importance of biology in training and the disjuncture between humans and the machines of war.

> Let us be more explicit in discussing the part which biology plays in warfare. . . . Let us remember that war is fought with machines, but more it is fought with men; and man is a biological product. Biologists of many sorts are concerned with rearing him and preparing him for war. . . . The hardening and breaking in process is in part a biological problem. In some divisions of the service very special physiological and psychological preparation must be given. The procedure must be developed by scientists with a knowledge of biology. . . .
>
> In some instances, the machines of warfare have been developed to a greater degree of efficiency than the men who run them. . . . The limiting factor in the height to which airplanes can fly is not in the mechanics of the machine itself. It is the ability of the human body to withstand the changed conditions at high altitudes even with artificial aids. . . . Clearly, if air superiority is an important factor in victory, the war may be won or lost according to how well the physiologist, physicist and physician can solve these problems. (1942, 206–7)

Butts sensed that war was becoming increasingly more mechanized and complex, and increasingly more difficult to survive. World War I and the challenges presented by new weapons of mass killing, and the sheer scale of armies deployed, meant that soldiers needed to be protected in new and novel ways. As a biologist, Butts realized that the new kind of war of the twentieth century was a war of biology. Sulzberger might not have known about Butts's talk (which was also published in *Bios* that same year), but Butts's statements would have clearly resonated with Sulzberger. Having experienced and examined the new "biological" battlefields of both World War II and Korea, and rather than thinking of medicine in a strictly palliative sense, Sulzberger made a fairly radical intervention by thinking about military medicine prophylactically and "loading" the soldier with medicines and biotechnology in order to keep the soldier healthy and in the fight, and prevent as much as possible the need for any kind of "after action" medical care. Sulzberger was writing at a time when there was immense excitement about the promises of scientific and medical advancements, and he saw the military as a natural area to exploit these advances, both for the good of the military and for the good of "mankind" through the development of dual-use medicines and technologies to enhance human performance and endurance in extreme conditions. This is reminiscent of Rigg's design for the soldiers of the "Futurarmy," as well as Manfred E. Clynes and Nathan S. Kline's (1960) work on cybernetics and the US space program, and the need to develop technologies that would allow "weak" humans to survive in forbidding and lethal environments. Rather than thinking of soldiers as expendable, or less important than hardware and weaponry, Sulzberger advanced what was then a fairly radical notion: it was very much in the military's interest to make the soldier into the hardware and the weapon. In effect, Sulzberger was ultimately arguing for an increased weaponization of soldiers in order to make them more reliable components of new, "syncretic"—or even cybernetic—weapons systems, fully merging them in a kind of complete violent embodiment designed to make them more easily produce and withstand violence. Idiophylaxis was to help the soldier survive any and all battlefield conditions, be they natural or manmade.

"Mr. Dermatology": Idiophylaxis and the Self-Armoring US Soldier

Born in 1895, Dr. Marion B. Sulzberger—known as "Mr. Dermatology" and named the "Dermatologist of the Century" by the *Journal of the American Medical Association* in 1983—was an American MD specializing in dermatology who saw "skin as a source of inspiration from which would flow the answers to many of the important problems of biology" (Goldsmith 2003, v; see figure 5.1). Sulzberger served in World War I as one of the first naval aviators and flight instructors in the US Navy; in 1961 Sulzberger was made a member of the "Order of the Daedalions," a fraternity honoring pilots from World War I (Hunter and Holubar 1984). After the war, Sulzberger began medical school at the University of Geneva, finishing his medical training at the University of Zurich (Hunter and Holubar 1984). During World War II, Sulzberger served as a lieutenant commander in the US Naval Reserves and directed a research team that developed and tested materials to protect against poison gas attacks and examine sensitization to chemical warfare agents (Hoffman 1983; MacKee, 1955). He also produced more than one hundred secret reports for the US Navy during World War II (Goldsmith 2003, v). In 1961 Sulzberger was made the technical director of Research, Medical Research and Development Command, Office of the Surgeon General of the US Army, holding the position until 1964, when he took a position at the Letterman Army Institute of Research in San Francisco (Sulzberger 1981, 503). Sulzberger directed research on tropical skin

Figure 5.1 Dr. Marion B. Sulzberger, 1962.

diseases, chemical warfare agents, insect repellants, and antifungal creams while at Letterman Army Hospital and on Guam (Hoffmann 1983). In addition to his military work, he also had a long and successful career as a civilian doctor and trained a large number of future dermatologists; he was a professor of dermatology at New York University's Bellevue Medical Center and later a professor of clinical dermatology at the University of California, San Francisco, and was also the founding member of the Society for Investigative Dermatology. Sulzberger died in 1983.

A driving force for Sulzberger and his call for Idiophylaxis was the recognition of the number of soldiers killed and incapacitated by disease during World War II (see figure 5.2). While advances in medicine—and military medicine—began to mitigate the effects of diseases and illness, diseases such as typhoid, malaria, and dysentery and various skin diseases and conditions continued to wreak havoc on soldiers in combat situations (Slotten 2014; Sulzberger 1962b; see also McNeill 2010; Pearn 2004). Sulzberger was influenced by T. C. R. Archer's 1958 article in the *Journal of the Royal Medical Corps*, "Medical Problems of the Operational Infantry Soldier in Malaya." Archer described his experiences training British soldiers in Malaya

Figure 5.2 US Army antimalaria poster, World War II.

over the course of two years, discussing the various medical issues and daily concerns of the soldiers, including disease, removal to treat medical issues, fitness (physical and mental requirements for soldiers stationed there), acclimatization, weight being carried, rations and water, and insects/pests. As he describes, disease is the largest threat, particularly tropical skin disease: "The chances of being killed or wounded by enemy action in this type of warfare are very small; the incidence of accidental injury and disease which requires evacuation from the jungle is a much bigger and constant problem" (1958, 6).

Military and civilian commanders and strategists recognized the need to develop ways to protect their soldiers not just from the enemy but against environmental conditions that directly impacted soldier health and performance as well. Idiophylaxis, in Sulzberger's conception, involves a broad array of medical interventions to provide "built-in protection" for the soldier: vaccinations, medications, psychological conditioning, and treatments to turn the soldier's skin into "armor." These biomedical interventions envision a soldier who is made to better withstand the physical and mental stresses of combat. For Sulzberger, these stresses included the anticipation and possibility of nuclear, chemical, and biological warfare; conventional warfare and combat conditions; and mundane but militarily important conditions like blisters and rashes that could keep countless soldiers from taking part in combat operations. Idiophylaxis was to embed protections against anticipated and imagined military and environmental threats directly in the soldier. "Idiophylaxis" is derived from prophylaxis, the Greek term for the "act of guarding." To guard something is to anticipate a threat to it and act to prevent any harm coming to it. It is a gaze into a dangerous future requiring a real-time solution in the present.

At the beginning of his 1962 West Point address, Sulzberger makes clear what he sees as the most important and urgent problem facing the US military, and the stakes involved in terms of comprehensively protecting the soldier, both internally and externally.

> All who have been connected with any aspect of military research and development realize that weapons systems generally consist of three parts: the man, the carrier or vehicle, and the weapon itself. Of these three, man is by far the most complex, most unfathomable and often most fragile. . . . I believe that man is also the most valuable military component, especially when trained and skilled in the various specialized crafts and intricacies of modern warfare. And, it is not just a matter of belief but one of record that in military campaigns . . . the component man is the one that fails the most often. Moreover, he most often fails not because of bullets or missiles or any enemy action, but because of the stresses of climate and food and anxiety and disease. (1962b, 317)

Sulzberger then explains what he and his collaborators mean by "idiophylaxis," and how this differs from standard forms of combat protection.

> The improvement and strengthening of the combat soldier's inbuilt self-protection by medical means is one of the central objectives upon which the United States Army's research and development program is focused. . . . I have given the name "idiophylaxis" to this form of protection. . . . We include under idiophylaxis <u>every form of protection that can be given to the soldier by preceding mental and physical preparation through medical means</u>. Thus, idiophylaxis includes mental conditioning,

the immunizing procedures, the chemoprophylaxis, the medicaments and the antibodies which we can cause to be embodied in the soldier's own person. It includes every protective capability with which we can medically endow him so that were he to be stripped suddenly naked, he still would carry substantial degrees of protection with him. (1962b, 320)

Sulzberger continues by explaining the rationale behind his conception of Idiophylaxis and the various forms of protection and biological armor making up his vision of the new US soldier:

Mental conditioning, i.e., psychic idiophylaxis, has been placed at the very top of my list because of the high priority which must be given to endeavors to equip our soldiers with the mind and the will to resist the terrible stresses which modern warfare brings with it. We must reduce his susceptibility to excessive fatigue and confusion, anxiety and mental breakdowns. . . . For, when the soldier feels the physical protection which we have been able to confer upon him coursing through his bloodstream or built into his own skin, he knows in his bones that everything has been done to protect him beforehand and everything will be done to help him if he gets into trouble later. (1962b, 321)

Militaries have long been concerned with the deleterious impact of disease, illness, and environmental conditions on soldiers, and their effects on combat operations and planning. J. R. McNeill (2010), for example, analyzes the devastating effect of tropical diseases on colonialism and colonial militaries—such as malaria and typhus—problems that continue to plague modern militaries. Environmental stressors and diseases, such as heat, cold, malaria, dysentery, and so on, constantly plague militaries, negatively impacting military campaigns and severely affecting soldiers and their ability to fight and survive (Cowdrey 1994; Harrison 2010; see also DeBruyne and Leland 2015). Indeed, the majority of military casualties are from disease and illness brought on by environmental conditions. In many ways, it is the "mundane" or the quotidian of the battlefield that knocks soldiers out of combat more often than not.

According to Sulzberger's calculations, US military losses due to skin diseases, for example, in World War II came to the equivalent of twelve divisions per day, resulting in the loss of four million "man-days" (Sulzberger's term) over the course of the war. (There is no evidence that these calculations were contradicted or questioned by the US military, at least according to his papers and a specific report; see Sulzberger 1962b.)

Sulzberger was very much aware that the military's need to combat disease and illness was an old and ongoing concern, and he attempted to devise new ways to deal with it that would be directed at the "armoring" of the biology of the soldier. From his analysis of disease and illness casualties in World War II and Korea, Sulzberger concluded that the soldier's "first line of defense" in combat was the soldier's own body, a body that needed to be steeled and hardened and fortified to withstand the demands of combat in ways heretofore medically and technologically unachievable. For Sulzberger, Idiophylaxis and its suite of internally embedded protective technologies and immunizations would turn the soldier himself into the armor he needed to survive on the new, possibly nuclear, and global battlefield.

Sulzberger then explains what he thinks is the most important component of Idiophylaxis, both for the soldier and for military medical research focused on protecting the soldier on all battlefields (these concerns will be directly addressed later by DARPA's Inner Armor program).

> Another, and perhaps the most militarily important field of all, is the idiophylaxis which consists in conferring immunity or heightening resistance to various types of <u>infectious diseases</u>. This is going on continuously with unremitting vigor, and our global effort in this can be divided into three main phases:
>
> 1 Gathering from every part of the world information and specimens of diseases which may be encountered there by our soldiers.
> 2 Research on the causes and carriers of these diseases, their microorganisms and viruses and vectors in laboratory and experimental animals, cell structures, etc., both here and abroad, and,
> 3 The endeavor to produce immunizing vaccines of all types and their laboratory tests and finally their clinical assays.
>
> In these efforts the Army's Medical Research and Development Command collaborates closely with our sister services, with the National Institutes of Health, and with numerous other agencies, both on this continent and throughout the world. (1962b, 321)

Following this recognition for directed biomedical preventative intelligence gathering, Sulzberger details many of the conditions that could then be covered by Idiophylaxis, those that could not but were soon possible, and those that were required but not possible at the time (see tables 5.1, 5.2, and 5.3, adapted from Sulzberger 1962b).

Table 5.1 Idiophylaxis Now Conferrable by Immunologic Measures (Vaccines, etc.)

adenovirus respiratory infection	mumps	Rocky Mountain spotted fever
cholera	paratyphoid A & B	smallpox
diphtheria	plague	tetanus
epidemic typhus	Q fever	tuberculosis (probably)
infantile influenza	rabies	typhoid
measles	yellow fever	whooping cough

Table 5.2 Idiophylaxis Now Conferrable by Chemoprophylaxis (Drugs) (Idiophylaxis May Soon Be Available)

anthrax	leptospirosis
botulism	Rift Valley fever
encephalitides (by certain virus)	Russian tick-borne fever
heat, humidity, cold, and altitude effects	tularemia

Sulzberger's lists of diseases, illnesses, and battle conditions are instructive, as they give a sense of the kinds of things the military views as detrimental to soldier health and performance. These conditions requiring intervention also highlight the kinds of areas and battlefields where US soldiers would or might be deployed. Following the places where these diseases occur is a way of mapping the possible areas of future conflict; in this sense, the disease is the battlefield.

Protection is about enhancing not just a soldier's chances of survival but a soldier's ability to labor and perform, on and off the battlefield. A main concern of Sulzberger's was making soldiers work harder, of figuring out ways to extract more labor from soldiers. Soldiering is a labor issue, and in many ways, soldiers are workers: they perform the work of combat and killing for the state and they perform the mundane work of garrison

Table 5.3 Some Examples in Which Idiophylaxis Is Required (Perhaps Possible but Not Yet Available)

battle psychoses	O'nyong-nyong fever
chikungunya fever	parasitic diseases (miscellaneous, worms, flukes, etc.)
common cold	radiation damage
dengue	relapsing fevers (tick-borne and louse-borne)
diarrheal and enteric diseases	schistosomiasis
encephalitides (various)	sleeping sickness
epidemic hemorrhagic fevers (various)	staph and strep infections
fatigue	thermal flash damage
fungus infection (various) (superficial and deep)	wound infections (clostridium, pseudomonas, etc.)
leprosy	

life. Idiophylaxis was a new way of thinking about and "enhancing" military labor, a new way of extracting more labor from soldiers, both in and out of combat. Soldiers must be healthy and able to perform a wide variety of tasks, with combat obviously being the most important. While disease and illness can incapacitate soldiers, environmental stressors like heat and cold can severely curtail a soldier's ability to work and fight. Sulzberger was concerned with disease and illness protection but also protection against the elements. Acclimatizing soldiers to heat and cold meant that they could perform more efficiently and effectively under these conditions. Sulzberger discusses the connections between acclimatization and military labor.

> In a recent test, 41 of our men were divided into two similar groups. One of these groups were trained, and in addition, acclimatized to heat while at Fort Knox in the United States. The other group was trained at Fort Knox at the same time and in precisely the same way but not heat-acclimatized. Both were then set down simultaneously in tropical Panama and put through the same military exercises and stresses. As had been expected and hoped, the heat-acclimatized men resisted the tropi-

cal heat and humidity much better than the men in the non-acclimatized group. In the 20 non-acclimatized men there were 10 casualties due to heat; while in the previously acclimated group there were none. Moreover, the heat-acclimatized men were able to carry out a substantially greater amount of work in the heat. For example, in a load-moving exercise task during a 90-minute period the acclimatized group were able to move 11,200 pounds more of water than the non-acclimated group. (1962b, 317–18)

Concomitant with his concerns about labor, Sulzberger was also very much concerned with the perennially pressing problem all militaries face: logistics. He saw Idiophylaxis as a way to both protect soldiers internally and lessen the logistics demands and stressors of battlefield medical problems: "Perhaps the best way to bring about a substantial reduction in personnel and logistics requirements is, of course, by individual preventive medicine—by endowing each soldier entering a combat zone with his own in-built capacity to protect himself against the prevalent diseases, stresses, climate, and other onslaughts" (1962b, 320). While he was happy with the results, as a dermatologist, Sulzberger was concerned with the toll that increased performance took on the soldiers' bodies.

In contrast to these expected and desirable results, an undesirable finding was that on the morning of the third day, 32 of the total of 41 men had blistering feet. The blistering occurred in 16 men in each group and was of equal severity in both groups; 4 men in each being incapacitated by the blisters.

Now blistering of the feet certainly affects both civilians and soldiers. But, while it is usually just a disagreeable and perhaps somewhat painful inconvenience to civilians, as a source of military incapacity severe blisters on the feet can result in the loss of a battle, a campaign, a cause. There is, therefore, an absolute mandate for military medical research to study intensively the factors and mechanisms which cause blistering—and how to prevent or minimize their effects in soldiers. (1962b, 318)

Sulzberger approached the idea of the enhanced soldier as a military doctor and researcher who understands the "everyday" and the mundane of military life, how the combined pressures of performance and environment play out on soldiers, and how things that we might take for granted—like blisters—can cause a military to lose a battle. Friedl, for example, writing about the US military's investigations of Benzedrine during World War II, notes that soldiers taking ten milligrams could stay awake for three days, but Benzedrine impaired their decision-making abilities, often motivating them to continue marching on blistered feet even if this risked greater injury (2015, S72).

Sulzberger also approached soldier protection and enhancement as a military researcher and administrator, with an eye to balancing protection, budgets, and funding. Protection becomes a kind of cost–benefit analysis: "built-in" protection not only protects the soldier; it protects the military's budget and the cost of caring for unprotected soldiers. Sulzberger was probably aware of the RAND Corporation's work on the market and nonmarket valuation of Air Force aircrews and the cost of military lives (Banzhaf 2014; see also Robin 2001 for a discussion of the importance of RAND's analysis during the early Cold War era). The military must trade off between protection and costs and logistics. For Sulzberger, Idiophylaxis was a way to address these calculations. As he makes clear, the more the military can do to provide soldiers with built-in protection, the greater the easing on military logistics and the need to deploy field hospitals, doctors, clean water, and so on. An important subtext of his talk is that military medicine, while important for the smooth functioning of the military, is also a logistics burden on the military. In other words, healthy and internally protected soldiers save the military money, material, and effort. Investing in the protection of the soldier before combat pays handsome dividends in the long run in terms of lessening the logistics burden of preparing for and carrying out combat operations. All of this, combined with the need to protect soldiers from disease and illness, formed the crux of his conception of the Idiophylactic Soldier.

Idiophylaxis was a combination of the mundane, the visionary, and the practical, a suite of interventions designed to protect the individual soldier, lessen the military's logistics burden, and promote military medicine and increase funding for military medicine and performance enhancement research. At the end of his address, Sulzberger lays out why the military must invest in and develop Idiophylactic Soldiers.

> In closing, I would like to assure you that we in the medical service are not so starry-eyed as to think that we will ever be able to confer upon the soldier a degree of idiophylaxis which will protect him against all of the attacks of nature or of an enemy, or to make his skin so tough that it will ward off bullets and flames, blast and radiation effects. However,

we do believe that we must develop the idiophylaxis of our soldiers to the utmost degree possible, and that we have every prospect of making him in this way the most effective and most resistant of all human beings and thus reduce the vulnerability of the most delicate component of our weapons systems—the trained man. (1962b, 326)

If, as Paul Stoller writes, "flesh both inscribes and incorporates cultural memory and history," then it also inscribes political policy and intentions, military necessity, military history, and military memory in the bodies of soldiers and creates new forms of military biomedical inscription (Stoller 1997, 47). From this nexus of memory and national security, new ways of imagining, making, and being a soldier emerge. For Sulzberger, Idiophylaxis—a program situated between memory and anticipation—was a response to the medical and operational history and memory of World War II and Korea, and the theorization and preparation of new forms of protection and new forms of warfare. Sulzberger's notion of Idiophylaxis was a call for a kind of visionary, operationalized medical intervention and research program that was much more active than passive: medical interventions would protect the soldier beforehand in ever-more encompassing and efficient ways.

Idiophylaxis, Military Medicine, and Belief Armor

While various forms of external armor were necessary and useful, Sulzberger saw the necessity of developing a kind of psychic "belief" armor firmly grounded in new biomedical technologies that would always be with the soldier, a belief anchored in the emergent biotechnological prowess of the United States, and a biotechnical belief that would both enhance and supersede "boldness" and counter weakness and timidity. Rather than simply dealing with medical issues and disease as they occurred, Sulzberger envisioned an applied military medicine ethos and focus that would use cutting-edge technologies and insights to develop soldiers who could "armor" themselves and thus prevent and mitigate the effects of combat, combat trauma, and disease. The changing nature of warfare also reflected his concerns about "manpower": increases in military technology demanded a different kind of soldier, so it was in the state's interest to better protect soldiers, as they were increasingly costly and time-consuming to train, and seen more as "investments," "assets," and "weapons" and less as mere cannon fodder (Banzhaf 2014).

Military performance enhancements are focused on imagining how to make the body useful for the military, and mitigating possible future negative influences and stressors on performance. Idiophylaxis would enhance the normal soldier by making him resistant to combat and environmental stressors that unenhanced soldiers would not be able to tolerate. The drive behind modifying or enhancing a soldier is to preclude certain kinds of actions and responses in the future; enhancements are intended to prevent a degradation of ability or functioning, based on anticipated events, stimuli, stressors, and biological/cognitive autonomic responses. If the soldier is the weakest part of the system, then the entire system is at risk. This is not to say that all enhancements are predicated upon a negative but to say that enhancements are about overcoming "normal" responses to things that would inhibit the unenhanced soldier from operating or carrying out the mission.

As Sulzberger makes clear, military doctors and biomedical researchers are not tasked simply with maintaining the health and well-being of soldiers, even if this is an important part of their jobs; rather, their task is also to produce, monitor, and intervene, and to incorporate technology *in* soldiers as a way to promote and enhance combat effectiveness, survivability, and readiness, and keep soldiers healthy and well—and in a state of readiness—when not in combat. This point is made very clear by the motto on contemporary Army Medicine ID badges: "To Conserve Fighting Strength." Combat readiness and the operational needs of the military come before the "personal" medical needs of the individual soldier. The goal of Idiophylaxis was to protect the fighting strength of the soldier in the face of new weapons systems, diseases, and biological hazards. By making the health of the soldier as strong as the machines around him, Sulzberger hoped to make the entire system unbeatable. For Sulzberger, Idiophylaxis was both an internal armor and a form of performance enhancement, as it would allow the soldier to "carry on" and continue fighting on the battlefield when normal, unenhanced soldiers could not.

"Body Armor": Skin as Metaphor, Protection, and Politics

We generally do not link "militarization," "dermatology," and "soldiers" together in any kind of semantic or technological chain, and we usually do not associate skin with actual military armor, even if our skin does protect us from the outside world. If these things are ever thought of in conjunction, it is usually skin requiring armor in order to be protected. And we rarely think of skin as militarily useful or as something that needs to be "militarized" or modified for military use on its own accord.

Predating Sulzberger, Rigg, in his war novel *War—1974*, discusses some of the reason the military needs to focus on "skin," and some of the technologies the military was attempting to develop to protect soldiers' skin.

> In an effort to make the American soldier more efficient, Army Quartermaster researchers are working on "artificial skin"—colorless creams designed to protect the soldier against the elements of nature and the effects of atomic weapons. One of the "skins" under development is designed especially to protect against blasts of heat such as would be experienced in close proximity to, but beyond the range of immediate lethal radiation, of a nuclear explosion. . . . Another type of skin under development is one for protection against acids and liquid fuels such as used in guided missiles. Next there are the arctic and sunburn creams, the former being an applied "skin" that would allow the soldier to work for brief periods without gloves in sub-zero temperatures. (1958, 242)

While Rigg was thinking of "skin" as a kind of appliqué armor, in Idiophylaxis, Sulzberger discusses two points about the need for the military to consider actual "skin."

> There are two points I realized only after I had seen this finished drawing [of the idiophylactic soldier]. One was that although it is to some degree a projection into the future, it does not appear to be nearly as fantastic as a drawing or description of our astronauts of today would have seemed to me only 15 years ago. The second point that I realized is that the majority of the protective capabilities indicated on this drawing have something to do with the protective capacities of the human skin. Perhaps this is why I, an old hand at dermatology, have been particularly interested in these problems. Not only does the skin serve as an accurate index and record of the immune capacities of the individual in the form of its many specific reactions to skin tests, but the skin is also a natural body armor protecting the individual in great measure against many of the onslaughts of his environment. . . . It would seem that the future soldier's increased protection or idiophylaxis would consist in some measure of a medically conferred augmentation of the already substantial inherent capabilities of man's skin to resist. (1962b, 323)

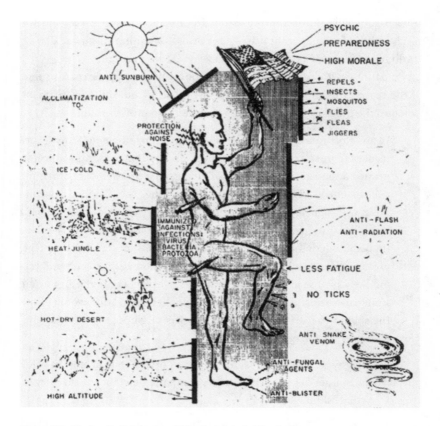

Figure 5.3 Marion B. Sulzberger, "Idiophylactic Soldier," 1962.

Sulzberger's focus on skin makes sense in light of his training as a dermatologist ("I, the old hand at dermatology"), and his concern is with the effects of combat and the battlefield environment on soldiers' skin (see figure 5.3). Skin is the thin line holding us together in the world, and on the battlefield, our skin is the target. Biological anthropologist Nina Jablonski describes the relationship between our skin and the environment in an interview discussing her work on human skin.

> Skin is the most important interface between [our bodies] and the environment. It bears the brunt of dealing with many environmental stresses—everything from sunshine and wetness to the chemical environment to abrasions and insect bites [to] microbes. It has been scrutinized by evolution to as great if not a greater extent than other

organs because it serves this unique function of protection, and yet it must remain sensitive—it can't just be [a] sort of armor plate of protection; it has to be somewhat porous, so that certain things can get in and certain things can't get out. So it's this very interesting, semi-permeable, resilient interface, and it has undergone tremendous scrutiny by natural selection in evolution. (Jablonski 2011; see also Jablonski 2004)

Jablonski explains why skin cannot simply be a kind of hard, impervious carapace, but it does have armor-like properties: "The skin comprises a sheet-like investiture that protects the body from attack by physical, chemical, and microbial agents" (Jablonski 2004, 585). These are properties that Sulzberger was well aware of and sought to exploit for the military. In Sulzberger's vision of the Idiophylactic Soldier, skin—already a kind of armor—needs only to be converted or augmented into a tougher, more militarily useful kind of armor to protect the soldier, even if/when other kinds of armor are unavailable or ultimately fail to protect the soldier.

In a report titled "Body Armor," Sulzberger writes about the easy supply of body armor at the US military's disposal.

There is now available a sufficient supply of full body armor satisfying the following specifications: to be negligible in cost; individually tailored to fit; extremely light, elastic, flexible and perfectly comfortable under most climate conditions, durable for life; corrosion, rust, and mildew proof; self-heating, self-cooling; self-thickening in response to repeated trauma and self-repairing in response to acute trauma; self-drying, self-humidifying, self-cleansing and self-sterilizing; practically impermeable to water, to grease and to most harmful chemicals; and equipped with thousands of slender antennae and telemetering systems to warn of approaching danger. For these specifications quite accurately describe the human skin—provided it is healthy and is not subjected to unphysiological and excessive attacks. (Sulzberger 1962a)

In "Body Armor," Sulzberger states the importance and necessity of focusing on skin diseases and the need to enhance soldiers' skin: "There is every reason to hope for better means of using the advances of modern physics, biochemistry, pharmacology, plastic and fabric technology to improve and reinforce soldiers' natural protective armor against the onslaught of heat, cold, moisture, infectious disease, insects, poisons, rays, and trauma" (1962a).

A September 1962 article by the Walter Reed Army Institute of Research (WRAIR) in the *Army Research and Development Newsmagazine* discussing Sulzberger's work, titled "Idiophylaxis: A Biological Armor for the Soldier" (see figure 5.4), explains how skin could serve as armor for the soldier: "By changing the man's chemistry, his skin becomes an effective repellant. . . . Pills are under study which would provide immunity from sunburn. Others someday may provide a measure of protection against nuclear radiation" (WRAIR 1962, 27). In Sulzberger's vision, the soldier's skin is to be made into a kind of "double" armor, a first line of defense that is superior to "normal" human skin; it has to be even more resistant to normal wear and tear, and it has to be made resistant to things that normal human skin is not. Skin is still the interface, as Jablonski describes it, but it is an interface that needs to protect and guard against mission degradation, and it must in fact become a kind of "armor plate of protection" in order to deal with the stresses and experiences and "interfaces" of combat. And while evolution has developed it this far, the skin of the soldier needs to be augmented and enhanced through Idiophylaxis to fit the needs of military deployments: "Perhaps more important than any of these will be the development of a material which when incorporated in the skin either after local application or when taken by mouth, would make the skin's surface and its secretions repellent to insects, flies, mosquitos, ticks, fleas, etc., and other vectors which are bearers of the most important diseases affecting military operations, including malaria, yellow fever, sandfly fever, hemorrhagic fevers, and so forth" (Sulzberger 1962b, 325).

The possibility of nuclear war changed the nature of conventional land warfare and conceptions of the survivability of the soldier in combat. This possibility also prompted the need to rethink battlefield protection, or at least ways of convincing the soldier that he was protected. The new operational and medical problems it presented to soldier survival on the battlefield influenced Sulzberger's thinking about soldier protection. Reflecting a major concern about the new forms of injuries presented by the threat of the wide-scale use of nuclear weapons in any conflict with the Soviet Union, Sulzberger also discussed the need to develop ways to change and protect soldier's skin from nuclear flash burns: "I have mentioned the prospects and efforts in idiophylaxis against flashburns. While this surely will have to do with increasing the resistance of the skin and the skin's surface, there is a large program endeavoring to develop better chemoprophylactic measures against the systemic effects of ionizing radiation, so that soldiers will be protected in sufficient measure to go into areas of fallout radia-

Army R&D Newsmagazine

Vol. 3, No. 9   September 1962

Editor . . . . Clarence T. Smith
Ass't Editor . . . . George J. Makuta
Editorial Ass't . Pfc Jerold Roschwalb

Published monthly by the Army Research Office, Office of the Chief of Research and Development, Department of the Army, Washington 25, D.C., in coordination with the Technical and Industrial Liaison Office, OCRD. Grateful acknowledgement is made for the valuable assistance of Technical Liaison Offices within the Technical Services and the U.S. Continental Army Command. Publication is authorized by AR 310-1, dated 15 May 1956.

Purpose: To improve informal communication among all segments of the Army scientific community and other Government R&D agencies; to further understanding of Army R&D progress, problem areas and program planning; to stimulate more closely integrated and coordinated effort among the widely dispersed and diffused Army R&D activities; to maintain a closer link from top management through all levels to scientists, engineers and technicians at the bench level; to express views of leaders, as pertinent to their responsibilities, and to keep personnel informed on matters germane to their welfare and pride of service.

Picture Credits: Unless otherwise indicated, all illustrations are by the U.S. Army.

Submission of Material: All articles submitted for publication must be channeled through the technical liaison or public information officer at installation or command level.

By-lined Articles: Accuracy and relevancy of contents of this publication to accomplishment of the Army R&D mission are of constant concern to the editors. Primary responsibility for opinions of by-lined authors rests with them; their views do not necessarily reflect the official policy or position of the Department of the Army.

DISTRIBUTION is made automatically each month based on requirements stated on DA Form 12-4, permitting changes as necessary.

Distribution requirements for the Office of the Secretary of the Army, Under Secretary of the Army, Assistant Secretary of the Army R&D), Chief of Staff, Chief of Research and Development, and Chief of Information will be submitted by the Office of the Chief of Research and Development.

All other Department of the Army agencies should submit their requirements through channels to the Army Publications Distribution Center servicing them.

Changes in requirements of other Government agencies should be submitted directly to the Army Research Office, OCRD, Department of the Army, Washington 25, D.C., ATTN: Scientific Information Branch.

SUBSCRIPTIONS. Public sale of this publication is authorized through the Superintendent of Documents, U.S. Government Printing Office, Washington 25, D. C. Single copies sell for 20 cents. Subscription rates (12 copies annually) are: Domestic (including APO and FPO addresses), $2.25; Foreign, $3.00.

Theme of the Month: Army Medical Research

By Lt Gen Dwight E. Beach, Chief of Research and Development

On Sept. 12, 1962, it will be my pleasure to participate in the dedication ceremonies for the new wing of the Walter Reed Army Institute of Research (WRAIR). The work of the research staff of the U.S. Army Medical Service all too often does not receive the attention and publicity it richly deserves. This dedication ceremony serves as a convenient vehicle to remind all of us of the problems as well as the accomplishments of Army medical research.

The great bulk of Army R&D is devoted to the development of those items we have come to call "hardware"—new cannon, new fighting vehicles, new logistical carriers. But the best-equipped Army in the world can become simply an impotent list of names if the men who serve and use these items are physically and mentally incapable of being present for duty.

As this Nation's worldwide commitments have increased, the job of Army medical research has expanded manyfold. No small part of this expanded mission has been the task of finding vaccines for, or means to control, the myriad number of exotic diseases indigenous to those areas where the American soldier is now or in the future may be stationed, be it Southeast Asia, Africa, or South America.

Today, with our increased assistance role to the underdeveloped areas and newly emerging nations, the problem of protecting our men from these exotic diseases is receiving urgent attention. We expect that the added facilities in the new WRAIR wing will increase our capability here by 25 percent.

Similarly, by means of the Army's first biomedical nuclear reactor in the new wing of WRAIR, Army medical scientists and technicians will provide us with the answers to many of the unknowns in the problems of man versus nuclear weapon radiation.

The United States Army stands today as a worldwide bulwark of freedom, prepared to fight with the most modern weapons and equipment under any condition of warfare, from conventional to nuclear, from a Special Forces team to full field armies. But we should never forget that but for the work of the civilian and military research staffs who contribute to the Army Medical Service, this readiness could be reduced to impotency.

Idiophylaxis: A Biological Armor for the Soldier

Prepared by Walter Reed Army Institute of Research

Many of the protective devices designed for the modern soldier are based on the concepts of cover and concealment. Whether defensive armor be the knight's steel mail or today's missile-resistant vest, the fighting man is still susceptible to the onslaught of enemies he cannot see, hear, feel or touch. The attack comes from the stresses and anxieties of a strange environment, unusual climate, peculiar forms of energies, strange foods or disease.

Just as vaccines can assist in protecting against the harmful effects of viruses and other disease-producing germs, so can the body be stimulated to develop its own protection against other potential hazards. This form of self-protection is called "idiophylaxis" by the U.S. Army Medical Service.

The protective coloration of certain animals is a form of in-built natural protection. The blotchy skin of the frog and the changing hues of the chameleon as it blends in with its environment provide some immunity from detection by enemies.

The pupillary reflex in man is another form of protection. When one exits from a dark theater into bright light, the pupil of one's eye—in the center of the iris—contracts to form a smaller opening. As a consequence, the amount of light that strikes the sensitive cells in the retina is sharply reduced. Conversely, as one moves into the dark from a well-lighted place, the pupil dilates and more light is permitted to enter the eye, thus giving better vision under dark conditions.

Examples like these show that biological organisms have natural mechanisms for defending themselves. Idiophylaxis is that form of natural protection which can be bestowed by medical means.

The middle ear muscles can be activated in a similar manner to protect the sensitive cells of the inner ear from too much sound energy. As high-intensity sound enters the ear, the muscles which move the little bones of the inner ear contract in such a way as to damp the ear drum. As a consequence, sound waves coming in are attenuated and the amount of sound to the sensitive cells in the inner ear is reduced. The action is called the "acoustic reflex."

A device to activate the acoustic reflex just before a soldier's gun goes off is now under study at the U.S. Army Medical Research Laboratory at
(Continued on page 27)

Figure 5.4 *Army Research and Development Newsmagazine, September 1962.*

tion which are still forbidden to the enemy" (1962b, 325–26). Sulzberger's idea that skin could be turned into its own armor against "flash burns" and "rays"—while fantastical and probably implausible—was an attempt to come to terms with nuclear war and strategize ways of keeping land warfare possible, survivable, and ultimately winnable.

For Sulzberger, the soldier's body is to be the soldier's own protection, the hardened projection of the soldier in the world, armored through and through, internally, externally, and psychically, and hardened in accordance with the military needs and technological advances of the time. Of course, much of Sulzberger's focus on skin is skin as metaphor; as Sulzberger concedes, there is no real way (in 1962 and, presumably, now) to *actually* turn skin into a kind of "armor" that affords the soldier protection to every kind of military and environmental threat. Skin can be fortified and strengthened and protected in certain ways against certain environmental factors and agents, and against some kinds of physical injuries. Again, in Sulzberger's formulation of a kind of biomedical "belief armor," the trick is to make the soldier think his skin is a suit of armor and not just simply his own unenhanced body, naked against the world. Soldiers are to think of their bodies as not just their own but as the state, armored and made indestructible by the biotechnical capabilities of the state, their safety vouchsafed by the state's directed interventions in their bodies.

———

A striking inclusion in Sulzberger's notion of Idiophylaxis was his discussion and vision of a kind of technological primitivism, of the soldier stripped down to his skin, naked and alone on the battlefield, seemingly unprotected and unarmored yet still powerful and undeterred, reminiscent of German artist Arno Breker's *Bereitschaft* (*Readiness*), a massive sculpture of a hypermasculine nude German soldier made in 1939 (see figure 5.5.). This is not to say that Sulzberger was in any way a fascist or a Nazi—he most obviously was not—but rather, when thinking about armored bodies with built-in protection, there are uncomfortable similarities, threads, and slippages running through these kinds of research projects. Sulzberger's notion of the Idiophylactic Soldier should be seen in the context of twentieth-century warfare and technology, and these ideas form the intellectual heritage of similar projects underway today. Sulzberger's Idiophylactic Soldier would be firmly locked in an image of the past while simultaneously embodying the technology of the future. At first glance, this seems to run counter to ideas of soldiers and body armor but makes perfect sense when the body, as Sulzberger saw it, was already a kind of natural armor that could be made even stronger with the right suite of interventions. As Sulzberger put forth in his address, his vision was to develop technologies for the soldier so that "were he to be stripped suddenly naked, he still would carry substantial degrees of protection with him" and would still possess a kind of innate armor and self-protection through vaccinations and other drugs and medications (1962b, 320). Sulzberger further explained: "I would like to emphasize that every protective measure with which we endow the soldier's body also contributes greatly to his mental idiophylaxis and his effectiveness and confidence" (321). Naked protection and biological armor also present the military with an extremely important logistical advantage: "All of these ideas have inherent the built-in, self-protection concept. All have the possibility of being controlled through medical knowledge. They have very great promise for very large savings in Army logistics. They do not require additional weight for the soldier to carry into combat; they do not require additional volumetric space in the ships or aircraft serving as supply lines overseas; they are part of the soldier—wherever he goes" (WRAIR 1962, 27).

Conceptions of the "naked warrior" revolve around notions of strength and weakness. Nudity—and the full exposure of the skin—is often associated with weakness, helplessness, and vulnerability (Norman Mailer's 1948 war novel, The Naked and the Dead, explores this connection) but can also be associated with strength, the unfettered use of one's powers, and authenticity (Berman 1975; Spotts 2004; see also Deakin 2014; Jablonski 2004). Naked bodies in the sun (in fascism) often represented strength, beauty, and innocence (Mangan 1999, 115), but for Sulzberger, bodies in the sun represented danger from sunburn and exposure, an exposure that demanded attention and intervention. Nudity also implies a kind of "blank slate," a body ready and open to manipulation and enhancement, tailored to specific goals or prepared for a broad array of possibilities, and a body devoid of equipment (Berman 1975). For Sulzberger, the "naked warrior" was a soldier who would be able to carry on and function on the battlefield because the blank slate had already been prepared and enhanced, confident in his own enhanced skin, knowing and feeling in his bones that the state is protecting him; he is cared for and protected, and still potent on the battlefield. The soldier is his own biological armor, encased in his own enhanced suit of "body armor."

The new soldier/laborer of the early twentieth century was envisioned as a body stripped of adornment, strong, alert to threats and danger, invincible

Figure 5.5 Arno Breker, *Bereitschaft* (*Readiness*), 1939.

on its own accord, predictable and efficient, "up to the task," and "ready for action." Twentieth-century conceptions of the internally armored soldier, like the protofascist New Man whom Jünger imagines, the armored body of the Italian futurists, Breker's *Readiness*, and the supersoldier serum-imbibing Captain America of the United States—all these conceptions and representations of the armored body were already circulating in the post–World War II cultural imaginary and can be seen in Sulzberger's conception of the Idiophylactic Soldier and its "Buck Rogers–like" possibilities as well as later iterations of US supersoldiers.

Even if the goals and intentions were different, in many ways, these concerns were seemingly also very much on Sulzberger's mind when he developed the Idiophylactic Soldier. Rather than just relying on soldiers as they found them, militaries could start to imagine ways to manipulate them and shape them in ways previously unimaginable or unattainable. It was a body that could be made to fit the ever-increasing needs of a military through technology and medicine—and new forms of weapons technology could be developed based on changes to the capabilities of the human body. The soldier would in many regards become the weapons system, be seen as a system (the "system man" in Sulzberger's phrasing), and fitted into a "system of systems" (Bickford 2008; Ford and Glymour 2014; Martinez-Lopez 2004). In essence, Idiophylaxis, the "armored" body, and human engineering are about imagining and designing a certainty and predictability of performance, armored against weakness and ensuring boldness, and of extracting as much labor and effort from the soldier as possible without "degrading" the ability of the soldier to actually function. As part of the Cold War US military's growing reliance on, and fetishization of, game theory, engineering logic, cybernetics, and algorithms, Idiophylaxis marks the emergence of an early systems engineering / cybernetics-meets-biomedicine approach to designing soldiers (Clynes and Kline 1960; DeLanda 1991; P. Edwards 1996; Erickson et al. 2013; Gray 1989, 1997).

As Sulzberger makes clear, the embedding of technology/medicines in soldiers would serve to protect them, but perhaps, most importantly, they would know and feel that they are protected, and feel like they were still supported and somehow not alone because of the sheer amount of technology "coursing through [their] bloodstream." Idiophylaxis was both protection and motivation, built-in armor and built-in willpower. Soldiers could continue to rely on the military, even if naked and alone, because they would know that the military had enhanced their bodies to continue to provide protection even without any other kind of armor. In many ways, the "insulated" body of the Idiophylactic Soldier mimicked the Cold War US obsession with "insulation" and a "closed world" of defense (P. Edwards 1996; see also Masco 2014): a state and a body insulated from the dangers of the world, armored from the inside against attacks and threats from the outside, the skin/borders presenting a (largely imagined) impermeable barrier.

The Cold War, Military Medicine, and Rethinking the "Component Man"

Idiophylaxis was a part of the logic of modernist technological development and advances and the constant attempt to improve capabilities and counter those of the enemy in an age of increasingly mechanized warfare. But in a key regard, it goes much further in embedding even more biomedical technology in the body of the soldier, of preparing the soldier for multiple contingencies rather than simply on an ad hoc basis. And rather than simply relying on "boldness" or "will" to ensure success on the battlefield, Idiophylaxis would augment willpower and belief and provide some certainty of performance through embedded protection. This continuum points to the ways in which metaphors of the "armored body" and the "man-machine" become both literal and applied over time, both partly ideological and partly productive.

Sulzberger wrote and theorized at a time when the Cold War, with its concomitant arms race and the space race—actually, a broader technology race with the Soviet Union—was in full swing. After the successful launch of Sputnik in 1957, there was a growing fear in the US defense community of a widening military and scientific technology gap with the Soviet Union. As each side prepared for war, the search for new ways of gaining any kind of military edge became a crucial national security concern. For Sulzberger, advances in military medicine and technology would enable the military to deal with medical concerns it was unable to cope with during World War II and enable the military to address and ameliorate operational and deployment concerns and potential problems brought about by the increasingly global battlefield of the Cold War and the matériel superiority of the Warsaw Pact over North Atlantic Treaty Organization (NATO) forces. Given the disparity in the size of NATO versus Warsaw Pact forces in terms of soldiers and matériel, NATO forces had to imagine and develop innovative ways to do more with fewer soldiers and keep the soldiers it had in the field, combat ready and capable for longer.

Idiophylaxis represented a fundamental difference in the ways the US/ NATO and the Warsaw Pact viewed soldiers and warfare: for the US, technological and medical solutions would carry the day and ultimately overcome any Soviet manpower and matériel advantages. Idiophylaxis would help counter Soviet tactics on the battlefield, such as massed armor and infantry attacks, or the expected use of tactical nuclear weapons (with the advent of both tactical and strategic nuclear weapons, soldiers had to be trained to contend with—and somehow, hopefully, survive—nuclear war and carry on with a mission after a nuclear attack). Of course, these concerns were not limited simply to Europe: the US and its allies also had to think about the Cold War on a global scale and prepare for a variety of battlefields and battlefield conditions in anticipation of the expected expansion of Soviet power and influence. As Sulzberger saw it, the embedded biomedical solutions of Idiophylaxis, and military medicine and new biotechnologies in general, would be the force multipliers of the Cold War, and the body of the

US soldier would increasingly mimic the high-tech solutions in military hardware favored by the US military.

The primary confluence of national security and science during the Cold War centered on major weapons projects and research, with "soldier-centric" research holding a second-tier position. Sulzberger's call for a focus on the soldier as a key priority of Cold War military scientific research ran counter to the prevailing interest in "big science" projects like nuclear weapons or other major weapons platforms (Creager 2014; DeLanda 1991; P. Edwards 1996; Gusterson 1996; Masco 2006, 2014; Oreskes 2014; Poggi 2014; Wolfe 2013) and was an attempt to put soldier-centric biomedical research on par with the "big science" national security prestige projects. Sulzberger was aware of the fact that weapons systems needed to be robust, but if soldiers could not keep up with the demands and stresses produced by the systems, then the systems would be fairly useless; military biomedical research would have to address and overcome the stressors to the "component man" that take him/her out of action. Describing science in general during the Cold War, but applicable to the kinds of research advocated by Sulzberger, science and technology historian Paul Forman wrote that science "effectively rotated . . . towards techniques and applications" (Oreskes 2014, 21). Idiophylaxis was to be a suite of directed and applied interventions and applications designed to prevent the "component man" from failing on and off the battlefield, and a suite of interventions that would give the military and politicians confidence that soldiers would not fail.

Rather than the somewhat slow, fits-and-starts evolution of military technology and improvements in soldier protection of the past centuries, the twentieth century—and the period after World War II—saw an exponential growth in biomedical protective capabilities and possibilities, a growth Sulzberger recognized and highlighted in his idea of Idiophylaxis. Military medicine was increasingly called upon not just for palliative care but for prophylactic armoring and advances, for preparing the soldier before the war, not just healing and curing during and after the war. Sulzberger, as a military physician, was of course aware of this mission and the differences between military medicine and civilian medicine. But he also saw that it needed to be forward thinking, and not just to cure but to enhance. Sulzberger was adamant in his belief that military medicine, while overlapping with civilian medicine in many ways, faced different challenges and demanded new and innovative responses to the types of conditions soldiers face on the battlefield. Sulzberger saw military medicine as a unique and increasingly important area of military technology and research and in his West Point address, he makes this very clear.

> The soldier's reliability, his mental and physical health, cannot be maintained except by a specially-oriented military medical research and development program, which is directly geared to every advance of science and at the same time rapidly responsive to the ever-changing military needs. The statement, self-evident though it is in relation to other military research and development programs, such as those in Ordnance, Signal, Transportation, Engineering, and the like is not quite so self-evident and requires a bit of explanation when it is applied to <u>medical</u> research and development. For medicine—the science and art of preventing, alleviating or curing disease and disability—would, on casual consideration, appear to be the same, whether it is to be applied to the man in or the man out of uniform. However, this is not the truth. All of us are kept fully aware of the billions of dollars which are being spent on civilian medial research . . . but despite the many and vast and varied programs of civilian medical research, there remain medical problems which are not now and will not in the foreseeable future be investigated by any civilian agency with a vigor commensurate to the magnitude and immediacy of the threats they pose to our Army's successful operations. These are the medical problems which are the clear-cut obligation of the Army's Medical Research and Development Command. (1962b, 317)

Near the end of his address, Sulzberger explained why military medical research is of the utmost importance to national security.

> We, in the medical service, who are responsible for the effectiveness of the component man are faced with Buck Rogers-Alice in Wonderland advances in technology; exponential expansions of scientific and medical knowledge; kaleidoscopic rearrangements of policies and plans; rapid-fire introductions of new kinds of weapons, new kinds of transportation and communication, actual and potential dispersion of combat and special forces throughout all regions of the globe; and our troops' consequent unbelievably sudden and rapid encounters with new types of hostile climates and environments, new types of animals, poisons, vegetation, microorganisms, virus and other causes of disease. These new conditions bring with them constantly new and constantly waxing stresses upon the capacity of our men to perform with reliability and ef-

fectiveness. They also present constant challenges, as well as opportunities for medical and scientific research. (1962b, 326)

This was Sulzberger's prescient realization that the speed at which soldiers would and could be enhanced—and would need to be enhanced if the US wanted to maintain its strategic and tactical edge—was rapidly accelerating. It was also a realization that this "embedding" would need to be positively embedded in the collective US social psyche as well. Technological innovation and advances of the past, Michael D. Bess writes, came about gradually, allowing people and social systems time to adapt (2008, 115). The changes brought about by World War II and the Cold War in military technology came at such a rapid pace that people did not have the same luxury of acclimating themselves to these new innovations and technologies. In this sense, Idiophylaxis marks this change in cadence and innovation with its dramatic, science-fiction-like implications and resonance.

Weakness and Strength, Boldness and Biology

Clausewitz's discussion of weakness and boldness helps frame the problems Sulzberger and later military biomedical researchers face and must overcome in order to produce bold, useful, and deployable soldiers. In the eyes of the US military, the human body is seen as a limiting factor in the prosecution of war—the basic weakness being the tendency of the "component man" to succumb to illness, fatigue, and trauma. Biomedical research will help the military learn to make the body do what it might not normally be able or even want to do. Where once the body could have been considered its own limit in the prosecution of war, through biomedical means, the body is to lose its self-limiting potential and allow for the continuous escalation of war through the continuous application of biomedical technology to sustain war. Overcoming the weaknesses and basic biology of the soldier allows for the deployment of the soldier; it is the reconfiguration of the soldier's own body to make her deployable, to promote boldness and readiness. In this conception of military health, the body is to cease being a limiting factor in the prosecution of war.

In both Sulzberger's and the contemporary US military's conceptions of the body of the soldier, the body is at once both powerful and weak, menacing and menaced. It must be strong enough to be deployed to counter any threat yet weak enough and threatened enough to require constant supervision and enhancement. Weakness is what drives a military, during both war and peace: the need to search for the enemies' weaknesses and to constantly be on guard for your own weaknesses, to think about your own potential shortcomings, flaws, and blind spots. Weakness equals intervention; power must spiral around and *in* the body of the soldier, constantly defining and redefining it, testing it and stressing it. The body is not only the "inscribed surface" of events (Foucault 1979, 1980) but also the inscribed and regulated interior of events. The soldier's body must be constantly prodded to expose its weaknesses, down to the molecular level: only then can the military know what a body might be able to do on the battlefield. As the US military Basic Training adage goes, "pain is just the weakness coming out." Finding, expunging, and armoring against pain is the crux of a military biopolitics of protection.

This biopolitical interior regulation is crucial to external politics, securitization, and warfare, and the health of the soldier in many ways becomes—and is—the health, security, safety, and protection of the state. As a military medical researcher, Sulzberger was well aware of the importance of the connection, and he closed his West Point address by echoing John F. Kennedy's message to Congress in 1962: "'The basic resource of a nation is its people. Its strength can be no greater than the health and vitality of its population. Preventable sickness, disability, and physical or mental incapacity are matters of both individual and national concern'" (Sulzberger 1962b, 327, quoting Kennedy's address to Congress, February 27, 1962).

For Sulzberger, only the internal reconfiguration of the soldier could make the soldier healthy, strong, and tough enough to withstand modern combat; the soldier would have to be made to fit the war. Idiophylaxis—and military performance enhancements in general—are the medicalization of national security concerns, carried out in and on and through the bodies of soldiers. Idiophylaxis is a term of both material and ideological production and is simultaneously a research, development, and production ethos and a metaphor for the augmented soldier and the high-tech military, the soldier carrying the cutting-edge technology of the state in his body. The enhanced soldier is a body that represents—and is—the high-tech state of the state on the battlefield, and the soldier represents the goals, aspirations, and capabilities of the state. The Idiophylactic Soldier of the 1960s can be seen as the prototype of an emergent high-tech, "flexible" soldier, a soldier made on an "as needed" basis for each and every contingency and embodying a "more with less" approach to warfare (Bacevich 2013).

The Legacy of Idiophylaxis: War, Medicine, and the Enhanced Mundane

The supersoldier has long been a staple of science fiction political imaginaries; Robert A. Heinlein's *Starship Troopers* and the superhero Captain America come to mind here. And like *Starship Troopers*, Sulzberger's neologism was an attention-getter with a definite futuristic ring to it: the "Idiophylactic Soldier" conjured images of high-tech soldiers who were far beyond mere 1960s "government issue" soldiers. Sulzberger's Idiophylaxis is a good place to start thinking about current efforts to produce supersoldiers, how they are imagined, what the military wants in and from them, and what they should be able to do. Idiophylaxis as a term and concept perfectly encapsulates the idea of the supersoldier, of the soldier pumped full of drugs and technology, protected even when naked and alone on the battlefield, knowing he is protected, and ready and able to carry on the mission.

As Ian Buchanan discusses in his overview of Gilles Deleuze and Félix Guattari's concern with the body, Deleuze and Guattari were interested in self-destructive practices like bulimia, anorexia, and masochism (1997, 75) and how bodies seemingly "willfully" destroy themselves (74). Of course, Sulzberger was not interested in these issues, but he was thinking about bodily injury and the destruction of the self. A focus on "self-destruction" allows us to view Idiophylaxis and performance enhancement and protection projects in a different light and think about the "self" and "destruction." Both are concerned with a body that does not self-destruct, and which resists destruction. In theory, this is what the "armored body" is: a body that in and through itself imagines, anticipates, resists, and is resistant to its own destruction and fragmentation (see also Theweleit's [1987–89] discussion of the armored body). But the internally armored body, from a military standpoint, is not a body that simply arrives on the battlefield; it is "made" by the state, by and through technology and medicine and training and ideology and capital investment. It is the soldier premade and pretempered for combat rather than the soldier who is hardened in and through combat. Sulzberger's vision of the internally armored soldier and the skin as a kind of armor entails a kind of "doubling" of the body, or a Cartesian split of the mind/body, where the body becomes armored to protect the body and the mind, and the mind steels itself to protect itself and the body. The "body" and the "self" blend together in one harmonious, unified, protected whole—akin to Theweleit's "totality"—which knows it is protected and can expunge its own pain and remorse (as Jünger called for). This is a "military self" created and enhanced to protect itself, and which knows that it is enhanced and protected.

Idiophylaxis is a neologism of both protection and proliferation. Just as Bruno Latour (1994) described Louis Pasteur's work on the microbe as requiring a large number of allies to make it official and socially established, Sulzberger's reimagining of the soldier requires a vast array of researchers and allies to bring it to fruition. Like "disease," "protection" requires a large number of people to agree on definitions and conceptions of potential threats and work together to develop solutions and countermeasures (Brown 2009, 167). Idiophylaxis—and protection and performance enhancement programs in general—works at a number of levels: at the level of the soldier, at the level of the researcher, at the level of the public, and at the level of the policy maker. At the level of the soldier, it is about getting more labor power from the soldier, and making sure that the soldier believes she is protected. At the level of the researcher, it is about creating research areas, agendas, centers, and, perhaps most importantly, budgets, in order to create the interventions for the soldier. At the level of the public, it is about convincing people that soldiers need to be protected in new and novel ways in order to respond to and fight new and novel opponents on new and novel battlefields. And at the level of the politician and policy maker, it is important to understand how they might believe that they have perfect military tools at their disposal. Terms like "idiophylaxis" act as a kind of performative (Austin 1975) in the sense that they bring something into being or at least make it seem like they exist. Idiophylaxis also acts as a kind of biomedical ontopower, bringing into existence—in the body of the soldier—concerns and anxiety around future threats and future security.

Sulzberger's Idiophylaxis never became a completely funded, independent research program (though his ideas reappear in DARPA's Inner Armor program in 2007), and Sulzberger later left his military research position and returned to private practice. But we can use Idiophylaxis as a way to situate enhancements and think about the links between the soldier and the macrolevel of political, military, and economic conflict. How do world political and economic and military rivalries and tensions drive science and military science, ultimately ending up in the bodies of soldiers? Is an enhancement the biomedical realization of crisis? How do abstract metastructures end up changing the body chemistry and neurology of someone pulled into a military? Is it ethical to embark on a suite of enhancements resulting in permanent change, when they are based on political/military contexts that are in flux and unstable? For Sulzberger, Idiophylaxis was a way to address all of the above, and it was an ethical and beneficial form of intervention, designed to protect the soldier and serve as a springboard for other kinds of medical advances, advances that could only be made through military medicine due to funding issues and the types of problems faced by soldiers.

Sulzberger's work also acts as a kind of corrective to the tendency to only think about performance enhancements and supersoldiers as "super high-tech." It expands our ideas and understanding of what military performance enhancements and immunizations are and what they are supposed to protect against: preventing illness and the mundane—like blisters and rashes and dysentery—is just as much a part of imagining and making enhanced soldiers as is creating soldiers with superhero-like abilities. As Idiophylaxis implies, the development of an enhanced immune system and body that can heal and protect itself—a kind of biological optimization—is the first step in creating supersoldiers; it is the "platform" upon which all other technologies depend. This point is often lost when we imagine supersoldiers, but the mundane is just as militarily important as the marvelous when it comes to designing the soldier of tomorrow.

Part III
Imagining the Modern US Supersoldier

SIX

"The Force Is with You"

An Army of One to the Future Force Warrior

Either *you* create your future or you become the victim of
the future someone creates *for* you.

» **Vice Admiral Arthur K. Cebrowski**, US Navy (ret.),
  director of Force Transformation, Office of the
  Secretary of Defense (Swofford, 2004)

In 2016, the dystopian science fiction/drama series *Black Mirror* broadcast
an installment called "Men against Fire." The episode follows a soldier
named Stripe and his unit as they hunt and fight humanoid "roaches." We
find out that the soldiers—both men and women—have all been enhanced
with a neural implant system called "MASS," which modulates their senses
and emotions, allows the military to manage and control their dreams
(soldiers who perform well on a mission are given explicit sex dreams as
a reward), and helps them deal with combat trauma. But the most disturbing aspect of the MASS system is that it allows the military to directly
control how soldiers see the world; rather than metaphorical roaches, the
soldiers kill what they actually see as monsters. The MASS implant gives
the military the ability to literally make soldiers see its vision of the world.
The "roaches"—which appear to the soldiers as horrifically mutilated
monsters—are in reality normal humans; the soldiers' task is to wipe them
out, as they are thought to be somehow contaminated and have impure
DNA. During a mission, Stripe's MASS gear malfunctions after one of the

"roaches" attacks him with an improvised neural disruptor. He is then able to see through the military's illusion—or hallucination—and realizes that he is not fighting mutants but normal people who are terrified of Stripe and his fellow soldiers. Stripe refuses to continue fighting but is eventually pressured back into combat by a military psychologist who threatens to prosecute Stripe and make him watch the video of the civilians he has killed, over and over. Stripe is also shown a video—the recollection of which has been wiped from his memory by the military—giving his consent to the MASS implant and neuroenhancement. The episode ends with Stripe discharged from the military, crying while looking at an illusion of a beautiful wife and house. He seems to know it is all an illusion, a kind of reward for his service, sent to him by the military through the implant in his brain. His implant may be able to make him "see" the enemy as bugs, but he knows it all to be a lie. As Simone Weil wrote in "The Iliad, or the Poem of Force," "the man who does not wear the armor of the lie cannot experience force without being touched by it to the very soul" (Weil and Bespaloff 2005, 36).

"Men against Fire" is a provocative dramatization of the possible uses and misuses of military performance enhancement technology in what seems to be the near future. It raises important questions of autonomy, agency, bioethics, military ethics, race, and class in an enhanced military. But of course, it is fiction, and it portrays an imagined account of supersoldiers even if it draws from current research projects. Just as Rigg imagined future warfare and future soldiers in *War—1974*, P. W. Singer and August Cole, in their novel *Ghost Fleet: A Novel of the Next World War* (2016), imagine future warfare and enhanced soldiers as well, and the United States Army Training and Doctrine Command (TRADOC) sponsors a military science fiction writing contest intended to draw from the public's imagination of future war.

Today, the US military is furthering the development of the hardened, durable, enhanced soldier through conventional means, such as more realistic training, improved command and control technology, and improved psychological motivation training. The "Army of One" was not only a pithy recruiting slogan but also a harbinger of how the military imagines and desires future soldiers and conceptualizes soldier performance enhancement projects: enhanced soldiers will function as an army of one. Increasingly, it is attempting to further the process of bodily mechanization, suppression of emotion, and certainty of control, through radically improved forms of biotechnology, all in the pursuit of performance, health, and readiness.

This chapter examines aspects of the major US supersoldier projects from the 1980s to today, detailing the focus of all projects on the increasing militarization and harnessing of soldiers' bodies and the increasing incursion of the military politics of anticipation into the inner reaches of soldiers. These projects encapsulate the strategic and tactical concerns of the US military, as early iterations of supersoldier projects attempted to provide solutions to Cold War problems; contemporary iterations show the long-term influence of Cold War concerns on present-day deployments and combat associated with the Global War on Terrorism and the "world as battlefield." The development of new and novel enhancement drugs, interventions in the wake/sleep cycle, remote pain management, hyperhydration, and "metabolic dominance," to name a few, are the signature "skin-in" technologies of all these programs. US military programs such as the US Army's Land Warrior, Objective Force Warrior, Future Force Warrior, Future Combat System, Ground Soldier System, Nett Warrior (named after World War II Medal of Honor recipient Colonel Robert B. Nett (Gourley 2012, 81), and Future Soldier 2030 were the major soldier-enhancement proposals of the 1990s and the following decade, with programs like Metabolic Dominance and Inner Armor taking place in conjunction with the broader suite of these other efforts (Brandler 2005; GlobalSecurity.org n.d. [Future Force Warrior]; GlobalSecurity.org n.d. [Objective Force Warrior]; Lin, Abney, and Mehlman 2013; Moreno 2012; United States Army Natick Soldier RD&E Center 2009). While some aspects and components of these projects have been fielded (like Land Warrior, and with limited success), most of these projects have not come to fruition, or if they have, then only in modified or limited forms, or only released to small groups of special warfare soldiers.

The soldier is a key component and focus of military biomedical "big science" research (Armstrong et al. 2010; Jacobsen 2015; Latiff 2017; Weinberger 2017), and the well-being of soldiers is militarily, politically, and economically important in ways that Sulzberger might have found surprising but most welcome. The growing concern with biology underpins new forms of military anticipation and responses to strategic and tactical fear (Masco 2014) and efforts to use cutting-edge biomedical research to make US soldiers unbeatable on the battlefield and more easily reintegrated when they return home.

Sulzberger's ideas for "built-in protection" continue to influence and course through research programs in the US military, and we can use them to think about and analyze current US military projects designed to protect and enhance soldiers, be they biomedical, pharmacological, psychological, or cybernetic. We can trace the connections between Sulzberger's idea of Idiophylaxis and today's representations and plans for supersoldiers, Inner Armor, and Iron Man suits—the idea of the armored and self-armoring soldier who can resist battlefield and environmental conditions, who is seemingly indestructible and "surgically" clean of the horrors of war, during and after conflict. We can also see a link in terms of military biomedical and scientific research, funding, and patronage, and the application of cutting-edge science to military problems, either contemporary or imagined for the future.

In 1962—the same year in which Sulzberger was developing and presenting his plans for the biomedically enhanced Idiophylactic Soldier and the expansion of military medical research focused on soldier performance enhancement and protection—Edward Shils (1962) first discussed the "governmentalisation" of science and the increased connections between the state, the military, and scientific research (see also Aronova 2014, 394; Shils 1972; Weinberg 1996). Today, this expansion of the state and the military into basic biomedical research can be seen in the soldier performance enhancement projects of DARPA (e.g., the Biological Technologies Office [BTO], the Natick Soldier Center, the Army Research Laboratory, the Oak Ridge National Laboratory, the United States Army Research Institute for Environmental Medicine [USARIEM]) and the increasing number of military-funded biomedical and psychopharmaceutical research projects carried out in US universities and private research corporations, such as MIT; Arizona State University; the Institute for Collaborative Biotechnologies at the University of California, Santa Barbara; and the defense contracting company Revision, to name just a few (Jacobsen 2015; National Research Council 2001; Weinberger 2017; see figure 6.1).

To talk about and analyze military performance enhancement is to obviously talk about war and combat, but it is also to talk about the hidden and not-so-hidden forms of military labor: labor in the military and labor for the military. Of course, the soldier appears to be a unified whole, but viewed from a different angle, the soldier—as the system of systems—is composed of a vast array of technologies and medicines designed and created by thousands of researchers and workers, spread across all fifty states. As former Chief of Staff of the US Army General Harold K. Johnson said, "The Army is like a funnel. At the top, you pour doctrine, resources, concepts, equipment, and facilities. Then, out at the bottom comes one lone soldier, walking point" (Kelly 1996, 16).

Figure 6.1 "The Supersoldier 'Big Bang.'" NSRDEC, "Future Soldier 2030 Initiative,"
2009.

We do not necessarily think of the biology of the soldier as the end point—and the rationale—of vast research and commodity chains that bring them into being. Embedded in the bodies of enhanced soldiers will be the work of countless thousands of scientists, technicians, and workers who will suspend the soldier in a military-industrial-biomedical web; the interior of the soldier is, and will continue to be, both the beginning and the end point of a vast commodity chain predicated on anticipation, preemption, protection, and performance. The soldier might not be autochthonous, but the technologies that make him seem to spring from everywhere. Each intervention in and on the body of the soldier represents a public-private venture, with potential patent spin-offs for the consumer sector. The body of the soldier becomes the proving ground—the platform for the "validity of concept"—for a variety of new technologies, each funded and driven by private concerns and companies, sometimes in tandem with the military or DoD and sometimes not.

Despite Sulzberger's attempt to rethink and redesign the soldier in the 1960s, little in the way of major soldier performance enhancement projects seems to have taken place in the late 1960s and 1970s, and little in the way of wide-scale modernization of US military equipment or the revamping of the US soldier was seen, with the exception of the introduction of Kevlar helmets and body armor. The Vietnam War, the incredible drain on funding for soldier-enhancement projects, and the subsequent loss of trust of the military in the United States contributed to the lack of interest in soldier-enhancement research and technology. Fundamentally, US military kit stayed pretty much the same as the Vietnam-era military, even if soldiers looked different after the replacement of the ubiquitous "steel pot" helmets of the World War II, Korea, and Vietnam GI. New camouflage patterns came about with the end of the green "pickle suit" uniform and the introduction of the "woodland camouflage" Battle Dress Uniform (BDU) of the 1980s. When I went through Basic Training in 1984, we were issued the old "steel pot" helmet of the World War II–Vietnam era, cumbersome body armor, and Vietnam-era M16 rifles, but wore the new BDU uniforms. When I eventually arrived in Berlin, we were issued the new Kevlar helmets and improved M16s. The result was a kind of hybrid image of the US soldier, with some modern equipment and upgrades but still recognizable vestiges of previous US soldiers. This equipment mélange was highly visible during the US invasion of Grenada and later in the first Gulf War, with different US units—Regular Army, Army Reserve, and National Guard—kitted out in different iterations and combinations of US military uniforms and equipment from different eras.

Missiles to Molecules: Making America Strong Again

US president Ronald Reagan's "rebooting" of the Cold War (P. Edwards 1996; Marzec 2015) and dramatic increase in defense spending in the 1980s, and the (re)building and modernization of the US armed forces after Vietnam played a major role in restarting US military plans for improved and enhanced soldiers. Importantly, the US military was keen on reasserting its dominance around the world after the loss in Vietnam. Reagan was determined that the US military would again be the preeminent military in the world and that the US military would regain its global footing and orientation. While projects like the Strategic Defense Initiative—"Star Wars"—were key to reestablishing dominance on the global stage and demonstrating US technological superiority to the Soviet Union, global power projection would also require soldiers who could deploy anywhere in the world, at any time, under any conditions (P. Edwards 1996; Marzec 2015).

The 1980s and 1990s saw plans for new kinds of soldiers drawn up, plans that drew from both emerging biomedical and materials technologies and from the military science fiction ethos of the Reagan era. While focused on countering alleged American "weakness," Reagan's rearmament programs promised to "make America strong again" (Edwards 1996, 280);

from missiles to molecules, the American body politics and the bodies of American soldiers needed to be rethought and redesigned for maximum performance. And like Star Wars, these plans would demonstrate US military biomedical superiority to the world; Star Wars was not simply about imagining an otherworldly missile defense—it was also about imagining otherworldly soldier/storm troopers and imagining the "Army of One."

The late 1980s, the 1990s, and the beginning of the twenty-first century saw a progression of US supersoldier projects, each building from its predecessors and promising even greater protection, enhancement, capabilities, destruction, and "overmatch" in the future, and each presenting new images and ideas of the improved and enhanced US soldier, increasingly referred to by the military as the new US "warrior." This is not simply a response to increased lethality aimed at US soldiers; it is the desire to achieve what is known as "overmatch": overwhelming firepower and combat capabilities that will ensure that the US destroys any and all opponents quickly and without loss to US forces. Instead of only focusing on increasingly lethal weapons systems, this will focus on making the soldier more lethal through enhanced technology. In other words, the soldier becomes the weapons system and ceases to be strictly a soldier. New technologies are to be developed that will keep the soldier in the field and functioning at a higher rate than what is currently possible. While these technologies are referred to as providing for the comfort and care of the soldier (which may be true), they will also ensure that these soldier/weapons systems stay in the field in order to fight.

In keeping with the American penchant to use advanced military technology to solve political problems, the Department of Defense and the various research and development units of the US arms community began drawing up plans for new kinds of soldiers, new kinds of interventions designed to counter personal and national weakness. In many ways, these plans represented a kind of Reaganesque Star Wars of the body, the direct application of new and cutting-edge offensive and defensive technologies in the bodies of soldiers. The soldier was to be not simply a soldier but a "system of systems," designed to increase the firepower and survivability of the soldier on the battlefield and allow the US military to—theoretically—do more, anywhere in the world, with many fewer soldiers.

Despite the lessons and costs of Iraq and Afghanistan—or perhaps because of them—the pursuit of a small, supersoldier military continues and in many ways is too appealing for the military and politicians not to attempt to create. Increased lethality means that the Army will potentially need fewer soldiers to undertake missions and control territory. This also means that war and conflict will become less of an economic burden on the government and the taxpayer. The utility of linking health, protection, the body, and readiness to the economic rationalization of war was clearly stated in the 1998 *Army Science and Technology Master Plan* (ASTMP).

> Combat systems will be designed to capitalize on human strengths and mitigate weaknesses while simultaneously improving sustainment and support of warfighting systems. Advances in warrior protection systems address concerns about casualties in conflict. By providing the personal protection and life support necessary to meet current and future threats, these technology efforts make the individual warrior more effective and achieve force multiplication. With fewer soldiers executing the mission, we decrease the tax burden and put fewer warfighters in harm's way while still achieving mission objectives. Advances in human systems interface technologies are essential for the services to meet their global commitments in combat and peacekeeping roles. (United States Army 1998, N2)

Of course, the dream of a smaller military is the dream of a more useful, powerful, and cost-effective military. The dream of a smaller—but exponentially more dangerous and effective—military reflects both the expectation that the US military will remain the dominant military force in the world far into the twenty-first century as well as the fact that the Gulf Wars and Afghanistan revealed myriad problems with soldier performance, survival, and resilience.

Anticipating Force in the Future: Land Warrior, the Objective Force Warrior, and the Future Force Warrior

Projects like Land Warrior (LW), the Objective Force Warrior (OFW), the Future Force Warrior (FFW), the Future Combat System (FCS), and Future Soldier 2030 all imagine and try to anticipate and determine the future of warfare, and we can see them not only as vast biomedical projects but also as vast visions and responses to a threatened and threatening future. Imagining the battlefield to come, these projects promise to actually make that imagined future real, as they control and dominate the battlefield through the development of technologies and biotechnologies that will allow for battlefield dominance on the imagined battlefield of the future—a kind of "blind, visionary conjuring of the future," as Jackie Orr (2004, 473) describes it, one that is experienced as a hallucination in the example given from *Black Mirror*.

But we need to be careful about going too far in thinking about military plans and contingencies as "blind" or some kind of completely false consciousness. These projects might seem fantastic and far-fetched, but they are deadly serious and will have deadly consequences for both soldiers and civilians if successful. The scenarios, weapons, equipment, and medical interventions designed by military planners and researchers might be imagined and revolve around a conception of play, but they are not necessarily a hallucination or a mere war game: weapons systems cause real injury to real people in the real world, and military biomedical projects will have both military and nonmilitary applications and implications. Nerve agents and other chemical weapons cause horrific deaths, and ballistic threats rip bodies to shreds; there is nothing hallucinatory about this. As we were told in Basic Training about the effects of a 5.56 mm round from an M16 on the human body: "it will homogenize your insides." Military planners and weapons designers know what these weapons can do to humans—soldiers and civilians alike—and plan and "wargame" scenarios accordingly around these "effects." The political situation or the foe might be imagined, but the actual effects of weapons are very well known.

The institutional history of each of these programs is complicated, representing the ebbs and flows of military funding and the revolving door of program managers and staff, but the trajectory of these programs and the different but overlapping iterations of each program were all part of a concerted effort to dramatically reimagine and change the US soldier. In many ways, all supersoldier efforts are fundamentally iterations of the same project, but with new names and new claims to dominance. Each version was to serve as the validity of a "concept" and as a building block for the next steps in creating the enhanced soldier. As each project ended, and as each new program manager assumed his or her new position, projects changed, budgets expanded or contracted, but the promise and goal of the enhanced soldier remained constant. Over time, programs were canceled, names were changed, subcomponent projects were revamped, and components were found to work well or fail in the field. Despite the names, and despite the general change in each project every few years, the fundamentals of all these programs remained the same: to armor and enhance the soldier internally and externally and develop ways to make the soldier stronger, faster, smarter, more resilient, and more "linked in" to fellow soldiers and command echelons than before through Command, Control, Communications, Computers, Intelligence, Surveillance, and Reconnaissance (c4ISR) systems.

The Land Warrior Program

The US Army's Land Warrior program of the late 1990s and early twenty-first century aimed to fully integrate the soldier into a series of overlapping communication and intelligence networks, provide better individual protection, and increase the firepower of the individual soldier. We can think of Land Warrior as the initial step toward a complete redesign of the US soldier, moving away from the basic equipment and overall look of the late or post–Cold War US soldier. Land Warrior was also the first step in enhancing the overall capabilities and survivability of the US soldier, and the first major step at attempting to integrate the soldier into the various weapons systems, intelligence systems, and protective systems—making a soldier a true system of systems—that would cocoon the soldier. In May 2006, the 4th Stryker Brigade Combat Team (SBCT) was equipped with the Land Warrior system in test trials, and in 2007 the 4th SBCT deployed to Iraq with 440 Land Warrior systems. In 2008 the entire 5th SBCT was equipped with the Land Warrior and deployed to Iraq, with generally less-than-positive results and opinions about the system (Schachtman 2009). The system proved heavy, often difficult to use, and not always reliable under battlefield conditions.

The Objective Force Warrior and the Future Force Warrior Programs

According to the Natick Soldier Center, the Objective Force Warrior program was part of the larger Future Force Warrior program, scheduled to come into service by 2025. The Future Force Warrior program itself is part of a much larger restructuring of the entire US military to prepare it for conflicts through the middle of the twenty-first century (United States Army 2005, 56–58). The unclassified 2005 Army report details the plans and goals of the Objective Force Warrior program and the research underway at various facilities, such as the Natick Soldier Center in Natick, Massachusetts. The Objective Force Warrior and Future Force Warrior programs were to build from the lessons learned from the Land Warrior program and advance the "proof of concept" of the overall projects. These new programs

Figure 6.2 Future Warrior
uniform prototypes,
Washington, DC, 2004.
Photo: Phil Copeland.

were to increase the amount and types of technology deployed—both skin-in and skin-out—and move toward the realization of the completely armored and enhanced soldier. Programs like Objective Force Warrior, Future Force Warrior, and Future Soldier 2030 are designed to maximize the combat effectiveness of soldiers by arming them with increasingly lethal weaponry, providing them with cybernetic technology and biomedical "improvements," and integrating them into an intelligence and data network that will monitor their health, ensuring they fight (see figure 6.2).

Fundamentally, each project and iteration of the supersoldier was to have improved ballistic protection and external armor, improved communications—with the OFW, FFW, and FCS having specialized helmets containing universal translators, integrated computer displays, targeting capabilities for "one shot / one kill" capabilities, integrated nuclear, biological, chemical (NBC) protection, and night vision. Soldiers would wear uniforms designed to hide their heat signature, provide ballistic and NBC protection, and have integrated heating and cooling systems, and the uniforms would have chameleonlike pattern-changing technologies to allow them to blend in to any background. To address the problem of the "overweight infantryman" who has to carry more than one hundred pounds into combat (Jacobsen 2015; King 2017), soldiers would eventually wear powered exoskeletons to help them carry greater combat loads, run and climb more quickly and efficiently, and keep them from tiring too quickly in combat. All these technologies—"skin-out" solutions—would require the soldier to carry improved batteries or other power sources (as it turns out, the major problem faced by all these programs lies with the hurdles associated with developing lightweight and long-lasting batteries; the technologies designed for the new soldier require significant amounts of power and are impractical unless small and powerful batteries are developed [Jacobsen 2015]).

Much like Rigg's soldier of the Futurarmy, the OFW program envisioned the development of special helmets that provide enhanced communications and night vision capabilities, and which would also allow for universal language translation. Helmets designed for OFW (and later FFW and FCS) would also come equipped with special "culture" programs to provide data on local customs and lifeways so that soldiers could readily make use of local culture to help determine friend from foe, quickly identify "enemy leaders," and provide constant and reliable "situational awareness." Indeed, the report states that the OFW "is deployable anywhere around the globe, anytime. The area of operations is the world" (National Security Directorate Oak Ridge National Laboratory 2001, 7). In the section titled "Cultural Awareness," the OFW report states that the goal is to "blend into the culture with ease" (National Security Directorate Oak Ridge National Laboratory 2001, 23). In other words, OFW technology would allow for perpetual, continuous war at any point on the globe. While such a capability could be touted as an increase in cultural awareness in the military, the intention is to mobilize cultural awareness as a sort of force multiplier, undercutting the stated intentions of this awareness; in many ways, the "culture helmets" would turn the soldier into a kind of on-demand "Human Terrain Team," the controversial US military plan to use anthropologists as combat cultural advisors.

"The Art of the Possible": We Can Rebuild Him

It is difficult for the soldier, exhausted, possibly wounded, sick, and mentally and physically broken, to be effective and heroic on the battlefield. How then do you "repair" this broken soldier to make him useful on the battlefield, again and again? How do you take the soldier "vessel" (Bickford 2011, 225–26; see also Bell et al. 2018 on the anthropology of repair), and in a manner reminiscent of the Japanese art of *Kintsugi*—repairing a broken vessel with gold to make it not only useful again but beautiful in its transcendent state—make him once again useful, and more than he once was?

While performance enhancement research is about discipline, it is also engaged with an ongoing fascination with repair and rebuilding. Indicative of how the US military imagines the next generation of supersoldiers, on October 12, 1999, the Army released information on the Objective Force Warrior program and its "vision for creating a force for the future that is strategically responsive and dominant at every point on the spectrum of conflict" (see also Douglas et al. 2001). In October 2001, the Natick Soldier Center released a report detailing the aims of the OFW program and the "vision" of how the Objective Force Warrior was to look and function. The Natick report blandly states, "Army Chief of Staff Gen. Eric Shinseki tasked the Natick lab to completely rebuild the combat soldier as we know him" (National Security Directorate Oak Ridge National Laboratory 2001; see also Shinseki 2001). This is a telling statement: soldiers are not to be retrained; they are to be rebuilt. This implies that soldiers—or rather, civilians who are to become soldiers—are weak, inefficient, or simply not up to the task. The key to this is the term *rebuilt*; it is generally only inanimate objects like machines that are "rebuilt" or "repaired." Of course, improved training and better equipment will remain important, but the soldier will be approached like any other piece of hardware, like any other "component" in the system. As such, soldiers as "machines"—unbreakable components in the weapons system—are required and desired and seen as the ideal. The OFW is the dream of making the perfect soldier or, as the OFW reports describes it, "The Art of the Possible." Over and over, the reports speak of ensuring "100% hit and kill," "one shot/one kill" technology, and protective uniforms that will make the soldier invincible and unstoppable. The reports also speak of developing technology that will allow the individual soldier to kill "without having to close with the enemy"—in other words, to kill without ever having to see the enemy and expose oneself to danger, much like in drone warfare (Gusterson 2016).

The Future Force in Action: *Assault on Normandy*

It is one thing to think about all the systems and subsystems of a new form and type of soldier, but it is another thing to see it in action and observe how all the systems and subsystems are to come together to make "the Force." However, since all these technologies are speculative, in development, or only partially deployed, the military can only imagine how all the systems of systems that will make and support the future soldier will interact and actually work in combat (see figure 6.3).

In the early 2000s, a short promotional film titled *Future Combat Systems: Assault on Normandy* gave an overview of how the Future Combat System and the Objective Force Warrior / Future Force Warrior programs were to function. The film shows how all the components of the "system of systems" would come together on the battlefield to provide the individual soldier access to cutting-edge intelligence and weapon system support, and it presents the overall advantages of the "netted" military. While the film is a promotional demonstration of how the Future Combat System would work in practice, it is also a celebration of the interaction and interdependence of the military and the defense industry.

The film portrays a small group of FFW soldiers in action against a group of unnamed terrorists (though the film implies they are somewhere in the Balkans). The film begins with an introduction by General Peter Schoomaker, Chief of Staff of the United States Army. General Schoomaker describes the progress in reshaping the US military for the future of warfare with the Future Force Warrior program.

> As we move from the current Army Modular Force to the Future Army Modular Force—which is our strategy—the Future Combat System is injected in here over this timeline so that we arrive at the Future Army Modular force with more and more of this FCS capability, and we're on a continual path of transformation. And as the Future Combat Systems become available to us, we insert them and we become more and more and more like what we envisioned in the past—but you know, we're never going to arrive someplace where we're going to stop: it's open ended. (*Future Combat Systems: Assault on Normandy*)

The Future Force, as imagined in the *Assault on Normandy* video, is a small, compact group of soldiers with skin-in and skin-out protection, supported by multiple echelons of fire support, intelligence collection, reconnaissance assets, advanced logistics, and remote medical assessment and

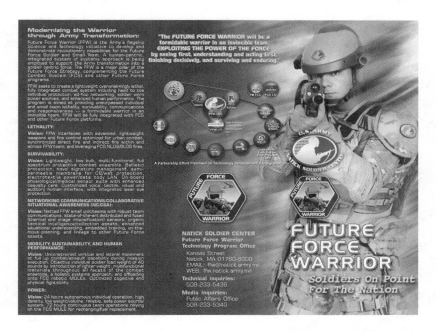

Figure 6.3 Future Force Warrior trifold, Natick Soldier Center, early 2000s.

intervention. Each soldier is enmeshed in multiple layers of electronic monitoring and is able to access real-time intelligence and situational data that gives him an immense advantage over the enemy, who is shown as both superior in numbers and basically cannon fodder for the soldiers calling upon the Force to support and protect them. The screen shots flash back and forth from the individual soldier to the remote command post, to drones, to satellites, to a command post in the United States: all working seamlessly to ensure the success and safety of the soldiers on the ground. It is the film version of how military planners and scientists imagine future warfare, weaponize anticipation, and make real "The Art of the Possible."

The use of in vivo technologies in soldiers will allow the military to both monitor and treat soldiers in ways heretofore impossible. A key component of the Objective Force Warrior and Future Force Warrior programs is the development of advanced soldier protection technologies, with medical interventions being a key component and goal. As described in the OFW report, medical interventions for future "soldier-systems" will include (but are not limited to) "implanted venous access port, physiologic monitoring, osmolality monitor to alert to fluid need, detect[ion of] sleep

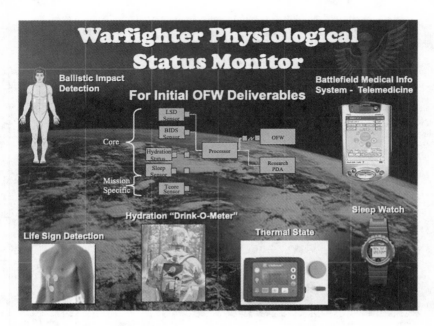

Figure 6.4 "Warfighter Physiological Status Monitor." Claude M. Bolton Jr., "ASA (ALT) Perspective: Military Medicine: Ready and Relevant," 2004.

deficit, EEG sensor—automatic stimulus for dozing, [and] pharmacology intervention for the wake/sleep cycle" (National Security Directorate Oak Ridge National Laboratory 2001, 21). Health monitoring systems are also in development; to keep track of a soldier's medical state, soldiers would be covered in biosensors designed to register and report any and all wounds and keep track of a soldier's vital signs, hydration, and stress levels (Wong 2013, 150 ; see figure 6.4). Combat uniforms would also function as a kind of wearable medic, able to harden like a cast, apply pressure like a tourniquet, and administer drugs when needed (Ford and Glymour 2014; Friedl 2018; National Security Directorate Oak Ridge National Laboratory 2001; Wong 2013).

Assault on Normandy provides a glimpse at how skin-in solutions and remote health monitoring would work in combat. At one point in the video, a US Future Force Warrior is injured. His condition is immediately relayed back to the remote headquarters, and the medics on staff initiate a set of procedures to assess and stabilize the soldier. As they determine his condition, a medic is heard stating over the communication network, "administering 10cc of diazepam" (diazepam is an anxiolytic). Through the implanted drug relay and reservoir systems, the soldier can be chemically stabilized and kept in the fight, or at least stabilized enough to stay calm. It also means that a medic need not be physically present to administer aid to wounded soldiers.

Research and development of a wearable physiological monitoring system for soldiers has continued apace. As Karl Friedl (2018) writes, wearable physiological monitoring is an important part of modern precision medicine and will be of great use and importance to the US military (Jenkins n.d.; Ford and Glymour 2014; NSRDEC 2009). A wearable physiological monitoring system will allow the military to both monitor and predict the health and performance of a soldier via their real-time physiological status monitor (RT-PSM) (Friedl 2018, 1147). Military applications of RT-PSM include the following:

1 Technological enhancement of performance by providing individual status information to optimize self-regulation, workload distribution, and enhanced team sensing/situational awareness;
2 Detection of impending soldier failure from stress load (physical, psychological, and environmental);
3 Earliest possible detection of threat agent exposure that includes the "human sensor";
4 Casualty detection, triage, and early clinical management;
5 Optimization of individual health and fitness readiness habits; and
6 Long-term health risk-associated exposure monitoring and dosimetry. (Friedl 2018, 1147)

The RT-PSM wearable monitoring suit encapsulates anticipation and preemption; as Friedl also writes, such technology will enable the military to focus directly on the individual soldier and not have to rely on "population-based predictions informed by human, mission, and environmental/ambient conditions" (2018, 1147). With the ability to monitor a soldier's overall physiological condition, the military can increase a soldier's performance through "technological doping" and the ability to use RT-PSM to pace and accelerate acclimation (1151). Friedl also notes that "monitoring soldier 'stress load' will be an important application of a neurophysiological monitoring capability. This application is an essential component of future man-machine interfacing" (1151).

While technology like a RT-PSM suit might save the soldier, it does something else militarily useful. Soldiers are faced with threats and technologies that are deadly, and as such, soldiers are compelled to confront these threats. In order to survive, soldiers must depend on, they are told, the most advanced defensive technologies available. Encased in futuristic combat suits and armed with the latest in destructive technology, the Objective Force Warrior and Future Force Warrior will be "netted" (the double meaning of which implies both connection and compulsion), connected via improved communications to one another, their company, a higher-echelon unit, and, ultimately, back to central command posts. Their vital functions will connect them to these command posts as well (Beidel 2010; Gourley 2012, 2013a), which will determine who receives medical attention, who is ordered to continue, and who is ordered to fight. Biomedical interventions for the Objective Force Warrior, the Future Force Warrior, and later iterations of US soldiers ensure both combat compliance and performance and envision a dramatic decrease or even elimination of traumatic experience.

But this also portends something else: the ability of the military, through medical assessment or necessity, to monitor each and every soldier's performance in battle, to know their exact location, their stress and awareness levels, and, perhaps most importantly, whether or not they are actually fighting and carrying out orders. A hallmark of military service has been the possibility for soldiers to not fire or fight, to aim to miss, to claim a weapon malfunction, and to come up with believable reasons for not fighting or firing in case they are questioned by their NCOs or officers. It seems that in the OFW "vision," soldiers will lose their autonomy of decision, their ability for free action and individual decision. There will be no excuses for malingering or cowardice: soldiers will become something like electronic chess pieces on the battlefield, monitored for compliance and combat by a control center. What starts out as a promise of "health" and "protection" will quickly become a method of monitoring who is fighting, who is really laying their lives on the line for the nation-state. The Art of the Possible will make it almost impossible not to comply and fight, to follow one's conscious. "Will," once the hallmark of the brave, fearless, heroic soldier, could be commandeered by biotechnology and monitoring. Medical monitoring will trump cowardice, malingering, and failure to follow orders.

Technologies of Enchantment: The Force Is with You

While presenting itself as an ultramodern fighting force, the US military draws upon myth and science fiction to present itself and inform and prime civilians in how to make sense of the technologies it is developing and hoping to deploy. It is also a way to present and craft a public image of the new supersoldier as superhero, one who is on the side of good, and not evil. Alfred Gell, in his analysis of technology and magic, wrote that the "technology of enchantment" is the most sophisticated "psychological weapon" we have to control the thoughts and actions of other human beings (1988, 7). Gell's argument is that technology is a form of magic, a way to manipulate desire, terror, wonder, fantasy, and vanity (and, as he writes, the list goes on) because it serves symbolic ends and codifies and formalizes the structural features of technical activity (7–8). Magic is a symbolic "commentary" on technological strategies of psychological manipulation and resembles and mimics children's play: "When children play, they provide a continuous stream of commentary on their own behavior. This commentary frames their actions, divides it up into segments, defines momentary goals, and so on. It seems that the superimposed organizational format both guides imaginative play as it proceeds, and also provides a means of internalizing it and recalling it, as well as subsequent exercises in innovation and recombination using previously accumulated materials in new configurations" (Gell 1988, 8).

Paradigmatic of this kind of magical play in US supersoldier research was the "guiding philosophy" of the Objective Force Warrior program as summed up by US Army General Paul Gorman, who—using language that the OFW report referred to as "elegant"—describes the Objective Force Warrior:

> *The soldier of today is thrust far forward.*
> *He is the point of the Army spear.*
> *It is very lethal and lonely out there.*
> *The soldier of tomorrow will never be alone and he will advance on his*
>   *enemy shielded by dominant information.*
> *His leaders will be able to say to him:*
> *Soldier, you are the master of your battlespace. You will shape the*
>   *fight. The network will enable you to see all that can be seen. You*
>   *will out-think, out maneuver, and out shoot your enemy.*
> *The Force is with you.*
> *You are one with the Force.*
> —National Security Directorate Oak Ridge National Laboratory (2001, 2)

Referencing and playing with material from the *Star Wars* universe, Gorman's "ode" mimics the play of a child—as Gell writes, "now I am doing this, now I am doing that, and now this will happen" (1988, 8)—and also evidences what Gell describes as the cognitive role of "magical" ideas: they provide a framework to orient technological activity. Technological innovations occur, he writes, not as attempts to supply wants but to "realize technological feats heretofore considered 'magical'" (8).

Gorman, who retired from the US Army in 1985 and began working for DARPA in 1990, had more to say and imagine about supersoldiers (Jacobsen 2015, 306). In a 1990 paper, he imagined an "integrated powered exoskeleton" (Jacobsen 2015, 306) and technologies that would turn the "weak" soldier into the supersoldier. As Annie Jacobsen describes Gorman's plans, Gorman's new soldier would incorporate "audio, visual, and haptic [touch] sensors . . . thermal imaging for eyes, sound suppression for ears, and fiber optics from head to fingertips. Its interior would be climate controlled, and each soldier would have his own physiological specifications embedded on a chip within his dog tags" (2015, 307). And as Gorman wrote, "When a soldier donned his ST [SuperTroop] battledress, he would insert one dog-tag into a slot under the chest armor, thereby loading his personal program into the battle suit's computer" (quoted in Jacobsen 2015, 307). A soldier's ID for death becomes the key or the chip that allows for the unleashing of death and violence more effectively.

Gorman's musing about the Objective Force Warrior and the enchantments of technology apply to all the US supersoldier programs. Merging fantasies and play of dominance, protection, and heroism with George Lucas's *Star Wars* mythology and dreams of computer-driven technological victory, Gorman envisioned a kind of Cyborg-Jedi-Superman-Warrior, alone on the front lines, the sharpest point of the tip of the spear, the lone soldier walking point, protecting us all but never alone due to increased network connectivity, superior technology, and "the Force." This is a fantasy and dream of a soldier so superior that only one is needed on the front line—the single soldier who *is* the front line, as his capabilities make him, in Timmerman's words, "three miles tall and twenty miles wide" (1987, 51)—and one that knows that only he is an Army of One. Alone and seemingly of epic proportions, the OFW soldier would be a wall between the US and its adversaries and nonmilitary threats (like immigrants). It might be "lonely out there," but to have another soldier there would take away the glory. In many ways, Gorman's call evokes an image similar to Breker's *Readiness*, the towering, glowering, all-mighty soldier poised to defend, dominate, and kill without compunction when ordered.

In the *Star Wars* universe, as Gorman is seemingly well aware, the Force is a mystical field of energy; as Obi-Wan Kenobi describes it in the original

Star Wars film, *A New Hope*: "The Force is what gives a Jedi his power. It's an energy field created by all living things. It surrounds us and penetrates us, it binds the galaxy together." Much like the Force, the new US military will be bound together by various forms of force, from the electromagnetic force of communications, nonhuman intelligence, satellites, targeting systems, "Blue on Blue" identification systems, NBC sensors, and medical sensors; the soldier will be both platform and sensor array. Surrounding and penetrating the soldier, it binds the military together. The new US soldier will be suspended in these overlapping fields of force that will provide superior force. The world around the soldier will also provide force for the Force; as we will see in chapter 8, DARPA hopes to harness the "energy field created by all living things" by identifying and extracting innate biological capabilities from humans and animals around the world and then transplanting them into US soldiers.

While this electronic "certainty" seems to promise quick and overwhelming victory for the US—maximum lethality directed out, maximum security for the US soldiers—what will it mean for those who are actually "netted," encased in these new combat suits, functioning as mobile weapons systems, acting as the interface between the enemy and massive amounts of weaponry? The soldier may indeed not even have to fire his personal weapon but instead simply focus the helmet sensors on the target and guide the new, improved "smart" weapons to the target. Like Gusterson's (2016) discussion on drones, this raises an important question: who will have done the killing? Or will killing become more of a collaborative event, "netting" many more in a sort of conspiracy of conscious but helping mitigate what it feels like to kill because one is netted into the Force?

In many ways, the Objective Force Warrior—and all iterations of the new US supersoldier—are very much an image and visioning of a "new hope" and the "New Man" for the US military. US soldiers will be so technologically superior on the battlefield that they will seem like Jedi Knights to the enemy. Soldiers will be "elevated" and "bound" by technology, but this is also a tacit admission by Gorman that technology is not enough; soldiers will still be weak unless they have a mystical power—magic—supporting and enhancing them. For Gorman, "the Force" is war magic in the guise of advanced technology. Potentially gone will be the days of uncertainty and unpredictability in combat; US soldiers will have a magical quality about them, tapping into the "force" of US technology, technology so advanced that it will seem like a magical force to its enemies. Like the Jedi, enhanced US soldiers—alone on the front lines—would be akin to "warrior-monks" (and reminiscent of the warrior-monks of Jim Channon's 1970s "First Earth Battalion," a group of Special Forces soldiers who would tap into, and use, paranormal powers; see Channon 1979; Gray 1989; Ronson 2009; Swets and Bjork 1990; as well as the book *The Men Who Stare at Goats*). Gorman's vision also evokes the quasi-religious nature of the Jedi and the First Earth Battalion, though this time religious order is a kind of technonationalist order, not tasked with peace but with war, and possibly more aligned with Darth Vader and the Sith (and we should keep in mind that Darth Vader wore a powered combat suit vaguely reminiscent of a World War II Schutzstaffel [ss] officer). Using the Force and sophisticated weapons and sensors, in Gorman's vision, the Objective Force Warrior would be unstoppable. Unlike the First Earth Battalion, which was to seek nonlethal means of conflict resolution, the Objective Force Warrior would be more like Ernst Jünger's audacious protofascist New Man, reveling in the remorseless destruction he leaves in his wake.

The Force is also a feeling of protection, connectedness, and strength, both for the soldier and for those protected by the soldier. We can sleep safe at night knowing that the Objective Force Warrior—or whatever the soldier will be called—is out there, standing watch, silent and heroic, bound to and part of a great cybernetwork of protection and security. The soldier of tomorrow "will never be alone" because they will be a part of the "system of systems," part of a broad and overlapping array of intelligence collection, sensors, satellites, and netted communications systems that will provide them with real-time information and connectivity and allow officers and other units near and far access to the information the soldier—the "soldier-as-sensor"—is registering and transmitting. The soldier will also never be alone because she will be monitored by the system of systems as well as the medical interventions designed to ensure her health and performance metrics.

Such are the musings and visions of desirable soldier systems by US military scientists, engineers, and biomedical researchers as they attempt to develop the technology to create supersoldiers. Under the aegis of "health" or defense, they discuss the bodies of soldiers as platforms, machines, "systems"—or, as Sulzberger referred to them, "components"—to be manipulated at will in order to achieve desired goals and outcomes. Just as the US military views "threat" civilians as "Collateral Damage"—as dehumanized objects—it seems to similarly view the bodies of its own soldiers as objects, machines to be redesigned, rebuilt, and enhanced. In much the same way that Carol Cohn (1987) and Gusterson (1996) describe the imaginative worlds of nuclear weapons scientists, and their ways of coping with destructive technology, here we see how US defense and biomedical intellectuals imagine the melding of the human body and machinery, all in the name of health, defense, and security. In many ways, these scientists resemble young boys playing with GI Joe toys or Transformers. As they design new types of soldier systems, they inhabit a world of deadly serious make-believe, in which there are no "real" people, only anonymous, "naked warriors" whose bodies are theirs to shape and make and improve with "skin-in" biotechnical solutions.

The supersoldier is a dream of preserving order, of trying to bring an imagined future of chaos into sharper focus and, through this focus, control it. Anticipation and preemption are about anxiety and control, and about holding on to and expanding what we have in the present. As Sheila Jasanoff notes in her discussion of E. E. Evans-Pritchard's work on Azande magic, witchcraft supported order by assigning inexplicable events to discernable social causes (Jasanoff 2015, 6). Military biotechnology—like witchcraft and divination as technologies of prediction—attempts to give some order and predictability to the inexplicable, to the known unknowns and unknown unknowns that the military will face. It is not just control, however, or the interpretation of unknown unknowns; it is also about projecting a vision of invincibility through superior technology. As Gell writes, "Technical innovations occur, not to supply wants, but in the course of attempts to realize technical feats heretofore considered 'magical'" (1988, 8). Our technology is so far advanced that it seems we can achieve the heretofore impossible or unimaginable, unless we imagined such things as the purview of magic and the magical. We might not know what we will face, but we can appear magically invincible in the present, which will hopefully somehow shape perceptions of us in the future. Imagining the magical potential of new biomedical technologies allows military planners and theorists to believe they have some control over the future of conflict.

The Tactical Assault Light Operator Suit

The Tactical Assault Light Operator Suit—or TALOS—is the latest dream of the hypertechnical US soldier as a kind of "battle-bot" or Terminator. In 2014 the US military released press information and videos related to its new TALOS project. The TALOS was a combat enhancement and protection suit under development for use by special operations forces. Research into powered exoskeletons and advanced forms of body armor like the TALOS fire the public's imagination and help us imagine Iron Man–like supersoldiers. Technology like the TALOS also allows the military to shape how we imagine the externally armored supersoldier.

While not part of the LW/OFW/FFW suite of projects, the TALOS marks a further step in the imagination and development of supersoldiers (see figure 6.5). After a US special operations soldier was killed entering a doorway during a mission in Afghanistan, Admiral William McRaven, the (now former) commander of Special Operations Command (SOCOM), was asked by a special operations officer why the US military had not developed technology to protect special operations soldiers during these kinds of missions; this question proved to be the impetus for the design and development of the TALOS.

Nicknamed the "Iron Man suit," the TALOS is named after the golem-like creation from Greek mythology that patrolled the shores of Crete to protect against pirates and that was "powered" by infusions of ichor from the gods (see figure 6.6). Talos was a hulking proto-man-machine, an early dream of a nonhuman superwarrior.

While not fueled by ichor, the TALOS is meant to give US soldiers almost godlike powers of protection and offensive capabilities. Fundamentally a powered exoskeleton covered in liquid metal armor, the Iron Man suit is to give US soldiers 100 percent protection against small-arms fire, have immediate medical responses such as tourniquets for wounds, have a heating and cooling system, and be "netted" into a vast sensor, intelligence, and drone network. Paul Scharre, Lauren Fish, Katherine Kidder, and Amy Schafer describe the protective capabilities of the TALOS as follows: "The current TALOS prototype models are battery-powered hydraulic rigid exoskeletons with a bulletproof outer shell. If developed as currently envisaged, the suit will increase protection by expanding the area of coverage of hard armor relative to current body armor. Additionally, the intent is for the suit to monitor the wearer through advanced medical technology, allowing for a supervisor to note potential risks such as dehydration or low blood sugar. Moreover, the suit could release wound-clotting foam should a breach of the suit occur" (2018).

Originally slated for field use in 2018, the program was canceled in early 2019; according to the "acquisition executive" of SOCOM, the TALOS was "not ready for prime-time in a close combat environment" (Tucker 2019). Persistent problems with the power supply made the suit unfeasible; lightweight and reliable power supply has been the Achilles Heel of most, if not

'Iron Man suit'

Concept suit from the animated video produced by the Army's Research, Development and Engineering Command

Head gear:
Live data feed projected on a see-through display inside the helmet.

Uniform:
Head-to-toe armor would protect the soldier from bullets and sharpnel.

Civil War | World War I | World War II | Vietnam War | Iraq War | Future

Pack essentials:
The prototype should be able to cure minor wounds with inflatable tourniquets. It would also carry an oxygen supply, cooling system and vital-signs sensors.

The suit would be connected with drones and satellite systems.

Pack weight:
Motors in the exoskeleton would allow a soldier to jump and run carrying 100 pounds or more.

Figure 6.5 "Iron Man suit." US military TALOS suit, 2014.

Figure 6.6 Talos at the Isle of Bronze. Film still, *Jason and the Argonauts*, 1963.

all, US exoskeleton/external armor designs and programs, including the Objective Force Warrior suit and the Future Force Warrior system (*Military Technology* 2006; Scharre et al. 2018; *Soldiers* 2006; Tucker 2019).

Regardless of the setbacks or the unrealistic design expectations of something like the TALOS, projects like this allow the military to advance supersoldier protection technologies, push the limit in what is possible in order to create possible armor and protection technologies and capabilities, and project an image of the US soldier as Iron Man or some other kind of invincible superhero. Projecting an image of invincibility, as Timmerman wrote, is the first step in defeating your enemy before even firing a shot on the battlefield.

The Naked Warrior Redux: Technology and Masculinity

Despite the development of advanced skin-out armor and technologies, and depictions of the Objective Force Warrior, Future Force Warrior, and TALOS soldier that look like something seen in a science fiction film, the US military continues to talk about the "naked soldier" and nude warriors on the battlefield. This might seem like a contradiction, but it shows that the military considers skin-in solutions to be the key to military success; body armor and exoskeletons will only get you so far and are prone to failure. Without an internally enhanced soldier, high-tech body armor and exoskeletons are merely shells; as Supersoldier Bob mentions in his letter home, he has to have special meals for days before he can actually wear his new OFW Mark 3 combat suit.

But the military must also worry about and contend with threats to deeply felt conceptions of military masculinity and heroism, and the threats to the hypermasculinity of the soldier that military performance enhancements and skin-out technologies represent. Military performance enhancement research has serious implications for military masculinity (in much the same way drones impact images and perceptions of hypermasculine fighter pilots in the Air Force [see Gusterson 2016]), but images of the naked ur-warrior conjure notions of the soldier enhanced not by technology but by his own innate and internal bravery.

At this point, it is useful to return to Sulzberger's Idiophylactic Soldier and his arguments about biotechnology and naked soldiers on the battlefield feeling protected through built-in medical protection. Enhance the body, and the soldier can continue the mission, even if naked and alone on the battlefield, as Sulzberger wrote. But plans for built-in armor and the "soldier as system of systems" underplay and in many ways negate the hypermasculinity of the supersoldier; if boldness and heroism can now be regulated through biomedical enhancements, what does that do to the conception of the brave soldier who rises above the rest? One way to counter these threats is through ideas and portrayals of naked soldiers and a kind of modern martial nudity. As James A. Mangan writes, the male nude is a symbol of martial masculinity (1999, 7–8). Mangan draws from Andrew Stewart and his work on the body in ancient Greece: "The supreme image of unfettered masculinity in Greek Art was not the collective killing machine of the phalanx but the individual warrior, represented as he was at that fateful moment: alone" (Stewart 1997, 2, quoted in Mangan 1999, 7–8). The Greek soldier as part of a phalanx—a mass combat formation that revolutionized Homeric-era combat—also meant that the warrior was consigned to the mass and only able to demonstrate his own innate bravery outside the mass. Conversely, only the "hero" was able to fight alone and outside the phalanx and the mass. Aloof, nude posturing—both ancient and modern—as Stewart writes, is a device to "elevate the man above time and space, particularity and decay" (1997, 24–25, quoted in Mangan 1999, 8). As Mangan puts it, "It allows the transcendence of the specific and contingent by the presentation of a superhuman beauty presented as an abstract image of male perfection" (1999, 8). We can think back to Achilles, who could never be constrained by the mass; few soldiers want to imagine themselves as anonymous cogs in a system of systems: they want to be the hero. This is also a fairly accurate description of Sulzberger's Idiophylactic Soldier and Gorman's Objective Force–Jedi warrior, not to mention Jünger's New Man and Breker's *Readiness*. They are all alone, on guard, walking point.

While Sulzberger mused about the naked soldier in 1962, the dream of naked warrior can be found again in a discussion of the "Naked Warrior" contained in the 2001 "Objective Force Warrior" report: "The group then took the unique approach of starting with what they called the 'Naked Warrior'—a warrior with no individual equipment or systems. Their logic was that before you could add technology to a warrior, you had to have a cultural strategy. Throughout all of the deliberations, they kept coming back to the concept of the Naked Warrior. There was a consensus that if the warrior did not have certain attributes, the addition of technology would not prove beneficial" (National Security Directorate Oak Ridge National Laboratory 2001, 2). Among the "attributes" deemed necessary for the successful melding of the "Naked Warrior" and skin-out technologies were "Brotherhood," "Confidence," "Adaptive/Agile," "Self-Discipline," "Initiative," and "Culture."

Ideas of nudity and mythic military prowess push back against counterhegemonic threats to military masculinity like biotechnologies and skin-out technologies. The naked soldier functions as a throwback to a premodern warrior and an antidote to cowardice. The naked warrior is perhaps the bravest of warriors or the ultimate hero: going into battle with only his own body as armor, the hero is pure "body" armor through and through, an armor that protects and broadcasts the hero's bravery. Naked and alone on the battlefield, this puissant warrior needs no external armor: his body is his own armor. Whether a naked Pict warrior painted blue, or Viking Berserkers, or other warriors who shed their armor and clothing in a flurry and blaze of naked violence and bravery, the modern US soldier is imagined by military and private researchers in much the same way, naked and alone, even as they are simultaneously imagined and trained to wear exoskeletons, improved body armor, and futuristic combat suits. Imagining the biologically enhanced soldier as the "naked warrior" allows for a reinscription of military masculinity in the face of biotechnical and biomedical emasculation. Naked and alone, this soldier does not need technology or the vast array of systems of systems that make it possible for him to function on the modern battlefield. It is a kind of prosthetic memory of a preprosthetic and preenhanced state of military masculinity and heroism.

"Naked" and "warrior" also help "reheroize" the soldier; while biotechnology can negatively impact conceptions of military masculinity, biotechnology can also make it possible for all soldiers to perform as what we would now see as heroes, thus emptying the category. We still want and believe in a military that is guided by traditional notions of masculinity, honor, bravery, selflessness—as do soldiers themselves—and we still like to believe in the moral and physical strength of the soldier. "Naked" and "warrior" help us—and soldiers in the military as well—maintain belief in what is increasingly becoming outmoded or anachronistic in the face of Revolution in Military Affairs and the embrace of biotechnology in the military. What before might have been some kind of idiosyncratic biological fluke of the individual soldier can now become a programmable and reliable fact at the tip of a syringe or encased in a pill for all soldiers.

Paradoxically, though, nudity continues to demonstrate the high-tech nature of the state: it armors the soldier from the inside, not the outside. The state can armor life itself and not just hang armor or protection on the soldier (even though it does this as well). The unseen armor of the naked soldier both highlights and obscures the political economy of soldier-enhancement research: it is "skin in," under the skin, unviewable, microscopic, a biological cypher. Nudity—for all its explicit openness and display—is intended to hide, conceal, and obscure military performance enhancements. Biotechnology will be hidden deep in the molecular workings of the soldier, who, having nothing to hide or be ashamed of, is imagined as naked on the battlefield, protected internally through the ministrations of the state that are not on display but are nonetheless known by the soldier. This logic leads us back to one of the early uses and intentions of nudity on the battlefield: to frighten the enemy. "Our" warriors are so brave, deadly, dangerous, and spoiling for a fight that they do not even want to or need to wear armor or anything that will protect or encumber them in their desire to get into the fight.

Nudity also simultaneously reinforces and counteracts modernist discourses of progress and the linear tale of perfection: it is a throwback, a recycling, a closing of the loop rather than a straight line. But it also affirms the ultimate triumph of modernist technology: it is so sophisticated that it does not even seem like technology any longer. Is it the soldier, simply naked on the battlefield, or is it the soldier, enhanced internally and made into a kind of human auto-armor? Is the soldier himself or now more than himself? Can we tell? Ultimately, perhaps, that is the goal: we will not be able to tell, until it is perhaps too late. It is just the body of the soldier, the naked soldier, steeled and alone against the world—the cyborg that looks just like any of us. We might imagine them as enhanced in all sorts of ways, as having brain implants that allow them to see what we want them to see and make it easier for them to fight and kill who we want them to, but if we imagine them as "naked," we can still think of them as human.

Nudity also implies a blank slate: in this case, a militarized tabula rasa upon which to build the supersoldier. Nudity connotes nature; rather than identifying actual recruits or soldiers who are to be "redesigned," the "naked warrior" erases the history, identity, or culture of the potential OFW soldier. Stripped down, the "naked warrior" is both the starting point of the OFW soldier and also a sign that the soldier is strong and powerful internally, even without external equipment. Embodying the attributes set forth in the report, the "naked warrior" will be the natural truth of the efficacy of the OFW program, a justification of the medical interventions necessary to produce a healthy and powerful soldier. The image of the "naked warrior" also implies a sense of rebirth as something new and improved; it is a powerful metaphor for a sort of technological virgin male birth. Nudity is also coupled here with a sense of parental control: given the semantic linking of "infant" with "infantry," the implication of "parental" control is strengthened. It is a vision of the technological male birthing of the dependable, compliant supersoldier.

As Elizabeth Grosz comments, in *The Genealogy of Morals*, Friedrich Nietzsche argued that every cultural group can be understood not only in terms of its social and cultural products but also in terms of how it arranges its corporeal and body ideals and the management, representation, and production of bodies (Grosz 2006, 188). Conceptions of the "naked warrior" work around notions of both strength and weakness. Nudity is often associated with weakness, helplessness, and vulnerability but can also be associated with strength, authenticity, and the "natural truth" of the body (Linke 1998, 29). Frederic Spotts, in a study of fascist aesthetics, points out that the "naked, virile male" was a prominent National Socialist symbol (2004, 111), and Benito Mussolini often appeared semi-undressed in official photos. In fascist aesthetics—and perhaps troublingly, in the imaginations of some US military researchers—nudity is seen as a source of weakness to overcome in order to attain strength, or perhaps the starting point from weakness to strength; ultimately, in both conceptions, nudity is the signifier of ultimate strength through the internal armoring of the psyche and the overcoming of physical and psychological weakness. Freed of cumbersome protective equipment and internally armored against all manner of threats, the most troubling possibility is the soldier increasingly resembling Breker's *Readiness*: stripped down and naked, armed and armored with only his own body against the world, potentially fearing and feeling nothing, like the ideal warrior Jünger envisioned.

Supersoldier, Superstate

The US military seemingly wants to play both sides of the soldier aesthetics game. The supersoldier must be human and more than human, someone who can come home as she once was and not as an enhanced supersoldier who is both more and less than human. But ultimately, and perhaps most importantly for the "home front" and recruiting, it might be easier to have an emotional connection to a naked warrior than an Idiophylactic Soldier or a soldier encased in a high-tech combat suit. If the enhanced soldier is portrayed as more machinelike than human and by implication can feel or suffer no pain (or possibly feel no remorse for their actions), we might have a very different image of them, and perhaps not find them admirable and ethical (Huebner 2008, 275–76). As a sign, the "naked warrior" creates a stronger emotional connection; "naked" still implies helpless—and human—while "warrior" implies the brave man who rises up to defend his kith and kin. The "Idiophylactic Soldier" implies something not quite human, something out of science fiction, something menacing, even if it is our soldier. The Army of One campaign paid a great deal of attention to mothers and their willingness to let their children enlist. It is perhaps easier to imagine a mother willingly allowing her son to become a kind of "naked warrior" over an Idiophylactic Soldier. Her son might still come home as her recognizable son if he is a naked warrior.

When you look at the soldier, you see the state. You see how the state thinks of itself—or rather, you see the actions of those in power who have the power to shape an image of the state and through this shaping create an image of themselves. When you look at a modern US soldier, you see a person covered in technology, enmeshed in technology, and increasingly constituted and "populated" internally by technology. You no longer see World War II's Willie and Joe (Gray 1997, 196; Huebner 2008, 275) or even a heroic or muscular soldier; the human is subsumed by the technology or simply gone. To look at the TALOS, for example, is to look at a kind of dream vision of the soldier-as-non-soldier, the soldier as nonhuman machine but somehow with a human inside to make sure we have not completely embraced something like the Terminator. It is similar to the Turk, the chess-playing robot with the human inside from 1770; you see the technology, but you do not see the soldier; he remains anonymous and protected, unknown and potentially unthought of, though we are to be somehow reassured by the fact that we think we know that a human soldier is in there, controlling the machine. You see the technology on display and in action, you see the system of systems interacting to achieve policy goals and "kill the bad guys," and rather than think critically about what is going on, we are supposed to "feel" that the soldier is protected and that the technology is really, really cool. Maybe something like the TALOS will eventually work as designed, and maybe the anonymous "operator" inside will be protected and fine. But it is not as if that is where all consideration of this kind of technology or "protection" or "enhancement" should end. Without an internally enhanced soldier, or a soldier who can withstand the battlefield through biomedicine or "will," high-tech body armor and exoskeletons are merely shells.

Technology like the TALOS fires the imagination and allows people to play out fantasies of war and combat and heroism, just like when playing video games like Halo or Call of Duty. Enclosed in a hyperadvanced carapace, the person is unstoppable and potentially unkillable. The problem is, however, that these things do not exist. And as Scott Neil, a former Special Forces operator, commented about the TALOS: "My sense is it is an up-armored Pinocchio. . . . Now the commander can shove a monkey in a suit and ask us to survive a machine gun, IED [improvised explosive device] and poor intelligence all on the same objective. And when you die in it, as it melts to your body, you can bury them in it" (quoted in Altman 2014).

Technology like the TALOS has other limits. While a powered battle suit might be useful in combat or hostage rescue situations, it might have serious drawbacks in counterinsurgency operations, where the goal is not to kill or destroy the enemy but "win the hearts and minds" of the local populace (Petraeus and Amos 2009). It might be difficult for a soldier—who for all practical purposes looks like a menacing robot—to win the love and affection of a village, even if she hands out soccer balls, bottled water, or DVDs of the latest *Iron Man* film.

Unlike Sulzberger's Idiophylactic Soldier, Breker's *Readiness*, or even Gorman's Soldier-as-Jedi, with something like the TALOS, you can see advanced body armor and external technology—and the soldier can take it off. We can imagine supersoldiers who can put on an enhancement or suite of enhancements and take them off at will, who can wear a kind of superskin and change their appearances. In this sense, the enhanced supersoldier is at-will and limited to the time the soldier wears the enhancement technologies. But what of internal, built-in biomedical armor that we cannot see, and which cannot possibly be taken off at will? We can encase soldiers in liquid armor suits, but the real goal of military performance enhancement research and supersoldier research is probably more akin to the Idiophylactic Soldier and *Readiness*: the soldier as its own armor, naked against the world, fearing and feeling—and possibly remembering—nothing.

Endless Transformation

In 2008 funding for the Objective Force Warrior program was scaled back, and some of the technology developed was to be integrated into the existing Land Warrior project. However, none of this should be seen as a failure, or that idiophylactic supersoldier research is a dead-end, no-win endeavor. Far from it: canceled projects often continue in different iterations of new projects. Each failure drives continued anticipation about possible threats to the soldier; anticipation is productive. Each "failure" drives new endeavors and highlights new areas to explore and exploit, and the dream of the "kill-proof" soldier—which might constitute the benchmark of success in supersoldier research—spurs continued research and development in the ever-increasing field of military biomedicine (Masco 2014). Biomedical research predicated on soldier protection and enhancement provides jobs, funding, and the circulation of resources, and like "Support Our Troops," soldier protection is a political "third rail" in the United States that is hard to fully counter (Jacobsen 2015; Weinberger 2017).

Regardless of success or failure, these projects are examples of the vision of the future of the US military and the steps the military is willing to take in melding biology and technology to make soldiers fit into a "system of systems" of supersoldiers. Projects like Land Warrior and the Objective Force Warrior never fully came online, and the US military, while clearly a "technological" force, is nowhere near the "modular" or "netted" force envisioned by the architects of these early projects. The interesting thing is not that these projects have "failed" but what they tell us about how the US military imagines and envisions the future, again and again. As General Peter Schoomaker said in the OFW promotional video, nothing will stop this move toward transformation. Projects will fail, but soldiers will remain weak and in need of protection, and so projects will continue, as US military researchers continue to dream up new and even more invasive attempts to enhance the body of the soldier in the name of protection and "the Force."

SEVEN

Molecular Militarization

War, Drugs, and the Structures of Unfeeling

On the battlefield of the future, there is no sleep but death.

» **US Air Force Research Laboratory**

Militaries have long wished to have soldiers who could fight longer, better, smarter, and faster than their adversaries, and soldiers themselves have attempted to self-medicate to meet the needs of the military and find ways to cope with the stress and horror of combat or simply the stress of boredom and military discipline. The use of drugs to enhance performance and control fear in combat is not a new phenomenon, and is perhaps as old as warfare, whether practiced by small-scale groups or modern nation-states (Bergen-Cico 2012; Caron 2018; Kamieński 2016a, 2016b; Kan 2009; Pugh 2017; Rasmussen 2011). Various drugs have been used for centuries to either inhibit pain or stimulate courage, and to promote "boldness" and inhibit weakness or timidity. The use of alcohol in combat—"Dutch courage"—has been a feature of militaries and armies for centuries (Gabriel 1987). During the Vietnam War, for example, American troops routinely used drugs and alcohol during combat and as a way to mitigate postcombat stress and trauma (Ebert 1993; Kamieński 2016b; Kan 2009; Shay 1995). According-ing to Anke Snoek, in 1971 the US military reported half of the soldiers in Vietnam had tried narcotics (heroin and/or opium), with 20 percent re-porting addiction issues; additionally, 92 percent of soldiers drank heavily, 69 percent had tried marijuana, 25 percent amphetamines, and 23 percent barbiturates (2015, 96; see also Kamieński 2016b; Rardin, Lawson, and Rush 1973). In other words, large numbers of soldiers were self-medicating to cope with the stress and horror of war.

Drugs were also a part of the Cold War US Army, though perhaps in unintentional ways. The Army decided that wisdom teeth were a possible problem for readiness, so almost all soldiers in my unit were ordered to have their wisdom teeth removed soon after arriving in Berlin. After the extraction(s), we were put on sick leave for three days to recover, and we all received large bottles of Percocet for pain, so much that it was impossible to take it all. Because it had been prescribed, there was not much worry about it appearing in the random drug tests we were forced to take. And again, boredom leads to invention: some people on my base in Berlin would grind up and snort lines of Percocet before heading out to the bars on the weekend. While not widespread, soldiers would sometimes resort to snorting Percocet and drinking as a way to cope with the stresses, boredom, and repetition of Army life and duty, and often put themselves in precarious situations. We heard a story of soldiers from another unit who snorted lines of Percocet, had a few beers, and then got into a major fight in front of an East German border guard tower while the Border Guards looked on in disbelief and amusement.

Paramilitary and "irregular" forces around the world use drugs as both performance enhancements and as forms of "recruitment" and rewards for fighting (Kamieński 2016a, 2016b; Kan 2009; Speckhard and Yayla 2015). Paramilitary forces often use alcohol and drugs like heroin, cocaine, and Captagon as a way to keep soldiers in the field, and child soldiers are often given drugs to coerce them to "enlist" and then are drugged to ensure they fight and do not run away. While alcohol and other drugs might be plentiful and cheap, they present a modern, professional military with more problems than they are worth. From a military standpoint, drugs need to be controllable, regulated, and provide the right kinds of enhancements and capabilities when needed. Drunk or drugged soldiers might be fearless, but they are not necessarily useful or controllable on the battlefield. Soldiers must be enhanced in such a way as to be clear-headed and effective in combat.

———

One solution to military performance enhancement has been the use of amphetamines as a "medical tool" designed to improve performance and morale. World War II saw the widespread use of amphetamines by both the Axis and Allied powers. US and UK pilots routinely used amphetamines during missions, and the Allies continued to use amphetamines throughout the war. Amphetamines were seen as a quick, easy, reliable, and controllable intervention, a drug that would keep the soldier going in the field under all adverse conditions.

On the Axis side, the German military did not leave it completely up to nonpharmacological interventions to create the new kind of soldier it needed to fight a new kind of war. In the early phases of the war, German soldiers were issued the methamphetamine Pervitin (see figure 7.1) prior to combat in order to make their bodies keep up with the pace of Blitzkrieg—"lightning war" (Kamieński 2016a; Ohler 2017, Pfaff 2017; Steinkamp 2003, 2006). According to C. Anthony Pfaff, the Wehrmacht ordered thirty-five million Pervitin tablets prior to the invasion of France in order to make sure soldiers could remain awake and maintain the operational tempo required to quickly overrun the French, British, Belgian, and Dutch armies (2017, 65). Blitzkrieg demanded soldiers who could stay awake and keep up with the pace of the new kind of relentless offensive warfare, with infantry and armored units on the move for days on end (Ohler 2017; Pfaff 2017; Steinkamp 2003, 2006). But the use of Pervitin, even if it did allow the German military to operate at a frenetic pace for days on end, was not without major problems. Prior to the invasion of Crete in 1940, German paratroopers were given amphetamines before jumping: many proceeded to jump without their parachutes (*New Scientist* 1991, 18). As Pfaff notes, German soldiers taking Pervitin often became anxious, nervous, and jittery, and one ss unit was easily overrun by Soviet troops because its soldiers fired at the slightest noise, expending all their ammunition before they were actually attacked (2017, 65–66). And as the war progressed, increasing numbers of German soldiers became addicted to Pervitin, and a number of German soldiers dropped dead from a combination of overuse and exhaustion (Kamieński 2016a; Ohler 2017; Steinkamp 2003, 2006). As a result, the Wehrmacht high command pulled Pervitin from front-line units and only issued it on an as-needed basis after late 1941. Near the end of the war, with concerns of long-term addiction no longer seen as a problem, the Wehrmacht developed a new drug called D-IX, which contained five milligrams of cocaine, three milligrams of Pervitin, and five milligrams of the opiate Eukadol (Ohler 2017; Ulrich 2005). This new drug was envisioned as a kind of wonder drug that would make German soldiers fight harder and longer, and thus win the war (or at least prolong it), without regard for short- or long-term side effects. Tests of D-IX on concentration camp prisoners showed that they could march up to

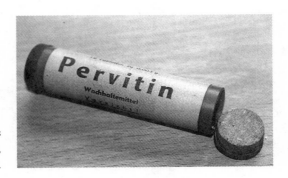

Figure 7.1 Pervitin tablets and container, Germany, World War II.

ninety kilometers per day while taking the drug, but many of the prisoners died during the trials (Krishnan 2018).

During World War II, the Korean War, and the Vietnam War, large numbers of American soldiers were given stimulants to improve their combat performance, despite the US military's awareness of the side effects of amphetamines like Benzedrine (Bergen-Cico 2012; Friedl 2015; Kamieński 2016; Kan 2009; see figure 7.2). Navy and Marine Special Forces soldiers in Vietnam stated that they were provided with the "best amphetamines" available (Gray 1989, 62); they described these drugs as producing a sense of "bravado," heightening every sound, and creating a feeling of being "wired in" (Gray 1989, 62–63). Troops were also provided with stimulants to keep them awake during ambushes (Ebert 1993, 251), and stimulants were part of the standard issue of equipment to US Army Rangers in Vietnam (Stanton 1992, 334).

The US military continues to use amphetamines, particularly for pilots flying long combat missions (J. A. Caldwell 2008; Krishnan 2018). The first and second Gulf Wars, as well as the war in Afghanistan, have shown that the military continues to use amphetamines for long-duration missions around the world. Pilots of B-2 bombers routinely fly missions more than twenty-four hours in duration, flying from bases in the United States to bomb targets in Iraq or Afghanistan. Without the use of amphetamines, many of these long-duration missions would be difficult, if not impossible, for the pilots.

But the use of "Go Pills"—dextroamphetamines—by US Air Force pilots to remain awake during combat is not without danger, which was brought into stark relief when they were linked to the Tarnak Farms friendly fire incident, resulting in the killing of Canadian soldiers by US pilots who were taking Go Pills in Afghanistan in 2003 (Annas and Annas 2009, 294;

Figure 7.2 US military ad for Benzedrine inhaler, Smith, Kline, and French Laboratories, 1944.

Krishnan 2018, 50). In an interview with ABC News, US Air Force General Daniel Leaf stated that amphetamines are routinely administered to pilots; as he said, "This is not a recreational drug. It's the use of a medical tool" (*Scotland on Sunday*, December 22, 2002). While this may be the use of a "medical tool," one serious problem with the use of Go Pills and with "No-Go Pills" (sleep aids to bring pilots down from Go Pills; see, e.g., J. L. Caldwell and Shanahan 1992 for an early discussion about these issues) is that this combination can cause "anterograde amnesia"—an amnesia of events and what the pilot/soldier has done while on the medication (Knickerbocker 2002). Side effects such as these raise serious issues for both command and control and the moral/ethical regulation of combat, targeting, and killing (Annas and Annas 2009; J. A. Caldwell and J. L. Caldwell 2005; Krishnan 2018; Snoek 2015). Armin Krishnan (2018) also notes that there is some concern that amphetamines can contribute to PTSD in soldiers (see also Farren 2010). The US military is moving away from amphetamines and exploring other options for soldier performance enhancement based on advances in biomedicine, synthetic biology, and genomics.

"Iron Bodied and Iron Willed": The Drug-Born Supersoldier

In the United States, the military's development and use of drugs to methodically enhance performance and modulate memory and trauma has advanced far beyond what might have seemed technologically impossible or cost-prohibitive in the 1950s and 1960s. Science-fiction-like enhancements have become increasingly imaginable since the 1980s, as biomedical technologies have progressed in an increasingly quick and expansive manner. The 1980s, with Reagan's massive rebuilding of the US military and defense programs, may have had Star Wars, Brilliant Pebbles, and vast missile-defense projects located outside the bounds of the Earth, but with advances in biotechnology, the microspaces of the human body were increasingly seen as an equally important area of national defense. Just like the *Powers of 10* film from the 1970s produced by IBM (and seen by millions of schoolchildren at the Smithsonian Institution's National Air and Space Museum in Washington, DC) that expanded into deep space and then snapped back into the molecular depths of the human body (see figure 7.3), military researchers began conceptualizing defense in much the same way, seeing the micro and the macro as the battlefields of the future, with each step promising ten (or twenty) times the danger, lethality, protection, and coverage.

As warfare and technology evolve, the battlefield recedes deeper and deeper into the body of the soldier while it expands farther and farther away from the soldier. The broader world of political and military threat is mirrored in the microworld of the body of the soldier, threats and anticipation telescoping back and forth between the two. Each and every biological system, subsystem, strata, substrate, connection, network, linkage, flow, ordering, and so on of the body is seen as weak but also crucial for defense and offense, and therefore enhanceable and necessary for military planning, strategy, and operations. The military's body problem is now the soldier as an infinite array of biostructures and possibilities. It is not enough to say "we do not know what the body can do"; rather, the military might now say "we do not know what all the various parts of the body, disarticulated and considered for military utility, operations, deployments, security, and resiliency, can do."

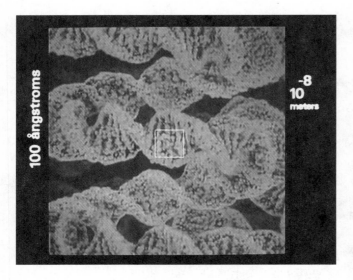

Figure 7.3 "The Emergent Pharmacological Battlefield." Film still, *Powers of 10*, 1977.

Even if the US military is not quite sure what the body can do, it has a fairly good idea of the kinds of soldiers/bodies it wants and needs and imagines. A report on US military biomedical research and the US military's Special Operations Command showed that military researchers hoped for performance enhancements to produce "iron bodied and ironed-willed personnel" (Knickerbocker 2002). While SOCOM soldiers are generally considered to be the elite soldiers of the military, we can see why the military wishes to make all soldiers, regardless of job or specialty, into soldiers who mimic the physical and mental characteristics of special operators.

To move toward this vision of a future army composed entirely of iron-willed and iron-bodied soldiers, the US military is examining technologies in enhanced cognition, memory suppression, "metabolic dominance," synthetic biology, genomics, neural connections, increased endurance, enhanced immune systems, automatic altitude acclimation, blood doping, synthetic blood, enhanced pain management, wound healing, enhanced clotting medications, and antifatigue interventions. All are projects and areas of research interest intended to manipulate the biology of the soldier and better use the biology and the inner depths of the soldier. As S. A. Cavanagh (2018) details, military performance enhancement drugs fall under a number of categories, such as psychostimulants, eugeroics, stimulants,

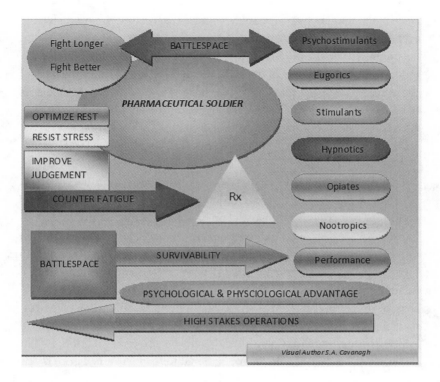

Figure 7.4 The Pharmaceutical Soldier—Performance Enhancing Drugs on the Battlefield. S. A. Cavanagh, "swj Factsheet," 2018.

hypnotics, opiates, and nootropics. Each broad category is to address and enhance stressors and soldier performance through the directed use of medications (see figure 7.4). The body of the soldier is a body pulled apart, each part analyzed and judged according to the needs of the military and analyzed on the potential for weakness or failure in the face of present threats or the imagined threats of the future. The soldier—the system of systems—is analyzed and conceived of as a biological system of systems, with each biological system and set of subsystems considered for different missions and battlefields, different combat conditions and contingencies. Each and every system of the soldier is seen in light of the battlefield: just as chain operator theory in archaeology "explodes" an object to analyze the myriad connections inherent in the makeup of and production of an object, so too does the US military "explode" the body of the soldier into biological subsystems to better understand and militarize each and every molecule in the soldier's body. The soldier comes apart before our eyes before he ever enters combat. In order to make sure the "component man" does not fail on the battlefield, the battlefield is brought inside the soldier: molecular militarization is the safety of the state, secured and anchored in the body of the soldier. This "pre-exploding" of the body is to ensure that the soldier is not pulled apart by all the weapons and threats she will face and might face. Each battle, each conflict, and, eventually, the fate of the nation rest on the ability of each biological subsystem to give its all—and more—for the state.

Like the "Rip Fuel" guzzling US Marine in *Generation Kill* (Wright 2008), the book and later HBO series about the invasion of Iraq in 2003, US soldiers are known to use a variety of off-the-shelf drugs and illicit/ nonprescribed drugs in combat and on base, such as diet pills, alcohol, caffeine, tobacco, sleeping pills, energy drinks, opioids, and steroids (though the use of steroids remains prohibited, and the overall value of steroids to the military appears to remain unknown [see Peltier and Pettijohn 2018]). In addition to off-the-shelf drugs, the US military investigated a wide variety of drugs to evaluate their usefulness in enhancing soldiers' performance; these investigations give us a good idea of the kinds of drugs the US military is interested in (Caldwell and Caldwell 2005; JASON 2008; Kelley, Webb, Athy, Ley, and Gaydos 2010; National Research Council 2001).

> Amphetamines and stimulants used to promote alertness, enhance cognitive function, and address combat fatigue:
>
> 1 dextroamphetamine
> 2 methylphenidate (Ritalin)
> 3 modafinil (Provigil)
> 4 caffeine
> 5 nicotine
> 6 donepezil
> 7 galantamine
> 8 ampakines
>
> Hypnotics and sleep agents used to optimize quality of rest, balance stimulant use, possibly counter combat trauma:
>
> 1 temazepam
> 2 zolpidem
> 3 zaleplon
> 4 propranolol
> 5 ketamine

The Objective Force Warrior, Future Force Warrior, and Future Soldier 2030 programs all identify skin-in performance enhancement technologies as key biomedical technologies for soldier protection and enhancement. Even though the OFW and FFW programs have been canceled, pharmacological enhancements currently being examined derived from these projects include trauma-blocking drugs for soldiers in combat, interventions in the "sleep/wake cycle" designed to keep soldiers on the go for seventy-two hours, specially designed performance enhancing foods, hyperhydration, new protective and information technologies, cognition enhancement and research into pharmaceuticals designed to "enhance situational awareness" and prevent the "degradation of decision-making," and military applications of synthetic biology.

The National Research Council Committee on Opportunities in Biotechnology for Future Army Applications 2001 report detailed the future uses of biotechnology in the Army. The expansive report imagined the myriad ways in which biotechnology will not augment but transform Army systems, combat, and, most importantly, soldiers. "Although soldiers in 2025 will look outwardly identical to soldiers today," the report states, "they will be stronger, have longer endurance, and will be more resistant to disease and aging. The capabilities of future soldiers may very well be augmented in ways that change the nature of individual and unit combat" (National Research Council 2001, 7). The report summarizes the ways in which biotechnology will be used to provide internal protection for the soldier as well as enhance soldier performance.

Functional Foods—Additives to improve nutrition, enhance digestion, improve storage characteristics, enable battlefield identification, reduce detectability; edible vaccines; fast-growing plants.

Health Monitoring—Devices to provide feedback on soldier status, enable remote triage, and augment a network of external sensors to provide intelligence on chemical, biological, or environmental agents.

Performance Enhancement—Cortical implants; computer input and display interfaces; prostheses control; sensory enhancement; antidotal implants; gene-expression monitoring; performance enhancing drugs.

Soldier Therapeutics—Drugs to counteract shock; genomics-based, directed therapies; optimized responsiveness to vaccines.

Vaccine Development—Reduced development and production times for small-scale requirements to respond to diseases encountered in exotic locales.

Wound Healing—Engineered skin, tissue, and organs; wound dressings and treatments to curtail bleeding and accelerate healing. (2001, 5)

Perkins and Steevens, in their analysis and discussion of military biotechnology programs and research foci, lay out perhaps the best overview of what is imagined, planned, and desired for the supersoldier of 2025, and how advanced biotechnologies will impact and enhance the soldier.

PERSONALIZED MEDICINE

- Prescreen soldiers for vulnerabilities/diseases
- Monitor soldiers to minimize injury
- Make soldiers stronger in order to allow for more intensive lifestyles/ training
- Gain personalized health understanding of soldiers in order to pick the right soldier for a particular assignment

MICROBIOME

- Through gut microbiome, control a person's mood, metabolism, and physical performance
- Use probiotics to improve performance (allowing for training to be shorter and more intense)
- Increase learning capacity, alertness, ability to perform in a stressful environment, enable integration of sensing in novel ways
- Probiotics could be used to alert soldiers to exposure to toxic chemicals or chemical/biological warfare agents by releasing a certain flavor in the mouth when exposure is detected
- Enable soldiers to eat grass or other plants as food sources

SYNTHETIC BIOLOGY

- Create synthetic biofuel and medicine
- Create organisms that "provide new mechanisms for sensing and responding to different signals (chemical, biological, magnetic, electric)"
- Organisms could be created that require little energy or create their own energy and are used to control simple devices, calculate events, and monitor environments
- Organisms could be created for helping soldiers adapt/survive in given environments

- Prevent common diseases
- Remove sensitivity to chemicals
- Allow soldiers to more easily work in urban areas where exposure to chemicals is more common (2015)

As Perkins and Steevens write, taken as a suite of collective measures, "this technology could be a game changer in 2025 if state actors with access to the technology are able to enhance soldier performance. The ethics and communication to the public regarding use of this technology will affect the Army's use of technologies for Soldiers" (2015). But Perkins and Steevens also note that the development of enhanced soldiers is one of the "controversial" and "nefarious" outcomes of biotechnology (2015). Their observation and warning harken back to the double-bind of military biomedical research, the double-edged sword of protection and compulsion. We might imagine these technologies protecting our soldiers and keeping them safe, but that might simply hide the dark possibilities and "nefarious" outcomes of internally enhancing soldiers.

Krishnan (2018), in his examination of military neuroscience, provides a very useful chart detailing information on known US military pharmaceuticals and the types of pharmaceuticals and their effects (see table 7.1). In terms of psychopharmaceuticals designed to prevent or mitigate the effects of combat stress, early research at USARIEM focused on the neurotransmitter tyrosine (Friedl and Allan 2004, 35), with the eventual goal to "compare effectiveness of neuropsychological health monitoring strategies in deployment" and the long-term goal to "explore behavioral strategies to regulate neurochemistry to optimize resilience" (42). At the Military Operational Medicine Research Program (MOMRP) at Fort Detrick, Maryland, researchers on the "Pharmacology Strategy Team" sought to "identify [the] cognitive performance impact of psychoactive drugs, such as the new nasal formulation of the Ketamine dissociative anesthetic and pharmaceutical fatigue countermeasures" (United States Army Medical Research and Materials Command 2004). Researchers at the U.S. Army Aeromedical lab also conducted a comparative trial on ketamine and morphine to "delineate performance decrements in basic soldier tasks comparing the effects of the standard battlefield analgesic (10 mg i.m. morphine) with 25 mg i.m. ketamine" (Gaydos, Kelley, Grandizio, Athy, and Walters 2015, 313). A nasal inhaler version of ketamine is now available, but the military—for now—is keeping it under tight control, using it only to treat depression (Carey and Steinhauer 2019).

Table 7.1 Stimulants and Supplements for Combating Fatigue and Enhancing Cognitive Functions

Class of Drug	Example	Effect	Military Usage
amphetamines	Dexedrine	increases stamina, physical strength, and alertness; euphoria; improves working memory	"Go Pill"—maintaining alertness and vigilance; reduced need for rest
nervous system stimulants	Ritalin	combats fatigue; improves working memory; improves performance on boring and difficult tasks	improved concentration during boring tasks
eugeroics	modafinil	promotes wakefulness; treats sleep disorders; enhances cognitive abilities	reduced need for sleep
nootropics	piracetam	combats cognitive problems and decline; improves memory	improved cognitive performance in tasks that require concentration
omega-3 fatty acids	docosahexaenoic acid (DHA)	combats cognitive decline; in high dosages improves cognitive functions; combats depression	sustaining soldier performance long-term

Source: Krishnan 2018, 49.

In an article published in the journal *New Scientist* concerning the "molecular strength" of US Special Forces soldiers and their ability to produce neuropeptide Y (NPY)—an amino acid that can lower stress and reduce cases of post-traumatic stress syndrome—the director of the US National Center for PTSD had this to say: "If we could bottle this, or if we could train people to mobilize their own Neuropeptide Y, that would be primary prevention for PTSD—a very exciting approach" (*New Scientist* 2003, 17).

A further study of neuropeptide Y, "Plasma Neuropeptide-Y Concentrations in Humans Exposed to Military Survival Training," noted that injections of neuropeptide Y acted as an "anxiolytic and buffer against stress" and that data "support the idea that Neuropeptide-Y may be involved in the enhanced stress resilience seen in humans" (Morgan et al. 2000, 902). And Esther L. Sabban and Lidia I. Serova (2018) discuss the usefulness of NPY in combating stress and PTSD, and the potential uses of an intranasal formulation of NPY. In other words, soldiers who can be made both idiophylactic and "auto-idiophylactic" are the soldiers seen as desirable, useful, and necessary for future US engagements. This is a clear overlap between aesthetics and anesthetics, biomedicine, and US military research: the body of the soldier potentially trained to produce its own anesthetic at will in order to withstand the stresses of combat and any potential postcombat problems.

"Living Foundries" and "Biological Control": Synthetic Biology, Genomics, and the Supersoldier

The following sections briefly discuss the US military's use of and interest in synthetic biology and genomics, amphetamines, cognition enhancers, and possible memory- and trauma-blocking drugs. Drugs can be used before, during, and after combat to prepare the soldier, maintain and enhance the soldier's combat performance, and bring the soldier back to "normal" after combat. Each time period calls for different kinds of medical and/or pharmaceutical interventions and a consideration of what the soldier will have to face and return to. The image of the enhanced soldier is not necessarily just one of survivability but one of control—before, during, and after combat (see Gray 1989, 1994, for a similar argument around cybernetics). It is an updated image of the New Man, biomedically armored, always ready and strong enough for combat, always promising predictability and success.

"Skin-in solutions" mean much more than drugs that improve combat and battlefield performance and survival. The military is actively investigating advances in synthetic biology and genomics as possible avenues of soldier enhancement; the military is also keenly aware that advances in genetic technologies could lead to new forms of "genetic warfare" (Appel 2009; Committee on Foreign Affairs 2008; Wheelis 2004; Wheelis and Dando 2005; see also Mukunda, Oye, and Mohr 2009; Niler 2017). Synthetic biology, the "design, construction, and characterization of improved or novel biological systems using engineering design principles" (Si and Zhao 2016, 258), is an area of biotechnical innovation of great interest to the US military (B. Adams 2016; Arrington 2017; Basulto 2015; Brady

2016; B. Edwards 2017; *Global Defense* 2016; Kuiken 2017; Lentzos 2015). As Joachim Boldt describes it in detail: "Synthetic biology . . . is characterized, first and foremost, by introducing engineering paradigms and methods into genetic engineering. Standardization and modularization of biological parts as well as computer-aided rational design of biological devices, systems, and organisms are prominent aspects of synthetic biology research. Generally speaking, synthetic biology thus can be understood as the systematic and rational design, creation, and modification at the molecular level of organisms and biological parts with predictable functions" (2014, 3052).

Synthetic biology promises to open up new areas of enhancement in soldier performance by intentionally engineering the biology of the soldier to meet certain kinds of performance and mission requirements. The military's interest in synthetic biology lies primarily in the development of new types of materials and fuels and the exploitation of new forms of molecular biology to make stronger armor using organic/inorganic nanocomposites, for example (Committee on Strategies for Identifying and Addressing Potential Biodefense Vulnerabilities Posed by Synthetic Biology 2018; Boldt 2014; Sund, n.d.; Si and Zhao 2016). But a number of synthetic biology projects focus on the soldier, imagining the reengineering of the soldier from the inside as a way to anchor anticipation and counter and preempt future threats.

An overview of some of DARPA's current synthetic biology programs provides a glimpse into the military's use and interest in synthetic biology and genomics, and the kind of future DARPA expects these technologies will create. DARPA's Biological Technologies Office (BTO) has a number of current projects examining synthetic biology, health, and protection for soldiers. DARPA is also pursuing a project in synthetic biology and genomics called "Living Foundries" (the name implies a kind of Frankenstein-like desire to literally produce new forms of life). The goal of the program is to "enhance methods for genome transplantation that will enable the engineering of complex functionality into human cell lines that are currently possible" (Buchner 2013, 42).

DARPA's current "Battlefield Medicine" program focuses on two main research areas: "Pharmacy on Demand" (PoD) and "Biologically Derived Medicines on Demand" (Bio-MOD). The goal of both projects is to develop "miniaturized device platforms and techniques that can produce multiple small-molecule active pharmaceutical ingredients (APIs) and therapeutic proteins in response to specific battlefield threats and medical needs as they arise" (Dugan n.d. [Battlefield Medicine program]). The Pharmacy on

Demand project is "aimed at developing and demonstrating the capability to manufacture multiple APIs of varying chemical complexity using shelf-stable procedures, while Bio-MOD research is focused on developing novel, flexible-methodologies for genetic engineering and modification of microbial strains, mammalian cell lines, and cell-free systems to synthesize multiple protein-based therapeutics" (Dugan n.d. [Battlefield Medicine program]).

The ominously titled Biological Control program seeks to "support a wide range of potential Department of Defense (DoD) applications by establishing design and control principles that lead to reliable performance in biological systems. Leveraging technologies developed under this program will enable consistent operation of systems that combat biological threats; speed healing after physical trauma; and support military readiness by complementing the body's natural defenses against emerging diseases" (Sheehan n.d. [Biological Control program]). "Reliable control in biological systems" could be directed at soldiers or at the biotechnologies that will be used and/or implanted in soldiers' bodies to help them heal more quickly and resist disease. And in what is perhaps the best example of a directed "skin-in" approach, DARPA's BTO is working on a project titled "In Vivo Nanoplatforms" (IVN).

> The In Vivo Nanoplatforms (IVN) program supports military readiness through the development of *in vivo* sensing technologies and therapeutics that facilitate optimal health and performance in individual warfighters. The program pursues technologies that provide early indication of physiological abnormalities or illness that can be proactively addressed with therapeutics or supportive care. The IVN program specifically seeks to develop new classes of adaptable nanoparticles for persistent, distributed, unobtrusive physiologic and environmental sensing. (Jenkins n.d. [In Vivo Nanoplatforms])

The IVN program is divided into two subprojects: the IVN Diagnostics (IVN:Dx) and IVN Therapeutics (IVN:Tx) programs. IVN Diagnostics "aims to develop a generalized *in vivo* platform that provides continuous physiological monitoring for the warfighter. Specifically, IVN:Dx investigates technologies that incorporate implantable nanoplatforms composed of bio-compatible, nontoxic materials; in vivo sensing of small and large molecules of biological interest." And the IVN Therapeutics program is focused on developing "unobtrusive nanoplatforms for rapidly treating disease in warfighters. This program is pursuing treatments that increase safety and minimize the dose required for clinically relevant efficacy; limit off-target effects; limit immunogenicity; increase effectiveness by targeting delivery to specific tissues and/or uptake by cells of interest; increase bioavailability; knock down medically relevant molecular target(s); and increase resistance to degradation. If successful, such platforms will enable prevention and treatment of military-relevant illnesses such as infections caused by multi-drug-resistant organisms" (Jenkins n.d. [In Vivo Nanoplatforms]).

While genomics and gene editing are seen as technologies with great military potential, they are also seen as potential weapons. In 2016 James Clapper, the US director of national intelligence, added gene editing to a list of potential weapons of mass destruction (Regalado 2018; see also Garthwaite 2016). In a move that indicates that DARPA fully anticipates new forms of genomic warfare and the weaponization of genomic technologies, the "Safe Genes" program appears to be an attempt to preempt US soldiers falling prey to genomic weapons and technologies.

> The Safe Genes program supports force protection and military health and readiness by protecting Service members from accidental or intentional misuse of genome editing technologies. Additional work will leverage advances in gene editing technology to expedite development of advanced prophylactic and therapeutic treatments against gene editors. Advances within the program will ensure the United States remains at the vanguard of the broadly accessible and rapidly progressing field of genome editing. . . . Overall, the Safe Genes program is creating a layered, modular, and adaptable solution set to: protect warfighters and the homeland against intentional or accidental misuse of genome editing technologies; prevent and/or reverse unwanted genetic changes in a given biological system; and facilitate the development of safe, precise, and effective medical treatments that use gene editors. (Wegryzn n.d. [Safe Genes program])

These projects propose the imbedding of technologies in soldiers as well as the ability to produce on-demand medications and to protect soldiers (and the homeland) from the presumed and anticipated weaponization of synthetic biology and genomic technologies. Synthetic biology will also allow the military to create vaccines and other medications on demand. As discussed in chapter 8, DARPA envisions the capability to station and forward-deploy small "factories" to produce medications as-needed on the battlefield; such an ability would provide an almost real-time ability to analyze and synthesize medications for soldiers as well as greatly lessen and shorten the logistics chain for medications.

Genomics

As defined by the National Human Genome Research Institute (NHGRI), genomics is "an emerging medical discipline that involves using genomic information about an individual as part of their clinical care (e.g., for diagnostic or therapeutic decision-making) and the health outcomes and policy implications of that clinical use" (NHGRI n.d.). Mauricio J. De Castro and Clesson E. Turner (2017) note that genetics and genomics have been a part of military medicine for the better part of fifty years and are increasingly integrated into the mainstream military health-care system, finding applications in clinical practice in a variety of areas.

As with synthetic biology, the US military sees genomics as a potentially important and powerful means of enhancing soldier performance, selecting soldiers for various missions, understanding how soldiers cope with stress, and discovering ways to better "make" the soldier through biotechnology. In the 2001 report *Opportunities in Biotechnology for Future Army Applications*, the authors called for the US Army to "lead the way in laying ground-work for the open, disciplined use of genomic data to enhance soldiers' health and improve their performance on the battlefield" (National Research Council 2001, 64; see also Mehlman 2012, 120). The report details the possible uses of genomics for enhancing soldier performance.

> In the future, genomic methods could be used to screen or supplement physical tests for qualities such as strength, endurance, marksmanship, or the ability to function when deprived of sleep; these predictions could be used to help in assigning individuals to perform appropriate tasks. The Army has long used physical characteristics, such as vision or physical size, to subdivide soldier populations and has used the outcome of physical and mental tests to determine who is qualified to pilot helicopters or join elite combat units. Experience has shown that some individuals cope with the horrors of combat better than others, but the basis for this difference is not understood. . . . Army experts believe that psychological screening may be used to improve soldier performance in close-combat units. . . . Genomic methods may eventually be used to supplement these performance-based tests. (National Research Council 2001, 63)

Maxwell J. Mehlman, who has written extensively on the ethics and policy implications of performance enhancement research, discusses a 2002 report by the Department of Defense Information Assurance and Analysis Center and observes that "because genomics information offers clues to improving human performance it could provide the Army with means of increasing combat effectiveness" (2012, 120). The JASONS, an independent group of scientists who have advised the US government on scientific/technical issues since 1960, issued a report in 2010 titled "The $100 Genome: Implications for the DoD" (JASON 2010). JASON researchers were charged with investigating the potential uses of genomic technologies for the military as these technologies become less expensive and more widely available; two of the areas the JASONs were tasked to examine were "What types of genetic information are likely to be most informative in personalized medicine relevant to military personnel?" and "What types of genetic information are likely to have tactical benefit in either offensive or defensive military operations?" (JASON 2010, 5). The report outlined an ambitious plan to employ genomic technologies to "enhance medical status and improve treatment outcomes," enhance "health, readiness, and performance of military personnel," and "know the genetic identification of an adversary" (JASON 2010; see also Lin, Mehlman, and Abney 2013; Mehlman 2012). According to Mehlman, as of 2012, the US military is reported to be spending $100 million a year on genomic research designed to counteract sleep deprivation alone (Mehlman 2012).

The JASON report also makes clear some of the possible advantages of genomics for the military. Genomic research and enhancement could

> determine which phenotypes that might reasonably be expected to have a genetic component have special relevance to military performance and medical cost containment. These phenotypes might pertain to short- and long-term medical readiness, physical and mental performance, and response to drugs, vaccines, and various environmental exposures, all of which will have different features in a military context. More specifically, one might wish to know about phenotypic responses to battlefield stress, including post-traumatic stress disorder, the ability to tolerate conditions of sleep deprivation, de-hydration, or prolonged exposure to heat, cold, or high altitude, or the susceptibility to traumatic bone fracture, prolonged bleeding, or slow wound healing. (JASON 2010; see also Mehlman and Li 2014)

Mehlman and Tracy Yeheng Li, in their discussion of the possible uses and ethical problems surrounding military genomics, also detail the possible benefits of collecting DNA already in place for identification (see also Wagner 2019 for the military's use of, and interest in, DNA for missing in action [MIA] accounting and identification purposes), using soldiers' DNA for the creation of biobanks and geno-phenobanks, personalized medicine, testing (for genetic diseases, physical traits, mental traits), gene-based therapeutics, and the enhancement of cognition, memory, muscles, metabolism, and sleep (Mehlman and Li 2014).

Designer Soldiers

While debates about the ethics of gene editing to create "designer babies" has captured the public imagination around the ethics of "playing God" with genomics and DNA modification, these debates are also ongoing in military bioethics circles about what is and is not possible and ethical for the military to attempt with genomics, gene editing, and clustered regularly interspaced short palindromic repeats [CRISPR] (Greene and Master 2018). While the ability of the military and DARPA, for example, to actually create "designer soldiers" is still the stuff of science fiction, military and nonmilitary bioethicists are beginning to consider what this might look like should it ever be possible, and what the military applications of gene editing might actually be. While the military is looking at gene editing as a way to protect against disease and illness, DARPA's Safe Genes research office is exploring ways to protect soldiers from gene editing; in other words, it is developing protections against weaponized forms of genetic editing that might be deployed against US soldiers.

Chillingly, Mehlman writes of a potential use of genomics that is similar to the debates around designer babies; this involves families and military recruiting, and the manipulation and exploitation of familial gene lines for military purposes: "In families with long traditions of military service, however, parents might be interested in installing traits that were conducive to a successful military career, and it is not that far-fetched to think that the government might encourage this practice, perhaps even subsidize it" (2012, 121). Mehlman continues, and adds an important caveat.

> Some parents, particularly those from military families, might be tempted to modify their children in this way to give them a better chance at a successful military career. Consider the Scotts. "We've had a soldier on active duty in the US Army in my family for more than 130 years," explains retired Army Major General Bruce Scott. . . . All six of their children are in the military, five in the Army; three attended West Point. Military ser-

vice, says General Scott, "is in my family's DNA." Families like the Scotts might feel that "optimizing" their children for the military was merely carrying the family tradition. Giving these children greater visual acuity or making them stronger, faster, and better able to survive battle damage might be acceptable, but not decreasing their moral intuition; powerful weapons should not be placed in the hands of soldiers who are morally compromised. (Mehlman 2012, 198–99)

However, as Nicholas G. Evans and Jonathan D. Moreno (2014) point out in their commentary on Mehlman and Li's article, there are still significant challenges and ethical issues the military must deal with before genomics can actually deliver what many military researchers and planners think it promises. The military's use of genomic screening of soldiers for entry into the military that Mehlman and Li discuss, such as a propensity to suffer from PTSD, bone fractures, or blood loss (Mehlman and Li 2014), and the suitability of a potential soldier for combat, might turn out not to be the best method of selecting soldiers, according to Evans and Moreno, since selecting soldiers for a mission is dependent on a wide range of criteria and contexts (2014, 3). Additionally, as Evans and Moreno argue, genomics might be a way for the military to discriminate against potential recruits, based on preexisting conditions (3). And in terms of cost, the "$100 Genome" would probably be more expensive in practice, and a simple "push-up test" might be a better and cheaper method of screening a soldier (3). Evans and Moreno also stress the problems associated with germ-line enhancements and the reintegration of a formally enhanced soldier into civil society. A soldier discharged from the military but still enhanced, they note, is still conceivably a partially militarized person who might use their physical or mental enhancements and advantages inappropriately (5).

Styx and Lethe: Protection, Performance, and Forgetfulness

Strong soldiers are not just physically strong or able: the military also needs mentally and emotionally strong and resilient soldiers, soldiers who can think clearly and quickly while under immense stress, and soldiers who can process and control their memories and traumatic experiences. All of this was very clear to Sulzberger when he discussed in his 1962 address the need to develop "mental idiophylaxis." New methods of developing resilient soldiers through training are important and necessary steps toward helping soldiers deal with combat trauma (see, e.g., Howell 2014, 2015; Jauregui 2015), but as with all conventional training methods, they leave much to chance. Direct biomedical interventions offer—at least in theory—the promise of direct, immediate, and predictable results. Two pharmaceuticals that have shown promise for military applications related to wakefulness, cognition, and trauma-blocking are modafinil and propranolol.

Modafinil is a stimulant currently used by the military to promote wakefulness and alertness and treat narcolepsy and sleep apnea. Modafinil is similar to Benzedrine but without the side effects (Annas and Annas 2009; J. A. Caldwell 2008; Cavanagh 2018; Krishnan 2018). Modafinil has been used by the US military since at least 2003, so it is not a new drug. However, possible counterindications show that modafinil could enhance the memory and cognitive abilities of soldiers (Brühl, d'Angelo, and Sahakian 2019; Kelley, Webb, Athy, Ley, and Gaydos 2012; Mereu, Bonci, Newman, and Tanda 2013; Scharre and Fish 2018; Seck 2017). Soldiers with enhanced or superior memory, speed of thought, and overall cognitive ability would be a boon to the military, given the increasing complexity of weapons systems. This would also be important for intelligence collection and analysis, planning, logistics, and overall combat performance. The benefits of modafinil as a cognition enhancer would be broad and far-reaching throughout the military, benefiting not just combat arms soldiers but combat support and combat services soldiers as well.

Alertness in combat also goes hand in hand with the military's interest in sleep and sleep studies, and designing ways to fundamentally militarize sleep and make it another weapon on the battlefield. Soldiers have always had to contend with exhaustion and lack of sleep, but if the military can develop ways to both keep soldiers alert and awake and cause and exploit the exhaustion and sleeplessness of the enemy, US soldiers would have a fundamental advantage on the battlefield (Ben-Ari 2005). As John A. Caldwell and J. Lynn Caldwell, writing about the benefits and side effects of modafinil and amphetamines, state: "Fighting and maneuvering around the clock is intended to wear down the enemy by minimizing or eliminating their recuperative rest breaks, thereby impairing effectiveness via the onslaught of severe fatigue. This fatigue-induction strategy has proven to work extremely well, but it can backfire unless US military personnel manage to effectively guard against sleep loss themselves" (2005, C39).

As Lin, Mehlman, and Abney point out, another possible issue with counterfatigue drugs—or attempting to induce fatigue in the enemy through round-the-clock operations—is the possibility that the enemy will have developed similar enhancements to counter any US advantage around sleep (2013, 7). Cavanagh, however, provides a much starker and bleaker quotation from the US Air Force Research Laboratory about the escalation of fatigue countermeasures and the use of wakefulness-promoting agents, of psychostimulant or eugeroic "Go Pills" on the battlefield: "Forcing our enemies to perform continuously without the benefit of sufficient daily sleep is a very effective weapon. . . . To win this war of exhaustion, we must manage fatigue ourselves. . . . We must drug our troops to outlast yours. You, in turn, must drug your troops to keep up. On the battlefield of the future, there is no sleep but death" (2018, 5).

This is fundamentally the same logic as Blitzkrieg: to engage in combat at such a high rate of operational tempo and use the violence of action to wear down the enemies and exhaust them into surrender and defeat. The weaponization of sleep—and other pharmaceuticals—is also to force the enemy to engage in a form of anticipation and preemption: Will the US be using the drugs in combat? How will we counter them? Should we also develop these drugs and use them in combat? The development of enhancements—even if they are not used in combat or fully developed—creates anxiety and uncertainty in the other side, which can also be an effective form of "soft" engagement (Masco 2014; Massumi 2015).

Propranolol is a beta-blocker that has shown some promise in blocking, or at least mitigating, the formation of traumatic memories (Bergen-Cico 2012; Glannon 2006; Henry, Fishman, and Youngner 2007; Jancin 2019; Kamieński 2012; Krishnan 2018; Lin, Mehlman, and Abney 2013; National Research Council 2008, 45; Snoek 2015; Wolfendale 2008, 30). As an anxiolytic (a drug used to reduce anxiety), propranolol has been used to help people deal with a range of anxiety disorders as well as tremors and angina. In addition to its anxiolytic properties, propranolol has shown some promise as a kind of trauma-erasing drug; that is, trials have shown that it can minimize the recurrence of traumatic memories and help people who have suffered trauma manage their trauma. If taken soon after a traumatic experience, propranolol might be able to block the short-term memory of the event, though this is not entirely clear (Henry, Fishman, and Youngner 2007; Kamieński 2012; Snoek 2015). From a military standpoint, this would be a very useful enhancement for soldiers: the ability to block the formation of traumatic memories would make it theoretically possible to block the formation of PTSD. If administered pro-phylactically, it could potentially create soldiers who do not register the trauma of war.

The proposal is to give propranolol—or a similar drug—to soldiers before they enter combat (Henry, Fishman, and Youngner 2007; Krish-nan 2018; Lin, Mehlman, and Abney 2013, 21). This would theoretically prevent them from developing traumatic memories and ensure—again, theoretically—that they did not suffer from PTSD later. Rather than relying on the innate resiliency of the soldier, the military would short-circuit the process and ensure that soldiers were not able to develop traumatic memo-ries. In a sense, this enhancement is not so much an enhancement as it is a form of repression, a kind of manipulation of selected areas of the neurology of the soldier to make the soldier more useful during and after combat.

The prophylactic suppression of memory is seen as a necessary step in the evolution of warfare. Even if memory is suppressed or repressed, soldiers could potentially develop forms of what Alison Landsberg (2004) calls "prosthetic memory," forms of memory that are taken on as one's own, even if you did not experience the event yourself. War could become both suppressed and imagined, a tangle of presence and absence, not knowing and imagining you know, of taking on the memory of another war or conflict, or someone else's experience of war and trauma to make sense of your own (non)experience after the fact. It could become a kind of programmed forgetfulness that will make war politically fungible and deniable. Interestingly, Sulzberger did not include memory suppression in the Idiophylactic Soldier; perhaps he thought this was a line that should not be crossed.

There are, obviously, a number of ethical issues and concerns around this, as well as the very real and distinct possibility that at least for now, this kind of clean and perfect suppression of memory is impossible. The impli-cations are immense, not just for the soldier but also for the "enemy" and victims of military violence. It also raises significant concerns for how we remember war and soldiers as a society, how the military remembers war and plans for future war, who will be allowed to remember and who will be made to forget, and how we historicize and analyze war and conflict (see, e.g., Hagopian 2011; Nguyen 2017; Piehler 1995; Wagner 2019; Wagner and Matyók 2018; Winter 2014 and their work on war, memory, commemora-tion, and society).

The medicalization of memory is a key part of enhancement programs, in terms of both augmenting the memory and cognitive abilities and suppressing the memory of soldiers. The memory abilities of the soldier are linked to questions of national memory, military memory, policy and memory, as well as commemoration and the memory of war crimes. To read US military plans and reports on war and memory is to read an ongoing fantasy of perfect, clean war. The reports tack back and forth between the supersoldier as Achilles, dipped in Styx for protection, and the possibility of soldiers being dipped in the River Lethe, the river of forgetfulness.

We generally think about the relationship between war and memory after the fact, after a war or conflict, how soldiers and civilians recall events and trauma, and how societies remember and politically shape "official" memories of war, or what can or cannot be remembered. We also think about how individual soldiers think about or remember war, and the nature of memory and trauma and PTSD. It is only in science fiction stories and films that we think about or imagine modulating the memories of soldiers before combat, before they experience the trauma and horror of combat and killing. Increasingly, the US military is engaging in this kind of imaginative play around memory, as it is seen as a key component in ensuring soldiers can make it through combat psychologically unscathed.

The Structures of Unfeeling: Time, Memory, and the Soldier

A friend who was a Korean War veteran said to me, "I killed too many, and I didn't kill enough." This is a kind of trauma that is almost incomprehensible. He killed as asked and ordered, killed "well," but did not kill enough to save his friends. This simultaneous excess and lack of killing and death defined each moment of his life after the war, as he constantly replayed his experiences and imagined what could have been, not only for himself but for his friends who did not survive.

———

Propranolol and modafinil and other forms of memory augmentation and suppression are linked to national memory and policy—reading between the lines, the message is that the management and medicalization of memory are increasingly important in not just the prosecution of war but the management of war and its aftermaths in the "homeland." Memory—as either an enhanced ability or a suppressed experience—is vital to national security, the ability to deal with and care for veterans (medically, culturally, and economically), and the ability of the military to continue to recruit volunteers for a future anticipated as one of never-ending war.

Much like *Black Mirror* imagines a future where military brain implants allow the military to control what a soldier sees and experiences in real time on and off the battlefield, the ability of the military to control or shape memories will change how soldiers relate to combat and violence and how they are able to recall and discuss what they saw and did in combat. If preemption—ontopower—is the key to the military's threat-response strategy, some form of memory and official accounting has to be operative for it to work.

Another recent television series that examined soldiers in combat was HBO's *Band of Brothers*. In episode 5, "Crossroads," Captain Richard Winters, the commanding officer of Easy Company, 2nd Battalion, 506th Parachute Infantry Regiment of the 101st Airborne Division, is shown writing a detailed after-action report of a series of engagements that took place over the preceding two days. The episode switches back and forth from Winter's recollections of the engagement—including Winters shooting a very young German SS soldier at point-blank range—to his sitting at a makeshift desk, recalling the fighting, which of his soldiers were wounded and killed, the number of the enemy killed and wounded, tactics, locations, and the results of the engagements. Winters is careful to write a detailed account of the actions, as detailed as his memory allows him to be, and as detailed as the flashbacks of the vicious combat and close-quarters killing allow him to be; his memory is in the processes of becoming official military history. At one point, his close friend and company intelligence officer Captain Lewis Nixon walks in and says to Winters, "That's not literature, just keep it simple. Try using the first-person plural; say 'we' a lot."

The fundamental paradox of plans to suppress soldiers' memories lies in the military's preoccupation with anticipation. How exactly can you anticipate something if you cannot remember what you have already done? To suppress is to foreclose the future, to make it nearly impossible to think about how you might anticipate and plan for the future if you cannot remember what you have done in combat in the past. Of course, not everyone will be "enhanced" to forget: battalion commanders and higher (for example) might be given cognition enhancers to help them understand combat and operations and think about and plan for the future (they might even end up functioning as a kind of Rhapsode, as the ones who remember and sing the tales of combat from memory, as in *The Iliad*). But how will you write after-action reports with combat soldiers if they cannot exactly remember what they have done? How will the archival knowledge of combat action reports, prepared by senior NCOs and junior officers, contribute to the long-term institutional knowledge of combat if those who prepare the reports have been enhanced to forget? Simply video recording combat in real time is not going to be enough to analyze second-by-second decision-making by junior leaders or NCOs, or individual soldiers. Fear and adrenaline shape combat action: to somehow short-circuit these responses will make it difficult to plan or train for combat later.

The memory ability of the future US soldier is to be both enhanced and suppressed, possibly at the same time. It is to be enhanced in order for soldiers to process more information, remember information and details necessary and important for an operation, and help soldiers operate increasingly complicated and complex technical systems and weapons. But memory will also need to be suppressed in order to keep soldiers sane and whole, to keep them from experiencing the full impact of war and trauma. They will be hyperpresent and hyperabsent, here and not here, aware and not aware. Jünger's ([1920] 2003) discussion of the need to develop a "second consciousness" to withstand the horrors of war comes to mind here, only this is not necessarily about developing a second consciousness but rather about suppressing consciousness of events, actions, and repercussions.

The suppression of memory is the loss of communicable experience (Huyssen 1995). Fundamentally, blocking memory means we do not have to listen to memories or experiences of soldiers, because if they cannot be recalled, they cannot be recorded. The war stories of old would disappear, and no longer would we listen to soldiers or veterans recount their experiences of war, combat, trauma, and terror. "Official" memory would replace individual memory, and the memory of defeat and loss, or of participation or witnessing war crimes, would disappear or be highly mediated. Of course, this is all dystopian fantasy, but without the memories of those involved, it is a possible future. We will no longer have to listen to someone talk and despair about having killed too many and killed too few.

However, despite the hype around propranolol, it does not actually erase memories or block trauma. Evidence shows that propranolol will not actually block out long-term memory. As James Elsey and Merel Kindt point out, there are a number of fundamental problems with the belief that propranolol, or a similar drug, could actually "erase" traumatic combat memories, or that a state that wished to create unfeeling supersoldier killing machines—or cold, unemotional interrogators—could do so with propranolol (2016, 233). For example, they make clear that the reality of threat in war poses further problems for the unlikely prospect of generating a "super-soldier" with far less fear, because reconsolidation-based interventions do not simply dull the fear system. Experimental work from our lab has shown that even after reconsolidation-based disruption of learned fear, the very same fear can be easily relearned with experience (Soeter and Kindt 2011). This suggests that where legitimate threats are routinely encountered, corresponding emotional reactions will also be relearned. Hence, if a soldier with greatly reduced fear of combat were successfully produced, that soldier would not be immune to developing new fear responses as soon as he or she were exposed to the dangers of real-life battle again. (2016, 233)

So, what would the soldier actually remember or experience? As Snoek (2015) writes, would the soldier know that she has killed but remain unfeeling and uncaring, and become a kind of unemotional, nonfeeling killing machine? If this is the case, Jünger's call for the development of a "second consciousness" to make the soldier unfeeling and unstoppable in warfare would seem to come true. But who would this benefit? If propranolol really cannot be used prophylactically to prevent or mitigate combat trauma, it will not be of much use to the soldier, unless, of course, these concerns were ignored, and it was used almost as a placebo, as both an anxiolytic and a promise.

This does not mean that it is not in the military's interest to continue to search for or try to develop trauma-blocking drugs or imagine ways to erase soldiers' memories. If not propranolol, there might be another drug or suite of drugs—or other neurotechnologies—that come along that hold the same promise. As military enhancement programs continue and develop, new ways of imagining "forgetfulness" will come into play, and possible new avenues of biomedical intervention into oblivion will be examined and possibly exploited. Blankness—oblivion—is militarily useful and beneficial, at least in some ways. Of course, to develop unfeeling soldiers is to develop the soldier who does not have the kinds of traits and values that we consider culturally appropriate to what we think of the soldier, of how a soldier should be and how they should be "bold" (see, e.g., Snoek 2015). Drugs might undermine what we consider—and value—as "courage"; George W. Bush's Committee on Bioethics addressed this point in 2003: "People who take pills to block out from memory the painful or hateful aspects of a new experience will not learn how to deal with suffering or sorrow. A drug that produces fearlessness does not produce courage" (Annas and Annas 2009, 290n28).

But this does not mean the military will not explore these possibilities or even attempt to deploy them if they become feasible and available. Considering the problems and dilemmas the military faces with PTSD, figuring out a way to block or mitigate combat trauma before it takes place is too important and tempting of a proposition for the military to ignore. While a drug or suite of drugs that could help former soldiers—and anyone dealing with trauma/PTSD—would be a good thing, the ability of the military to modulate and influence how memories are shaped and formed before combat in order to block traumatic memories arising from combat or other military-related actions raises a variety of issues and should give us all pause. Mehlman, while aware of the potentially serious problems associated with cognition-enhancing drugs, believes that their use by the military might nonetheless be ethical, given the intense pressures placed on soldiers: "What about the military? Military service can subject individuals to extraordinary risks, even death. But there are limits to the extent of these risks. For example, in the absence of special circumstances and a presidential order, soldiers cannot be required to participate in medical experiments. Yet the exigencies of combat probably justify requiring soldiers to use cognition-enhancing drugs unless they are highly dangerous" (2004, 501). However, as Leon Kass points out, "Altering the formation of emotionally powerful memories risks severing what we remember from how we remember it and distorting the link between our perception of significant human events and the significance of the events themselves. It risks, in a word, falsifying our perception and understanding of the world. It risks making shameful acts seem less shameful, or terrible acts less terrible, than they really are" (2003, 226; see also Taraska 2017).

Łukasz Kamieński, in discussing propranolol, notes that soldiers taking it may in fact remember what they have done but will feel nothing about it; their memories will be rendered "toothless," as he writes (2012, 401). Propranolol will result in memory stripped of emotion, leaving behind a kind of affectless artifact of combat and killing. As they discuss what they have done and while wondering about the "liberation" of Iraq and the people they have killed in the process, one of the Marines in *Generation Kill* says, "A priest told me it's not a sin to kill if you don't enjoy killing. My question is whether indifference is the same as enjoyment."

Having experienced the rapid development and use of increasingly lethal weapons and tactics during World War I, Jünger observed that the increase in weapons technology and lethality on the battlefield engendered the need to create a "second consciousness" in those deeply involved in this technological growth; the second consciousness is for those involved to "stand outside of the zone of pain" (Buck-Morss 1992, 33). Jünger later described this need to develop a second consciousness as a way of nullifying physical feeling and pain: "it almost seems as if the human being possessed a striving to create a space in which pain . . . can be regarded as illusion" (quoted in Buck-Morss 1992, 33). Without explicitly stating it, both Jünger and Timmerman (see chapter 2) pointed toward one of the central concerns of military training, military medicine, and performance enhancement research: the need to manage, block out, and expunge feelings and experiences of pain and trauma, the need to make the soldier "merciless"—and hence, unfeeling—toward himself and his experience of war and trauma, and toward his enemy, in order to complete the mission.

Pain and fear must be deferred, for both impose their own teleology on the body: pain calls attention to itself and demands attention, attention that can detract from one's attention to the goals and contingencies of the mission (Leder 1990, 77; see also Scarry 1985), and fear can cause a soldier to act irrationally or often not at all. The deferral of pain and fear can be considered to be the top priority in mission completion; soldiers must not be distracted from the task at hand. As the catch-phrase of the defense contracting firm Revision makes clear in the introduction to this book: "Rely on the human body alone, and you may need to pick between mission and safety. Combine innovation and the human body, and you have an unstoppable capability." At the level of national policy, individual pain can impede the political goals of the state. The quote makes one thing clear, even with a seventy-year gap and a giant leap between "will" and biomedicine: the idea that soldiers are weak and need to be made strong and enhanced to survive and thrive in modern combat requires a fundamental redesign and rethinking of the soldier.

Pain is the nexus between "willpower" and biotechnology: willpower will allow you to fight through pain and carry on; biotechnology might make it possible for you to never experience pain, be it physical or mental. And here seem to lie the troubling links between fascism and biotechnology: the suppression of pain can create a kind of military/political utility to indifference and possibly an enjoyment and celebration of war through indifference. What the US military is attempting to achieve through medical and pharmacological interventions bears an uncomfortable resemblance to what Jünger believed was necessary to survive modern warfare: a form of armored life that allows no space for experiencing pain or emotion, in both soldiers and civil society, a numbing forgetfulness that makes war possibly easier and politically palatable. Chemical enhancements like propranolol could make the pain and trauma of war and killing seem like an illusion: known but not felt; seen but stripped of terror.

If an important part of the new forms of warfare and counterterror operative in US military strategic planning is the modulation of "fear" (Masco 2014), the need to block memory and fear might not necessarily be focused on the soldier but on civilians, a kind of pan-anxiolytic to help people support the military. We need to believe that soldiers can make it through war and combat, if not unscathed then at least somehow "returnable" to a sense of normalcy and with the possibility of reintegration. Perhaps propranolol will work after the fact and actually help veterans—and other victims of war—manage their trauma and have some semblance of a normal life. While militarily useful, the danger of a fear-blocking drug is more ideological: it is to convince us that we can collectively forget, or if we cannot forget, we do not have to feel.

Skin-In Solutions and the Ethics of Enhancement

A major ethical conundrum of soldier-enhancement research is whether or not the "skin-in" enhancements will be temporary or permanent (Annas and Annas 2009; Breede 2017; Lin, Mehlman, and Abney 2013; Mehlman 2014; Moreno 2012). Unlike external armor—which the soldier can put on or take off when necessary and the military can take away once a soldier leaves the military—"internal" armor provided by the military might stay with the soldier for life; she will always be the internally armored supersoldier and an enhanced veteran in ways that current veterans are not (Breede 2017). This opens up a number of ethical issues for not only the enhanced soldier-veteran but for society as well: How will the enhanced veteran cope with having his enhancements in a (presumably) nonenhanced environment? And how will civil society deal with the presence of enhanced former soldiers in the workplace, at home, in school, in sports, and so on (Annas and Annas 2009; Braun, von Hlatky, and Nossal 2017; Gross

2006; Gross and Carrick 2013; Lin, Mehlman, and Abney 2013; Lin, Mehlman, Abney, French et al. 2014; Singer 2008; Tracy and Flower 2014)? Will there be a place for them in society after their service time ends? Or, as Evans and Moreno point out, will the military see enhanced soldiers as a technology security risk and attempt to keep them in the military? According to Evans and Moreno, "The typical strategy of restricting access to 'dual-use technologies' is to control their export, sale, and transfer. And unlike many other occupations—and warfighting is increasingly a professional occupation—we typically privilege the military's interests over the warfighter's rights. Yet the troubling move here, that the military could very well attempt to exercise its prerogative over a soldier beyond her enlistment in the interests of protecting against technology, cannot be overlooked" (2014, 6).

Unlike external enhancements, internal—"skin-in"—enhancements cannot be taken off and represent the direct intervention of the military and the state in the body of the soldier. Until—and if—the military can ever develop a fully mechanized "battle suit" like the TALOS, the body of the soldier and the soldier's ability to resist the pressures of the battlefield will be the key to military success. But this success will probably come at a price for the soldier. These kinds of internal, unseen, "built-in" enhancements raise a plethora of ethical questions. Fundamentally, soldiers might not always have the option to say no (and soldiers are conditioned to follow orders from officers and NCOs without hesitating). For example, while Navy and Air Force pilots can refuse to take amphetamines before a mission, if they refuse, a flight surgeon could potentially mark them as unfit for the mission and ground them, which would have a serious impact on their careers and their ability to fly later missions (Snoek 2015, 6). US Navy medical guide NAVMED-6410, "Performance Maintenance during Continuous Flight Operations," includes the following paragraph under "Informed Consent for Operational Use of Dexedrine."

> My decision to take Dexedrine is voluntary. I understand that I am not being required to take the medication. Neither can I be punished if I decide not to take Dexedrine. However, should I choose not to take it under circumstances where its use appears indicated, I understand safety considerations may compel my commander, upon advice of the flight surgeon, to determine whether or not I should be considered unfit

to fly a given mission. . . . I understand that a copy of this notice shall be inserted in my medical record. If I have any questions with regards to the administration of Dexedrine, I will raise them with the flight surgeon. (United States Navy 2000, 24)

Jessica Wolfendale and Steve Clarke, in their discussion of military enhancement and paternalism, write that consent plays a very small role in military life; having enlisted, the ability of the soldier to exercise autonomy is severely curtailed (2008, 338). They provide a quote from the military ethicist John Pearn on informed consent in the military: "In normal military service, whether during training or on operations, the theme of free or informed consent is almost never relevant. Duty is duty and command is command, and the Clausewitzian principles of 'the definition and maintenance of the aim,' irrespective of discomfort or risk, take precedence over any individual discretion in the military doctrines of all sophisticated forces" (Wolfendale and Clarke 2008, 338, quoting Pearn 2000, 352).

We should keep in mind that while MPE is open to the imagination, not all enhancements are legal, at least theoretically. Within these checks and fail-safes lie a great amount of flexibility and possibility as to the shape and form of MPE projects. And military contingencies can make these boundaries pliable, stretching the limits of ethics in times of need (such as the use of the anthrax vaccine or the prophylactic use of pyridostigmine bromide pills against the nerve agent Soman during the first Gulf War) (Fulco, Liverman, and Sox 2000; Moreno 2012, 157–59; Parasidis 2016; see also McManus et al. 2005 on informed consent in the military following the first Gulf War and the issuance of emergency research waivers). Even though the US military and government agencies like the Central Intelligence Agency (CIA) have conducted clandestine, covert, and unethical medical experimentation on US soldiers in the past, like the MK-ULTRA experiments with lysergic acid diethylamide (LSD) in the 1960s (Kinzer 2019; Lederer 2003), as Annas and Annas point out, US soldiers cannot now be forced or required to participate in medical experiments, according to 10 U.S.C. §1107(f) (2004, 501). However, as they also point out, the contingencies of war and combat can place a great amount of pressure on soldiers to allow themselves to be enhanced or given experimental drugs that have not been fully tested and vetted (501). The ever-present danger with pharmacological enhancements is that military medicine becomes a form of iatrogenic medicine for soldiers. As Moreno discusses, US military performance enhancement research is guided by the "Common Rule," designed to protect human subjects, ensure consent, and ensure that there is proper vetting and oversight of military biomedical research projects (2012, 196). In their overview of human performance enhancement projects in the military, Scharre and Fish point out four guidelines developed by Colonel Michael Russo of the Army Aeromedical Research Laboratory regarding cognitive-enhancement drugs.

1 Use is voluntary—the soldier has given informed consent;
2 The treatment is safe for the intended operational use;
3 Dosage and use are consistent with its intended function; and
4 Nonpharmaceutical agents have been fully explored. (2018, 8)

However, Pfaff, in his discussion of military bioethics and the moral autonomy of the soldier, makes the important point that "in the military context, respecting freedom and autonomy is less concerned with whether one should be allowed to receive an enhancement as much as whether one may be *forced* to receive one" (2017, 69). As Scharre and Fish point out, "voluntary use" is particularly difficult in the military, as soldiers are particularly vulnerable to coercion—real or perceived, implicit or explicit—from their NCOs, officers, and other soldiers (2018, 11).

Command and Control: The "Nondepleting Neurotrop"

The use of certain drugs in combat can often have a negative effect on combat performance, not to mention a deleterious impact on command and control; even the ubiquitous amphetamine could not be relied upon to keep the soldier mentally focused and in control of his senses. From the military's point of view, the key is developing a drug that will suppress fear and anxiety, but which will allow the soldier to otherwise function normally. It is the search for a drug that Richard A. Gabriel, a military psychiatrist, has called a "nondepleting neurotrop," a drug or combination of drugs designed to interact with neurological receptors without side effects; "nondepleting" refers to the ability to keep the soldier coherent and mentally alert during combat (Gabriel 1987, 143; see also Gray 1997; Kamieński 2012). While his research is a few decades old, Gabriel sums up the potential cultural, political, and ethical problems with US military biomedical research on fear and anxiety-depressant drugs, and what is at stake for the future of warfare: "If the search is successful, and it almost inevitably will be, the relationship between soldiers and the battle environment will be transformed forever. . . . If they succeed, they will have banished the fear of death and with it will go man's humanity and soul" (1987, 184; see also Gray 1989, 50).

Concerns with the pharmacological battlefield and supersoldiers are not simply an American problem; other militaries are working on it as well. This aspect of modern warfare came up during my work with East German Army officers. An NVA special forces officer, whom I worked with in Berlin mentioned that East German Special Forces soldiers were routinely issued a medical pack containing six syringes. "We knew what the first three were for," he said, "but the last three—we were told never to use them unless ordered, and that they were only for use during an actual war in order to keep us going." If the East German military had these sorts of performance enhancing drugs available, we can assume the Soviet military, and the rest of the Warsaw Pact, had access to, or knowledge of, these drugs.

Skin-in and skin-out enhancement programs are underway in a number of militaries around the world. Programs and systems under development around the world that are similar to the Land Warrior system (and presumably expandable to future systems similar to the Objective Force Warrior or Future Force Warrior system in the United States) include the German Bundeswehr's Gladius / Infanterist der Zukunkft (IdK) (Future Soldier) system; in France, the FELIN (Fantassin à Équipements et Liaisons Intégrés) system; in the UK, the FIST (Future Integrated Soldier Technology) program; in Spain the COMFUT (Combatiente del Futuro) program; in Norway the NORMANS (NORwegian Modular Arctic Network Soldier) program; in Switzerland the IMESS (Integrated and Modular Engagement System for the Swiss Soldier) program; the Indian military is working on the F-INSAS (Futuristic Infantry Soldier as System); and the Russian military is developing the Ratnik (Warrior) soldier system program (SoldierMod.com, 2019; Gourley 2013b).

Like the US military, militaries around the world are also looking at different suites of pharmaceuticals to enhance their soldiers (Bergen-Cico 2012; Cavanaugh 2018; Kamieński 2016a, 2016b; Kan 2009). Most states are looking at drugs to counter sleep loss, such as modafinil (Saletan 2013), and China is developing a drug it calls "Night Eagle" to allow its soldiers to stay awake for seventy-two hours (Cavanaugh 2018; Kamieński 2016a, 2016b). And all militaries have to contend with the use of drugs by nonstate actors; apparently, the "drug of choice" for the Islamic State of Iraq and Syria (ISIS) is Captagon, a stimulant that "promotes alertness, enhances strength, numbs fear, and induces bravado" (Cavanaugh 2018; Kamieński 2016a, 2016b; see also Kan 2009), though there is skepticism that the drug could actually produce the effects claimed by fighters who take it (Anderson 2015).

The US currently holds the lead in all these research efforts in terms of research and funding, but that does not necessarily mean that the US will always have the lead on the battlefield. Given the ethical concerns around psychopharmacology and other forms of biomedical technology in the US military, even as it tries to gain every advantage and come up with new "force multipliers," there may be enhancements the US military will not pursue for ethical reasons while other states or groups do. Masco's analysis of the new counterterror systems in place in the US also points to the fundamental problem of all emerging supersoldiers: "Every system has built into its infrastructure a future crisis" (2014, 13). As states attempt to out-enhance the others' soldiers, we have to hope that ethical constraints remain a barrier to an anything-goes milieu of military biomedical research. Military performance enhancement is a Pandora's Box that has been opened and cannot be shut again. The biomedical and pharmacological arms race currently underway among the world's militaries means that just as weapons systems will continue to evolve, so too will biotechnologies designed to make the soldier more effective on the battlefield and put the enemy at a disadvantage by exploiting any and all weakness in their bodies. Drawing on skin-in solutions, synthetic biology, and genomics, if the US military has its way, kill-proof soldiers will not be the soldiers sleeping the sleep of death on the battlefield.

EIGHT

"Kill-Proofing the Soldier"

Inner Armor, Environmental Threats, and the World as Battlefield

It is my goal to provide our men and women
with an *unfair advantage* over the enemy.

» **Michael Callahan**, "Inner Armor"

Sulzberger's Idiophylactic Soldier and DARPA's Inner Armor bookend the decades-long concern with environmental and disease threats in the US military and present varied but related ways of how the US military imagines and develops different built-in and embodied solutions to constant battlefield problems based on advances in biomedical technology (Bickford 2018). As I discuss here, US military biomedical research is intended to provide soldiers with protections to allow them to deploy in any condition or climate around the world and protect them from any and all pathogens they might encounter on the battlefield. As the US military increasingly sees the entire world as a battlefield, it must anticipate, imagine, and design new ways to protect soldiers in order to make them deployable anywhere in the world. Projects like Idiophylaxis and Inner Armor highlight the shifting biomedical, political, and cultural imaginaries and forms of

Portions of chapter 8 appeared in Andrew Bickford, "'Kill-Proofing' the Soldier: Environmental Threats, Anticipation, and US Military Biomedical Armor Programs," *Current Anthropology* 60, no. s19 (February 2010), s39–s48.

anticipation at play in military performance enhancement research and how visions and perceptions of diseased battlefields (and, even if unmentioned in military reports, people) are translated into military biomedical projects and "solutions," which are then embedded in the bodies of soldiers. Military medicine and biotechnologies are key components of the anticipation/imagining/planning nexus, of the ongoing attempts to ensure that the soldier does not break down and fail on the battlefield.

Sulzberger envisioned applied military biomedical projects that would anticipate all infectious disease and environmental threats to the soldier and use cutting-edge biotechnologies to develop soldiers who, through Idiophylaxis, would be both internally armored and continually self-armoring, and thus prevent and mitigate the effects of disease, environmental stressors, and combat trauma. Four decades later, plans for providing built-in armor against the environment and diseases around the world, and the importance of medical anticipation and imagination in protecting US soldiers, would be broached again, but this time with the added promise of the "unfair advantage" of deathlessness on the battlefield.

War Play

Performance enhancement research allows the military to engage in a kind of imaginative play around questions of future conflict, battlefields, weapons, and enemies; performance enhancements act as a kind of deus ex machina, or rather, a kind of "miles ex machina" intervention that can be imagined as neutralizing military and environmental threats to soldiers and units. As Masco writes about affect and fear in the US imaginary during the Cold War and the War on Terrorism: what if? Masco focuses on the "what if?" of enemy action, but what if you switch the focus and think about the possibilities of soldier enhancement? "What if?" opens up a space for the serious play of imagining a threatening future and developing all sorts of responses to these threats. Imagining threats becomes an incitement to play and imagination, albeit serious and dangerous play.

If you can imagine the enemy and where you might have to fight them, you can start to imagine and war-game scenarios in which you think about, anticipate, and plan for the kinds of soldiers you might need for the future engagements. As Massumi remarks, "potential threats call for potential politics" (2014, 12–13); we can think of these "politics" extending into the politics of military imagination. Whether these soldiers exist in the here and now is immaterial; you can imagine how you can "make" or produce or shape the kinds of soldiers you think you will need, and then look at the available drugs and biotechnologies and those in development to start to imagine and plan for future conflict.

"Kill-Proofing" the Soldier: Inner Armor, Environmental Hardening, and the World as Threat

Far ahead of its time in terms of what was actually medically possible, the goals and insights of Sulzberger's Idiophylactic Soldier live on in current projects designed to create biological armor for the US soldier. As the "Mad Science" research branch of the US government, the Defense Advanced Research Projects Agency is charged with creating cutting-edge technologies that are far in advance of what is available at any given time. As a result, DARPA fully expects at least 90 percent of what it funds to fail, though of course these "failures" are simply a part of advancing future projects and technologies (Jacobsen 2015; Weinberger 2017).

At DARPA's Twenty-Fifth Systems and Technology Symposium held in 2007, Dr. Michael Callahan, program manager of DARPA's Defense Sciences Office, gave a presentation titled "Inner Armor." Highlighting the US military's ongoing concern with the impact of environmental conditions and infectious disease stressors on soldier performance and breakdown, Callahan's plans for new, enhanced US soldiers focus on protecting the soldier against both the enemy and the world, blurring both to produce "threats" to the soldier.

> We have made extraordinary advances in the *external, physical armor* that protects our Soldiers from most of the enemy's weapons. There is one flank that remains unprotected, and it is this gap that is responsible for continued unacceptable levels of morbidity, illness, injury and death. Not ALL of the threats encountered by our deployed Soldiers are inflicted by the enemy. The dramatic increase in the number of exotic, primitive and tropical battlefields brings the modern military into extreme contact with the world's most hostile environments—and most dangerous threat agents. As a DARPA program manager and physician-scientist, it is my vision to address all of these threats, and to leave NO PART of the soldier unprotected. . . . It is my goal to provide our men and women with an *unfair advantage* over the enemy. In the next 2 years, I am developing technologies that will extend the soldier's personal protection

beyond bullets and bombs, to include protection against environmental threats, infectious diseases and chemical, biological and radioactive weapons. . . . The objective is to fortify the *entire* soldier against attack from the enemy—or from the environment. I call this comprehensive protection *Inner Armor*.

In order to counter what Callahan sees as the innate—and from his point of view, unfair—biological "immunity advantage" of the "enemy," and to allow US soldiers to fight on "exotic" and "primitive" battlefields by mimicking organisms found in the world's most toxic environments (and in the process, equating the human enemy with deadly organisms), Callahan intends to develop "kill-proof" US soldiers and give the US military the ultimate advantage of biological supremacy.

> I will talk about two focus areas of Inner Armor—*Environmental Hardening*, which will allow Soldiers to excel in the world's harshest environments, and *Kill-Proofing*, which will protect them against chemical, biological, and radioactive weapons. . . . Today's wars require our military to deploy with minimal delay, to far-off, remote, and austere environments. These operations often require small, lightly provisioned teams capable of engaging an enemy that is fleet, camouflaged, skilled, and insidious. Under these conditions, casualties resulting from hypothermia, heat and altitude illness can have devastating consequences to life, to limb, and to mission success. . . . My job is to prove that high altitude acclimatization can be *transplanted* to Soldiers arriving from sea level, allowing them to immediately engage the enemy in the vertical environment. . . .

At this point in his talk, Callahan moves into issues of imagination, anticipation, and preemption, and circles back to some of the concerns that Sulzberger had about the impact of disease on soldiers and combat operations, striking a tone reminiscent of the focus and parameters of Idiophylaxis:

> The second focus area in Inner Armor that I want to share with you is Kill-Proofing. As of today, our Soldiers are vulnerable to diseases to which the enemy is immune. When a single soldier is infected, the mission is jeopardized and often, terminated. Let's first look at ways to "kill-proof" our Soldiers against chemical and radioactive weapons. Over the last 2 years, surveillance studies of the world's most toxic places, including nuclear waste and chemical weapons dumps, reveal that these ecological niches are teeming with life. The organisms growing in these areas have developed compensatory biological

mechanisms to deal with radiation and chemical toxins. . . . Many of the enzymes under study share properties with drugs the physician uses to treat the side effects of radiation or chemotherapy. It is our intention to mimic these natural successes in the human body by producing synthetic vitamins and safe preventive drugs that will forestall the onset of radioactive and chemical injury.

Throughout recorded history there has been no greater natural threat to the soldier than infectious diseases. Currently, we prevent infections from exotic and tropical diseases through daily or weekly doses of microbial inhibitors and poisons, such as those used to prevent malaria. Today's military vaccines only protect our Soldiers against 7 of the 44 highly dangerous pathogens that our Soldiers encounter in today's conflict zones. . . . I envision that we will preposition universal immune cells that are capable of making antibodies that neutralize tens, perhaps hundreds, of threat agents. Imagine that in the future, a universal immune cell can be quickly given to any non-immune soldier who is going into harm's way, which will provide stand-by protection against any tropical infection, or agent of bioterrorism. . . . Over the last 15 years, 16 new killer pathogens have emerged, and most of these occur on foreign soil, including in regions which harbor terrorists. . . . What we need is to preempt a pathogen's emergence with an effective vaccine.

Callahan then lays out his vision of making US soldiers kill-proof against all potential enemies and the world,

I DO NOT accept that our Soldiers cannot physically outperform the enemy on his home turf. My DARPA vision is that we have the drive, motivation and resources to environmentally harden our Soldiers to allow them to outperform native combatants in the harsh environments in which they were born, raised, and now wage terror. We must also work to make our men and women Kill-Proof against infectious disease, radioactive and chemical threats delivered from intentional man-made or natural sources. (2007)

Projects like Idiophylaxis and Inner Armor are predicated on disease-mapping the entire world to make sure there are no surprises on the battlefield. In both projects, the fearful anticipation and visions of diseased and dangerous battlefields for which US soldiers are not prepared lurk just under the surface. In terms of counterterrorism planning, Masco (2014) states that anticipation is the opposite of surprise (see also Caduff 2008). But it is not just counterterrorism that relies on forms of anticipation; military biomedical anticipation is based on concerns about unknown disease vectors and battlefield pathogens and coming up with ways to counter these threats. Callahan's plan to "pre-position universal immune cells" to produce antibodies on demand is a form of anticipation and imagination: the military will not be surprised by any "threat agents" to the soldier and will have immunizations ready to go, wherever and whenever needed. It also shows how the military is already anticipating and imagining areas as future conflict zones; to preposition biomedical supplies—biomedical bases—is to imagine an area of the world as already a battlefield. Anticipatory biomedical research and performance enhancement research is to take the uncertainty out of combat through the direct intervention of the state in both the terrain of the "enemy" and the biology of the soldier. In the imagination of the US military, if a project like Inner Armor is successful, environmental stressors and diseases that have hampered or prevented US military operations in the past will cease to be a hindrance.

Weaving through both projects is a kind of ongoing military-environmental-biological orientalist fantasy: the environmentally hardened killproof Idiophylactic Soldier with his own inner armor will handle the exotic and primitive—and presumably Third World—battlefields and enemies of Sulzberger's and Callahan's fearful imaginations with ease. It is a long-term fantasy of biomedical-cum-security anticipation and preparation played out in the bodies of soldiers.

Drunken Sherpas, Bird Men, and Sea Lion Soldiers: The World as Enhancement Imaginary

DARPA and the US military have conducted decades-long research projects aimed at harnessing animals and insects for national security and military usages, like bee drones and counterterror dolphins (Schachtman 2007; Singer 2008). What is new is the desire to somehow identify and extract the natural abilities of certain humans and animals around the world and transplant them into US soldiers as a way to counter battlefield climate and environmental stressors. Soldiers have to contend with the atmospheric conditions of the battlefield as well as the pathogenic conditions. Indeed, as Sulzberger made clear, soldiers who are not acclimated to battlefield conditions are at a significant disadvantage to those who are. Afghanistan has proved difficult for US soldiers because they are usually not acclimated to combat at sixteen thousand feet in mountainous regions while carrying more than one hundred pounds of combat equipment and weapons, while the Taliban and other fighters are acclimated and carry little equipment (we can think back to Rigg's "soldier of the Futurarmy" and his extremely lightweight equipment as a solution to this problem).

Imagining and drawing from the "natural" world also means drawing from both the local world of indigenous inhabitants and the animal world of local taxa. As part of the Inner Armor program, Callahan envisioned soldiers who can act like people and animals in their natural habitats and who are enhanced to be immediately acclimated to any and all battlefield conditions.

> Meet Apa Sherpa. Apa Sherpa is a middle-aged Nepalese highlander who lives above 15,000 feet—*and who likes to drink beer*. Apa Sherpa <u>also</u> set the world speed record for ascending Mount Everest, which is 11,000 feet <u>higher</u> than the mountains of Afghanistan. He set this ascent record without using supplemental oxygen. On the summit of Everest, Apa was breathing only one-FIFTH of the oxygen that we have in this room. This feat is accomplished by triggering the local production of a <u>natural</u> molecule called nitric oxide, which increases *organized* blood flow in the lungs, thus improving total oxygen transfer capacity to the blood. This adaptation *is also* found in non-Sherpas who ascend to altitude but the effects may take weeks to become elevated. We do not as of yet know how beer contributes to this achievement.
>
> My job is to prove that high altitude acclimatization can be <u>*transplanted*</u> to Soldiers arriving from sea level, allowing them to immediately engage the enemy in the vertical environment. Such a capability would radically advance high-altitude military operations, and perhaps air combat safety and performance, by accelerating the <u>natural</u> physiologic changes of altitude acclimatization currently found in the world's most elite alpinists, the Sherpas.
>
> High altitude environments also impact other physiologic processes which degrade mission readiness. At higher elevations, soldiers have a reduced ability to fight infection, maintain muscle mass, and think clearly. Insomnia reduces alertness, saps strength, and degrades morale. This is unacceptable for those that must respond quickly and decisively during life and death situations. (2007)

Having extolled the abilities of Sherpas to quickly climb mountains, drink beer, and excel in low-oxygen environments at altitude, and codifying them as just another "species" to emulate, Callahan moves on and discusses the military's need to mimic the abilities of animals to improve military operations. He first discusses the male bar-headed goose.

> Preventing this deterioration requires inspiration from some unusual places. For example, my DSO [Defense Sciences Office] team is working to replicate solutions provided by animals that excel in these extreme environments.
>
> Meet the Male Bar-Headed Goose. This is a species known to crash into jet aircraft at altitudes over 34,000 feet. In April, this male goose took off from the lowland swamps of Southern China. Over the next 3 days, he was tracked by transmitter as he flew continuously, increasing altitude to cross over a 22,000 ft pass near Mount Everest. Two days later he reached the lakes of Central Siberia. You might be impressed to know he flew this distance for 5 days without eating or drinking, and crossed the highest mountains on the planet. And after landing 3000 miles later, he started looking for a *date*. Now that's conditioning! (2007)

Engaging in an overtly sexist fantasy of equating courtship with combat, Callahan waxes poetic about the incredible abilities of the bar-headed goose to travel an extreme distance at extreme heights for days on end and still have the strength and endurance to mate at the end of its odyssey. This is the kind of stamina and conditioning that Callahan imagines for US soldiers in combat.

> Scientists have only now started to understand how the bar-headed goose is able to transiently adjust his hemoglobin, the red cell protein which carries oxygen for high altitude flight, and alter his metabolism to allow for continuous physical activity without rest. In my programs to improve performance during high altitude and high atmosphere operations, I will be looking into the clues provided by Apa Sherpa and the bar-headed goose. I will borrow from their success to develop transferable, transplantable acclimatization that speeds the body's natural adaptive process in a manner that allows an Army Ranger from Georgia to deploy to Afghanistan, and immediately give chase and engage the enemy without delay, limitation, or health consequence. (2007)

Callahan also imagines how DARPA and the military could draw from the abilities of aquatic animals to improve underwater operations.

> Military operations underneath the water pose even more daunting challenges. Water is 11–15x more effective than air at pulling heat from

off the body. Also, the metabolic activity required for underwater operations results in limits set by the oxygen supply, the onset of cold, dehydration, and consumption of energy stores. Attempts to extract oxygen from water have been limited by the energy requirements and the poor efficiently of current systems.

Meet the Steller Sea Lion.

During deep dives, the sea lion has developed the capacity to redirect blood flow away from non-critical organs, thus reducing oxygen demand. One strategy, then, to improving oxygen use by our Navy divers, may *not* be to increase oxygen supply, but rather to do what the sea lion does: *reduce total body oxygen* DEMAND.

The sea lion does more than preserve oxygen for use by the most critical organs such as the brain, heart, and lungs: he is also able to slow the heart rate during deep dives. Recent studies show that humans also have a residual capacity to slow the heart rate and redirect blood flow during dives; however, this response is unstable, blunted, and difficult to control. What has recently been discovered is that both the sea lion and human oxygen-preservation dive reaction or "dive reflex" is in part neurally-controlled. Imagine the advantages of reproducing the natural compensation mechanisms of diving mammals to conserve oxygen by 30–45% during military dive operations. In a time not too distant, our military divers might wear a device that provides a push-button controlled "dive reflex" allowing for a reduction in the total oxygen consumption during loiter activities but which is turned off when divers need to perform at high levels of exertion. (2007)

Essentializing and equating indigenous peoples and their "natural" abilities with animals, and seeing the animal world as just another enhancement imaginary opportunity, Callahan presents a view of military performance enhancement as a type of extraction and bioenvironmental dispossession of biological potential, a dispossession of abilities from people and animals for military potential in order for them to possibly later take these same lands and areas more easily (West 2016). Seemingly enchanted by his own biomedical vision, Callahan's dream is in some ways similar to Gorman's vision of the supersoldier as Jedi Knight: it is the serious play of enchantment and magic, of technology allowing humans to play at becoming animals, of doing things animals can do, of becoming superhero human-animal hybrids to perform the unimaginable (Gell

1988; see also Massumi 2014). It is a vision of a magical transference of animal abilities into humans and the transference of human abilities seen as somehow more than human into regular, "normal" humans. Humans and animals all have potentially useful biomedical adaptations that US soldiers must have if they are to survive on the battlefield. US soldiers will have these abilities "transplanted" in them, abilities that will allow them to shortcut the usual acclimation period and enter combat immediately. This seems to be DARPA's version of the superhero and supermythologies, and the institutionalized symbolic commentary on technologies of psychological manipulation and the realization of previously unimaginable technological feats seen as magical (Halvaksz 2016; see also Gell 1988): soldiers designed to resemble and function like animal-inspired superheroes like Wolverine, Man Bat, The Rhino, King Croc, Killer Shark, Spiderman, and Aquaman. Through the transplantation of adaptations, the "battlefield" will be implanted into the soldier and made real in the soldier before he ever sets foot on the battlefield. Air, land, sea: it is a dream and vision of a kind of automatic weaponized indigeneity and "naturalness," an automatic "passing" of the soldier in the world as all things and all peoples. If the entire world is to be the battlefield, the abilities and ecologies and adaptations of all living things in the world need to be translated, synthesized, medicalized, and transplanted into the bodies of US soldiers. Anticipation and preemption transform the world into both battlefield and laboratory in the visions and imaginations of US weapons scientists, presenting a kind of tautological proposition: people and the world are dangerous, but both possess abilities we can use against this danger. Therefore, we need to take from both in order to fight against both, but fighting and extraction create new dangers, so we have to keep imagining and taking from people and the world. Rather than viewing the world as unified, as "one world" in a positive sense (Miller 2015), DARPA and the US military view it as one unified threat, as an assemblage or "system of systems" of bioenvironmental threats to US soldiers and US security interests. The world is an open-ended source of sociotechnical imagination, play, risk, security, extraction, and control.

Both Sulzberger and Callahan discuss the need to surveil and collect infectious disease specimens and other environmental and chemical threats from around the world in order to discover all possible threats to the soldier. These humans and animals could be of use if only we can first catalog and understand them, and only if we can figure out how to synthesize and transplant their presumed abilities. Through this military biomedical/toxicological discovery and appropriation, all the biological systems of the world are to be made known and understood (see Malet 2016 and Wang 1998 on DARPA's "phage" library to develop antibodies to all possible strains of infectious agents), grasped by the military through a kind of biomedical optical tactility of dispossession (Feldman 1994). Medical surveillance and collection will create a map of military potential of the world, the world as military medical threat and possibilities. The new optics of military dispossession is not just of infectious disease but of human and animal abilities as well, abilities the military wishes to discover, mine, translate, and transplant into the bodies of soldiers. Enhancements are fundamentally about extracting more labor from the soldier, to make him or her exceed what the normal, unenhanced human can do on the battlefield and in the barracks, whether as Sherpa or goose-man. The military is prepared to imagine human-animal hybrids to ensure that as much labor power as possible can be mobilized. Military biodispossession is not simply the taking of resources; it is the taking of potential in order to further the possible taking of resources. With the world as battlefield, the soldier, through translation and transplantation, will increasingly resemble the world.

War Play Redux: Humans and Animals

In his extended essay on animals and politics, Massumi discusses the differences between play and combat by analyzing how wolf pups play fight, and the difference between a nip and a bite. Wolf pups play at fighting but never fully try to kill one another in this play; as such, Massumi calls this "combatesque" (2014, 9). Wargames also play at war, mimic war, and engage in the combatesque. They are not war but the preparation of war—almost-but-not-quite-war—in the sense that if it were war, this is what we would do. Wargames are the serious play and rehearsal of existential threat (Masco 2014, 165); it is the wolf pup play bite that is a bite but not a bite, as Massumi writes (2014, 4). They play at fighting, and mimic fighting, and each move is what they would do in a fight, but it is not a fight. The play wolf pups are like the play of a soldier in a war game; a war game is preparation but not a full opening up of possibilities, the opening up of oneself to the full, serious play of combat. In a sense, the nonenhanced soldier—at least in the eyes of military researchers—is like the wolf pup: playing but held back, still engaged in the "-esqueness" of combat and not the full serious play of combat. Performance enhancement, whether "capacity-restoring" or "capacity-increasing" (Caron 2018), will open up the soldier's capabilities, make her go beyond the contradiction of mere play-at-war, and allow her to be fully in and at war.

Performance enhancement drugs have the potential of opening up the drug-induced soldier to the "full play" of combat. Performance enhancing drugs and trauma-blocking drugs have the danger of opening up soldiers to a kind of gregarious, ebullient embrace of war and violence, a kind of bliss state of the "New Man" replacing fear with joy in destruction. If the soldier is afraid, this holds him back in combat; to activate the kind of "boldness" that Clausewitz mused over is to move from fear to play, to the play state of simultaneous awareness and non-awareness, of being so in the game that you forget that you are playing a game, despite the rush. Drugs might allow the soldier to fully lose fear and embrace one's capabilities of destruction, to fully open oneself up—or be opened up—to the ludic possibilities of war. That is, drugging a soldier might allow her to feel no fear and embrace war as fun, just as the wolf pups nip and bite (Massumi 2014). This seems to be what Jünger, Marinetti, Gumilev, and those who celebrate the beauty of war were getting at, and of course, the complete "giving over" of oneself to war and combat in the way Jünger describes it is to embrace the love of destruction and death, to find joy and beauty in death and destruction like the Futurists or even the Freikorps. The soldier who feels no fear is no longer constrained by his own fear—or humanity, or cultural or ethical brakes on killing—and can realize the full potential of war, war devoid of feeling bad about it, and just having fun with it. These soldiers will not have to engage in the merely combatesque; they can finally fully engage in combat with all systems and subsystems of their body fully ready and committed to victory. The imagined hero of the wargame becomes the real hero of enhanced warfare—at least in simulations of how enhanced warfare will be realized. Of course, none of this is to say that unenhanced warfare is not deadly or dangerous: it most obviously is, and soldiers routinely die in wargames. But the conceit of military performance enhancement is to imply that there is more that soldiers can do, more they should do, and more they will be able to do, if only it can be drawn out and extracted from them. This "more" implies that all combat and all soldiers heretofore have only been playing at war: enhanced soldiers will show us how it is really done.

The Pharmacological Battlefield: Climate Change, Infectious Disease, and Environmental Threats

"Global health security," as Andrew Lakoff writes, describes a sociotechnical imaginary and framework for identifying, responding to, and potentially preventing catastrophic disease outbreaks (2015, 300), As he explains, "At the heart of the regime of global health security is a sociotechnical imaginary concerning the future problem of infectious disease and its possible solutions: it is a future in which outbreaks of novel diseases continually threaten human life, but catastrophe may be averted if such events are detected and contained in their earliest stages" (300).

Despite the official US government rhetoric that minimizes or outright denies the impact or existence of climate change, the impact of climate change on global military and political strategy and tactics has long held the attention and imaginations of US military planners, and the changing map of diseases and the changing constellation of security issues brought about by climate change has been on their planning agenda for decades (Bickford 2015; CNA Corporation 2007; Department of the Army 2015; Marzec 2015; United States Navy 2010; White House 2015). Despite attempts by the Trump administration to minimize the military impact of climate change (White House 2017), we can assume military officials tasked with planning and preparation will nonetheless continue to take it seriously. As climate change reshapes the global disease map, the US military will try to track and predict the new contours and overlaps of infection, deployment, and conflict. Writing about globalism and environmental research, Clark A. Miller observes: "As science has become capable of monitoring and modeling Earth systems in intricate detail, globalism has become the basis for locating insecurities as the product of complex, interacting social, ecological, political, economic, and technological systems operating at global scales. Globalism thus transforms the Earth from a place that people live to a set of global systems that they inhabit and shape and that, in turn, imposes limits to which people must increasingly adapt themselves and their actions" (2015, 278).

In a report on "medical intelligence" as part of NATO planning (and drawing from US military medical intelligence protocols), Rostislav Kostadinov (2009) stresses the need for medical "situational awareness" around adversary actions, endemic and epidemic disease, environmental pollution, local flora and fauna, climate, and geography, among other areas. In other words, both offensive and defensive aspects of military medical planning and operations are key aspects of fighting on the modern battlefield.

Thinking about and analyzing global systems and climate change means thinking about and analyzing new kinds of medical changes and "terrains," and thinking about new kinds of security concerns. Tracking the spread of diseases through disease mapping and spatial epidemiology is important for protecting civilian populations (Caduff 2008, 2012; Lakoff 2015, 2017), but it also has military applications that are not necessarily defensive. Spatial epidemiology and disease mapping—from a military standpoint—are exercises in security and conflict mapping, of planning for possible deployments into an area with particular medical "stressors."

We might not generally think of vaccines and immunizations as performance enhancement technologies, but in the military, they are essential for enhancing and enabling soldier performance and internally armoring the soldier to deploy and fight in diverse battlefield settings (Benenson 1984; see figure 8.1). From a military standpoint, it is not an exaggeration to say that without these very basic enhancements, modern warfare might not be possible. Despite concerns and controversies about the safety and efficacy of vaccines and immunizations, as well as questions of informed consent, for example the military anthrax vaccine of the first Gulf War (Friedl, Grate, and Proctor 2009; Howe and Martin 1991; Lin, Mehlman, and Abney 2013; McManus et al. 2005; Moreno 2012; Sidel and Levy 2014a, 2014b; Terry 2017), and the rise of the "anti-vaxxer" movement in the US, military physicians and planners continue to see them as essential tools in their armamentarium.

The first Gulf War provides a good vantage point from which to explore the effectiveness of the fear generated around certain forms of weapons technology and the pushback the military can encounter when deploying new forms of protection. By citing military intelligence reports concerning possible Iraqi NBC capabilities, the US was able to institute a widespread program of experimental vaccinations against these weapons. The war provided a testing ground for gauging how far military medical authorities might go in coercing men and women—once again, among both soldiers and civilians—to accept new definitions of health and protection, predicated on security and defense. For example, an experimental anthrax vaccine was administered to US soldiers, and soldiers were ordered to take untested or counterindicated medications, such as pyridostigmine bromide ("PB pills"); long used as a treatment for myasthenia gravis, the military believed PB pills could be used prophylactically to protect soldiers from the

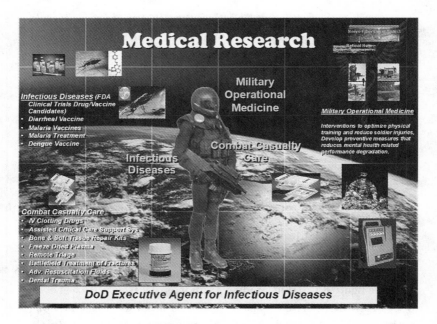

Figure 8.1 "Infectious Diseases and the Soldier." Claude M. Bolton Jr., "Military Medicine: Ready and Relevant," 2004.

nerve agent Soman (Cory-Slechta and Wedge 2016; Fulco, Liverman, and Sox 2000; see also Friedl, Grate, and Proctor 2009).

The issues and controversies surrounding the military's use of untested or counterindicated drugs and the urgency of imagined threats illuminate how the military sees and imagines threats and solutions, how it imagines what it needs to do to soldiers in order to keep them safe and useful, and how it needs to manage the optics of experimental vaccine or biomedical programs. Since the widespread pushback against the anthrax vaccine by both soldiers and civilians, as well as the concerns about the links between the vaccine, PB pills, and Gulf War Syndrome, the military has tried to gauge the public's comfort or unease with these programs and come up with strategies to cope with societal unease.

> Insofar as the military mirrors the larger society, such social concerns [about vaccinations and refusing anthrax vaccines] are an important factor in successful vaccinations programs. The public discussion of the Gulf War Syndrome reveals a widespread distrust of the protection provided to American personnel shipped to strange lands and subjected to

foreign risks. Whether justified or not, the concerns are real. Anxieties about vaccinations in both the military and general population are likely to persist. A long-term approach to ameliorating this concern could include systematic collection of genomic data to monitor the response of participants in vaccination programs. (National Research Council 2001, 62–63)

Vaccines and pharmaceuticals are generally "dual use": that is, they benefit both civilians and the military and are usually developed by joint military and corporate/private-sector research initiatives, if they are not "off the shelf" drugs used for different indications by the military (Armstrong et al. 2010; de Almeida 2015; Greenough, Holmberg, and Blume 2017; Terry 2017). Founded in 1969, the US Army Medical Research Institute of Infectious Diseases (USAMRIID) has been tasked as the "lead laboratory for medical biological defense research," with the core mission to "protect the warfighter from biological threats [and] investigate disease outbreaks and threats to public health. Research conducted at USAMRIID leads to medical solutions—therapeutics, vaccines, diagnostics, and information—that benefit both military personnel and civilians" (USAMRIID 2014). Reminiscent of Sulzberger's list of threats against which the military should develop idiophylactic measures, USAMRIID is currently attempting to develop vaccines against anthrax, botulism, the plague, Ebola and Marburg hemorrhagic fevers, hantavirus, ricin toxin, and staphylococcal enterotoxin B (USAMRIID 2014). USAMRIID also develops new diagnostic instruments and technologies to use with "forward field medical laboratories" and the Joint Biological Agent Identification and Detection System (JBAIDS), which is used through the Department of Defense (USAMRIID 2014).

DARPA and the Walter Reed Army Institute of Research (WRAIR), for example, have both also been at the forefront of the development of a dual-use Ebola vaccine (Pellerin 2014; Smith 2014; Tucker 2015; US Military HIV Research Program 2016; the Chinese military also developed an Ebola vaccine, which is slated to go into mass production [see Winsor 2015]). DARPA also began its "Blue Angel" program in 2009, designed to speed up the mass production of strategically important vaccines (Lo 2014). As discussed in chapter 7, DARPA's Battlefield Medicine directorate is working on ways to improve battlefield logistics and the capability to produce on-demand/as-needed pharmaceuticals in remote battlefields through the Pharmacy on Demand and Biologically Derived Medicines on Demand projects. These "miniaturized device platforms" will make it possible for the military to respond quickly to existing and emergent battlefield medical threats as soldiers encounter them, without relying on lengthy medical supply chains.

The military's identification of climate change as a top security and strategic priority for the coming decades suggests future changes in strategy, tactics, and doctrine; planning and operations; and technology, research, and development funding. As climate change impacts the global landscape, it will also change the global security and conflict "scape." In turn, the US military will attempt to come up with dual-use vaccinations and other kinds of medical "force multipliers" to deal with these changes. While saving and protecting civilians—and perhaps helping to stave off unrest, upheaval, and conflict—vaccinations also open up spaces to the military that might otherwise be closed off. If new forms of built-in armor are made available in the (near) future for soldiers, deployments once considered unimaginable due to climate and/or terrain issues could be anticipated and imagined as possible.

Advances in military biomedicine allow the military to imagine new forms of armor and deployments and think about and plan for combat in what it sees as diseased and dangerous "primitive" and "exotic" battlefields, a conflation that tells us how the military imagines the world, anticipates danger, and justifies the need for immunizations and built-in armor. A vaccine is both a response to and a predictor of a physical/medical space. Military vaccinations are embodied spatiotemporal markers for potential conflict: they prepare the soldier to enter environments that disease and other forms of health risks might prevent him from entering. As climate change exacerbates the intensity and spread of diseases (Cho 2014) and public health crises, ever-greater areas of strategic interest and importance to the US and its allies could theoretically become off-limits (Lakoff 2017). Vaccinations and other medications prevent diseases— like dysentery or malaria, for example—from becoming a kind of area denial weapon. Even if the disease in question has not been weaponized, it can still "aid" the enemy if the military does not have a way to counter it. Beginning with George Washington's order to inoculate American troops against smallpox during the Revolutionary War (Lin, Mehlman, and Abney 2013, 5), the devastating effects of disease on both sides during the Civil War (Sartin 1993), and concerns with battlefield losses due to diseases like yellow fever, dengue, hookworm infection, and malaria during the war with Spain, in the Philippines, and during World Wars I and II (Slotten 2014), the US military has long been concerned with the impact of illness and infectious disease on troop strength and combat capability. Threatening from within and without, the enemy is not only the human enemy but the world of microbes, pathogens, and environmental conditions that attack the soldier.

There is the ever-present fear that as diseases evolve and new threats appear, the military will not have the necessary or appropriate vaccinations on hand to allow for safe deployments, or conversely, it will have to deploy into an area knowing that soldiers will have to contend with exposures and illness later. As such, these "nightmare scenarios" (Masco 2014, 196) and deployment possibilities will drive military medical research and development into militarily effective vaccines and countermeasures. Paying attention to which vaccines the military investigates and develops is a way to anticipate those areas of the world that the US military is thinking about for possible deployments.

The US Army Medical Research Directorate-Africa (USAMRD-A) is the "premier US Department of Defense (DoD) infectious disease laboratory in sub-Saharan Africa" (WRAIR n.d.). As part of WRAIR, the USAMRD-A is tasked with developing and testing "improved means for predicting, detecting, preventing, and treating infectious disease threats important to the U.S. military and host nation" (WRAIR n.d.). Consider Ebola: the recent widespread outbreak(s) in Africa give us a chance to think about how the US military is preparing for future outbreaks of its kind in Africa and elsewhere, and how this influences programs designed to provide US soldiers with inner, unseen armor to negate these outbreaks. Given the growing importance of Africa in US strategic thinking, and the increasing presence of the US in Africa via the United States Army Africa Command (AFRICOM) and the expansion of US military bases throughout the continent, the quick development of an Ebola vaccine is of great interest and use to the US military as well as government officials and nongovernmental actors (Lakoff 2015, 2017; Terry 2017; see also the Ebola Response Anthropology Platform, Social Science for Emergency Response n.d.). Without a viable vaccination at hand, large parts of Africa could effectively become "no go" zones for US forces (for the medical requirements mandated to enter AFRICOM, see United States Africa Command Instruction 2019). The creation of an effective vaccine would be a very welcome development for people in countries impacted by Ebola, but it could also become an important pharmacological tool and weapon in the "great game" of influence and power projection in the parts of Africa impacted by Ebola outbreaks (Abramowitz 2017).

Preparing the Soldier, Making the Battlefield

US military doctrine calls for various ways of "preparing the battlefield" for deployment and combat. One kind of preparation is the "medical intelligence preparation of the operational environment (MIPOE)" (United States Department of the Army/United States Department of the Navy 2014) in the sense of monitoring health conditions and stressors of a potential battlefield and preparing soldiers to be able to fight and survive there. The deployment of US troops to help with the Ebola outbreak and provide humanitarian aid can also be seen as a kind of trial run for dealing with an outbreak of this kind. The military can observe how soldiers cope with a deployment into an area with a deadly disease outbreak, see if the contamination and decontamination protocols in place are adequate and effective, and determine if new medical preparations, protocols, and procedures need to be developed.

While vaccines help protect both civilians and soldiers, they also allow military planners and policy makers to imagine deployments and develop contingency plans they might not otherwise consider. Climate change will affect the military-medical calculus of risk, deployment, and research and will go hand in hand with the new and plastic logics of disease prevention, pharmaceutical production, security, and military performance enhancement. Dual-use medicines benefit civilians, but they also help extend the military's reach to all points of the globe. The slogan for Walter Reed Army Institute of Research in many ways makes this perfectly clear: "Soldier Health. World Health."

While seemingly defensive in nature, this built-in armor would also allow the soldier to take part in offensive operations in hostile environments and on "exotic" and "primitive" battlefields that previously either hindered or prohibited engagements. In a world anticipated and seen as one of perpetual struggle and war, in the imagination of military researchers and in accordance with the needs of military planners, soldiers must be armored, physically and emotionally, internally and externally—but most importantly, internally—to make them useful to the military and the state.

Examining how the US military imagines environmental threats and disease—and imagines solutions—we can see how the military simultaneously imagines the "component man" and the world and presents militarized visions of terrain and tissue, environment and biology, threats and enhancements. Each new anticipated battlefield and each new imagined intervention to prevent death will open up new questions, new threats, and new avenues for "unfair advantages" and "kill-proofing." Far from being a kind of military "exotica," these research efforts—even if unsuccessful in their "pure" forms—will continue to drive the development of new types of protection, countermeasures, and weapons to overcome these countermeasures. We might want boots on the ground, but we do not want bodies in the ground. Dead soldiers are a political liability in the new conceptions of clean and perfect war; as the *Army Science and Technology Master Plan* made it perfectly and cynically clear, dead and wounded soldiers are real "war stoppers" (United States Army 1998, Q1). Part of the appeal of enhanced soldiers is that they are seemingly invincible, do not easily die, and are always victorious. Preparing for war is an ever-increasing struggle over anticipating, imagining, and manipulating the biology of the soldier. Despite the ring of science fiction, the idea of "pharmacological soldiers" preparing to fight on the pharmacological battlefield is the increasingly real terrain of military biomedical research, operational planning, and combat.

The Tip of the Spear: Delegates, Protection, and Deployments

The supersoldier exists in the present moment and imagination of an already dangerous and threatening future. Much like the discussions of future threat and affect provided by Masco (2014) and Massumi (2015), the battlefields of the future that the supersoldier will encounter, and through encountering, make, are fraught with unknown hazards and stressors that will test the physical and mental limits of the soldier. Born out of the need to counter Soviet numerical superiority, NBC weapons, and the global battlefield of the Cold War (Nardulli and McNaugher 2002), the supersoldier has morphed into the flexible platform of both neoliberalism and the War on Terrorism era. The new soldier will be one that can be made to fit any and all contingencies, internally armored and armored on demand by psychopharmaceuticals, prepositioned vaccines, and vaccine-production capabilities. Through projects like Peak Soldier Performance and Metabolic Dominance, and the biodispossession dreams of Inner Armor, the soldier might be able to fight—and work—for days on end without sleeping, eating, or drinking (Lin, Mehlman, and Abney 2013, 7; Moreno 2012). Nothing will impinge upon the continuous and predictable extraction of military labor power.

As military officials and politicians are fond of saying, soldiers are the "tip of the spear" of national policy. In this sense, they are the "tools" of policy makers and the tools by which policy is enacted. In order to be effective, tools must be well made, honed, kept in good shape, and protected. Latour's notion of "delegates" allows us to cut through the ideological and semiotic fog of "protection" and think about what it means to be made into a tool of policy. Mark B. Brown, in his discussion of Bruno Latour, technology, and delegates, states that "whenever people want a particular task to be performed but would prefer not to do it themselves, they can delegate it to technology" (Brown 2009, 172; see also Latour 1992 for his discussion on technology and delegates). By embedding technology in soldiers, Inner Armor and other military enhancement projects are directed toward making soldiers into better, more efficient, and more reliable "delegates" of policy and force projection. Following Clausewitz, if "war is a mere continuation of state policy by other means" (1976, 40), then technology turns the soldier into the delegate of the politician and policy maker in order to affect this continuation.

Technology transforms the person into the soldier/delegate of the politician and policy maker, the tool to address and counteract political-military anticipation and fear, to allow us to think we can "secure the future." In turn, the soldier becomes the fulcrum point of research, scientific development, and budgeting and acquisition. Of course, the soldier is still human, but he is now enmeshed in multiple, overlapping areas of imagination, anticipation, power, discipline, and concern, the point of extraction and abstraction, the point of protection and power projection, power projected internally to allow for the external projection of the soldier. While soldiers may be protected by the technologies developed to protect them, "protection" also becomes a kind of protection for the research and development regime of soldier protection. Embedded technologies in the body of the soldier turn the soldier into a kind of "double delegate" of policy makers who want their ends achieved but cannot or will not perform the actions required themselves and so delegate soldiers to do it for them, and develop and deploy technologies to help the soldiers better accomplish the task at hand and achieve the desired policy goals. These projects are not neutral, even if the term *protection* implies a kind of political neutrality predicated on safety, and even if "safety" and "protection" are afforded the soldier. This is a "safety" with an intention behind it, a purpose, and is in no way neutral or apolitical.

Biomedical-enhancement research in the military is geared first and foremost toward enabling the soldier to successfully complete the "mission," that nebulous concept of getting something done on the battlefield, whatever that something might be at a given time and place (Masco 2014). As Masco writes, "the [counterterror] state is loading new capacities into the future as well as the conditions of possibility for new nightmares not yet realized" (2014, 13). Masco's observation holds true for military performance enhancement research as well: enhancements both address perceived weaknesses and create new areas of concern for future mission failure—nightmare scenarios caused by environment and illness—that need to be addressed and "corrected" in the body of the soldier.

Soldiers are both metaphorical and literal "tools" of national security and defense policy and goals. The soldier/delegate becomes the focus of military labor extraction and enhancement, the focus of power projected internally to allow for the external projection and deployment of the soldier, and the focus of continued research to ensure that she continues to be a reliable, effective, and deployable delegate. Protective technologies, while potentially protecting the health and well-being of the soldier, are also directed at the protection of future policy possibilities and contingencies. As biomedicine makes possible performance enhancements and vaccines that could allow the soldier to fight in any and all climates and resist any and all pathogens, the entire world becomes a battlefield. This is a major, if unspoken, implication of Sulzberger's Idiophylactic Soldier and DARPA's Inner Armor programs: the imagined and anticipated battlefield needs the soldier who can stand up to its challenges in order for it to be a battlefield.

Military enhancement projects designed to counteract environmental and infectious disease stressors help us situate military performance enhancement research in general; they also help us think about the links between soldier health and the macrolevel of political and military necessity and conflict, and the impact of climate change on military medicine, operations, and planning. If military biomedical research is about anticipation, we need to anticipate how civil society and everyday life might be impacted by these kinds of projects. Military performance enhancement research opens up troubling questions about the militarization of everyday life for both soldiers and civilians, even if military researchers see their research as ethical and necessary engagements with biomedicine, creating beneficial and dual-use medicines directed toward saving lives around the world, though, admittedly, the lives of soldiers first (Annas and Annas 2009; Beam 2003; Gross 2006; Howell 2017; Lin, Mehlman, and Abney 2013; Mehlman, Lin, and Abney 2013; Moreno 2012).

These projects also let us think about the broader implications and uses of military biomedical "armor" and "protection." What interests me is the ambivalent nature of projects like Idiophylaxis and Inner Armor: US military biomedical and pharmacological performance enhancements both protect and compel. They represent a kind of defensive and offensive conundrum of protection: biotechnology and performance enhancements may in fact protect and/or save the soldier, but they will also compel soldiers to fight, lay their lives on the line in combat, and expose themselves to continued—and perhaps even greater—risk. Both Idiophylaxis and Inner Armor are concerned with a kind of freedom from injury and death and a strategic-level freedom from operational worry. But it is exactly this deployment of "freedom" that binds and constricts the soldier in a regime of health and turns her into a delegate of national security and power projection; military health must ensure that the soldier is constantly made "free" of weakness through application of new technologies, pharmaceuticals, and equipment. It is not a conception of health that seeks to "restore" the health of the patient; rather, it is the military's use of "health" to produce something new: a soldier-delegate potentially immune to wounding and—fantastically—to death.

Returning to Gell and his discussion of technology and magic, we can see how "kill-proofing" is a kind of "ideal" technology: an ideal technology is one that can be practiced with "zero opportunity costs" (1988, 9). "Kill-proofing" and making soldiers "idiophylactic" are both a kind of magical endeavor to develop and make an ideal technology, one that is "costless in terms of the kind of drudgery, hazards, and investments which actual technical activity inevitably requires. Production 'by magic' is production minus the disadvantageous side-effects, such as struggle, effort, etc." (Gell 1988, 9). This is a good description of the symbolic production and visioning of supersoldiers, of victory and success without cost to the soldiers and society; there is no drudgery and struggle, no opportunity costs in the form of dead soldiers. Except this is not the play of children but the transference of a kind of serious play to military biotechnology, to imagining real-world effects and real-world impacts. Mimicking the bloodless, perfect war of children's imaginative play, it is the serious play of fantasy warfare where you die and never die, can immediately morph into whatever form you imagine, heal yourself instantaneously, and are always the victorious hero in your own mind, returning to the fight and to glory again and again.

NINE

"Catastrophic Success"

Back to the Futurarmy

Coming full circle, Robert B. Rigg's "Soldier of the Futurarmy" lives on, serving as the inspiration for TRADOC's Mad Scientist Science Fiction Writing Contest. This competition invites soldiers and civilians to take part in and shape a militarized technoscientific imaginary (Jasanoff and Kim 2015) and to imagine what war will be like between 2030 and 2050. "Mad Scientist" and the *Mad Scientist Laboratory* blog are a US Army TRADOC "initiative and community of action that continually explores the future through collaborative partnerships and continuous dialogue with academia, industry, and government. Through this initiative, the Army shapes future multidomain (i.e., Land, Air, Sea, Cyber, and Space) operations in its role as a thought leader in the future of warfare . . . envisioning the Deep Future Operational Environment!" (TRADOC n.d.).

An initiative like the Mad Scientist Competition is both a chance to excite people about future military technologies and a "crowd sourcing" exercise for the military and Department of Defense. It is both the fun, somewhat ridiculous play of military wargamers—"Mad Scientists"—and the deadly serious exercise of planning for new military futures. Contestants were tasked with "looking for ideas that are unorthodox and outside of what the Army is already considering about the future of warfare and technology," and the contest rules list ten areas of potential interest, such as "synthetic biology," "mobile and cloud computing," "climate change," and "anti-access/area denial," but contestants were not bound by these areas (AUSA 2016).

Specifically, the contest asks entrants to think about the following, and to be mindful of the "laws of physics."

- We are looking for ideas that are unorthodox and outside of what the Army is already considering about the future.
- Be mindful of the time frame—We are looking for ideas about Warfare in 2030–2050 that could have an influence on the world in 2050. This means technologies that will be mature enough over the next 35 years to approach real world application. Now, we want you to push the edge of what might be feasible by 2050. However, avoid ideas that violate the laws of physics. In DoD parlance, we are looking for ideas that could reach Technology Readiness Level (TRL) 5 or 6 by 2050. (AUSA 2016)

Calling on the public to imagine future enhancements, weapons, platforms, and conflicts, the military wants to use the public's knowledge and imagination—and access to ideas and information it might not be privy to—to help it anticipate what is to come in the next twenty to thirty years. But of course, the Army anticipates some unease around this; in the FAQ section of the contest, the organizers anticipate contestants wondering what the Army will do with the stories submitted to the contest.

What is the US Army going to do with these stories?

Glad you asked. In the immediate term, your stories will be used as input into the Mad Scientist Initiative, ASA (ALT) (Assistant Secretary of the Army (Acquisition, Logistics and Technology) and ARCIC (Army Capabilities Integration Center). These stories are being used to explore fresh ideas about the future of warfare and technology. **The Army is specifically looking for unconventional thinking, which is why we want you to participate!** (AUSA 2016)

TRADOC was apparently very happy with the results and the submissions of the "Mad Scientists" who took part; the "Executive Summary" of the Mad Scientist competition states:

In November 2016, the US Army TRADOC Mad Scientist Initiative launched its first Science Fiction Writing Competition, with the topic "Warfare in 2030 to 2050." This contest sought unconventional thinkers and was open to people from all walks of life. One of the founding ideas inspiring the contest was the notion of "Science Fiction as reality." Science Fiction has been historically predictive of future technologies and ideas. One example is the prevalence of mobile "smart devices" and advanced communications in popular films and television such as *Star Trek* and *Back to the Future*. These kinds of forward-looking ideas and themes help the Army think about and prepare for future challenges

Figure 9.1 Image from TRADOC's "Warfare 2030–2050" military science fiction writing contest, 2016–2017.

and opportunities in conflict. . . . We experienced "catastrophic success" with over 150 submissions from authors in 10 countries. . . . This
diversity in authors presented us with a wide variety of thoughts and
ideas on the future Operational Environment and warfare. Through the
art of storytelling, the Army was able to visualize the known, probable,
and possible challenges and opportunities that the future holds. (Shabro
and Winer 2018)

Military crowdsourcing competitions like the "Mad Scientist" challenge
are increasingly common, and the US Department of Defense intends to
do more with crowdsourcing, hoping to tap into "creative thinking" as a
way to better imagine and plan for difficult scenarios and futures in the
coming decades (see figure 9.1). From this, the Pentagon hopes to produce
three "Performance Objectives" around crowdsourcing.

a   Identify alternative futures and global and regional security environ-
     ments in the 2020–2025 timeframe that considers military, sociologi-

cal, economic, scientific, technological, and environmental trends and potential shocks with implications for the Department.

b   Generate innovative scenarios that present pathways to a crisis or conflict that is antithetical to US national security interests. Scenarios will provide a narrative description that captures a representative potential future national security challenge and includes the following key elements: identity of key actors, their interests and objectives, primary drivers to conflict and rationale for key actors' decision-making and actions, key capabilities they could use in a crisis or conflict, description of representative activities they would take (i.e., the manner in which they would use their capabilities to achieve their objectives), and role of third parties. Scenarios should remain within the bounds of plausibility.

c   Develop and provide quick-turn analyses exploring the implications for the Department on new and/or potentially game-changing military capabilities of the adversary identified in the alternative futures environment and/or the innovative scenarios to inform the development of alternative strategies and force planning options to mitigate the impacts of the capabilities. (Mark Thompson 2015)

The US military has recently crowdsourced ideas for the "detection of underground voids (tactical tunnels)," and DARPA has sponsored a number of crowdsourcing events around robotics, geo-locating (its "Red Balloon Challenge" in 2009), amphibious tank design, cube satellites, and the use of online games to "accelerate the verification of software" (Tilghman 2015).

In September 2015, DARPA hosted an event called "Wait, What? A Future Technology Forum" in St. Louis, Missouri. The idea of the forum was to imagine ways DARPA could "throttle up science into an even more powerful engine of discovery and technology than it is now" (DARPA News, September 29, 2015). The meeting covered "new ideas in the technoscape," such as new optical technologies, neural interfaces to control prosthetics, and new forms of artificial intelligence to better understand genomics, the human brain, and the "Internet of Things"; more than 1,400 people attended and took part in the breakout discussion sections (DARPA Outreach, September 29, 2015).

Inviting people to imagine all sorts of interventions for new kinds of soldiers and warfare involves them in collective brainstorming; it is the creation of a virtual psychosocial space designed to shape how people imagine and fear the future by socializing them to military narratives, terminology, and framing devices (Masco 2014, 54). Crowdsourcing is a way to allow people to think that they have some possible say in how the military imagines the future and designs new technologies to control and assuage anxiety about the future. And it allows the military to tap into the technoscientific dream worlds of people it would probably never know about and involve them in the imagination and visioning process of designing future war.

If Bronisław Malinowski's instruction to budding anthropologists was to engage with the "native" in order to "see his version of his world" (2014, 24), then the military's idea of vision is the exact opposite: it engages us so that we learn to see its vision of the world. Military crowdsourcing games are to help us learn to see like the state, how the state wants us to see what it sees and imagine the future as it imagines the future. These crowdsourcing activities allow TRADOC, DARPA, and other military biomedical security experts and professionals to set the terms of the future: they decide what the terms are, how they relate to the main areas of concern, and, in doing so, imply that these are the real threats and areas most in need of attention (Bigo 2008; Goldstein 2010). They have the authority and resources to set the terms and frame the future of security through the use of terms like *anti-access/area denial*, and in the process teach us the vocabulary of security and enhancement. We become attuned to the terms and framing vocabulary used by the military to frame the future of war and enhancement; we might have a large degree of freedom in how we imagine war of the future but a limited degree of freedom in the categories we can use.

Crowdsourcing promotes a positive affect around military technologies. You can engage your creative muse and dream up a story about supersoldiers using all sorts of innovative and fantastic technologies and biotechnologies (and in the process, perhaps fulfill your own biotech fantasies about performance enhancement in the future, like Gorman's fantasy of being a Jedi Knight). The military can draw upon a diverse range of people to imagine supersoldiers, enhancement, biotechnologies, new battlefields and environments, new missions, and new challenges. It is not only DARPA that can imagine kill-proof Sherpa-dolphin soldiers or TRADOC that can play at military science fiction: we can all play, and we can all be part of the collective anticipation and anxiety of the new pharmacological battlefield. Like the mass alert drills of the Cold War that bound all US citizens together in a performance of fear and preparation (Masco 2014), crowdsourcing, while on a smaller scale, allows people to engage with defense and security. Most importantly, the play of crowdsourcing can make all the military's anticipation and preemption work seem not quite dangerous, as something not quite like war and the reimagining of human society and potential (Povinelli 2011). None of this is any cause for concern, as none of it is real; it is simply brainstorming, playing around with "wouldn't it be cool if . . ." and imagining how technology might change us. It is simply a fun and entertaining exercise in the "Art of the Possible."

We really do not know what will happen if all the US military's various plans for enhanced "supersoldiers" come to fruition, but it is a safe bet to say that these projects will dramatically alter what it means to be a soldier and how we think about soldiers and warfare. If the operative question of the Cold War and the present biosecurity moment is "what if?," the follow-up question might be "what then?" As one participant in the DARPA forum observed about the "far out" ideas put forth at the forum and technology in the future, "Everything is Sci Fi until it happens." In the case of US military performance enhancement technologies, if chemical heroes come to be, what then?

TEN

Natural Cowards, Chemical Heroes

Keen Odysseus, do not try to make me welcome death. I
would rather live on earth as a hireling of one who was but
poor himself than to be the king of all the ghosts there are.

» **Achilles**, *The Odyssey*

The idea of a "chemical hero" is something of an oxymoron: we usually do not think of our heroes as taking drugs to turn themselves into heroes. Even if they are taking unauthorized drugs in combat, we still like to think of our heroes as clean and honorable and wholesome, *authentic*, somehow pure and untainted, even as they wade into the thick of killing and combat. All too often, we imagine that it is the cowards—both enemy and friend—who are on drugs in combat, using them to unfair advantage or to compensate for a lack of martial masculine prowess and courage. We like to think of our heroes as natural and normal, and we like to think of heroism as something intrinsic in the person, something that was always there, simply waiting for an opportunity to emerge for it to be expressed. Heroism is a kind of "moral fiber"—the intrinsic "will" of the person—that allows the person to perform heroically when called upon, when faced with a situation that the majority of people could not face and could not engage with or overcome. We imagine heroism as something in all of us, even if it is ephemeral: "we can be heroes / just for one day," as David Bowie sang about lovers kissing in front of the Berlin Wall.

But lurking in each of us, and lurking in the background and dark recesses of all US military performance enhancement research, is a specter: the specter of cowardice. While never directly addressed, it is there in the form of concerns with strength and weakness, boldness and anxiety, performance and failure, and this specter informs and shapes much—if perhaps not all—of what counts as military performance enhancement research. Cowardice can be expected of all humans in combat; heroism is special because it is unpredictable, but it could become much more militarily useful if it were predictable, and if cowardice could be eliminated with precision.

The baseline by which heroism is measured—at least in a military setting—is cowardice (Walsh 2014). Officially, the US military codifies cowardice under Article 99 of the Uniform Code of Military Justice (UCMJ). Article 99 covers a broad suite of behaviors, like failing to act or to perform one's duty, shirking one's responsibilities, wavering in combat or in the face of fire, running away to safety, abandoning one's position or comrades, surrendering, throwing away ammunition. But these acts are also normal responses to the death and devastation and terror of war and combat. If these are normal responses, but normal is not militarily useful, how do you create a more militarily useful "normal" that is, for all practical purposes, "heroism"? Or, can you medicalize cowardice and the weakness that causes it and is caused by it, and eliminate it or at least protect against it? Like a militarized Occam's Razor, would you be left with—*perforce*—heroism?

To read US military biomedical performance enhancement plans and reports is to read a long, extended narrative implicitly about worry, anticipation, and cowardice. Will the specter of cowardice—always present, always menacing and looming, lowering and glowering—sweep through our ranks and destroy the trust we have in our soldiers? It is in this space that enhanced supersoldiers are imagined and designed. Cowardice is a kind of infectious disease in the military, and guarding against it are forms of anticipation, preemption, and imagination. If the military can think of cowardice as a disease—similar in its devastating effects to something like malaria or dysentery—how then can it medically expunge it and preemptively "cure" it?

Heroism—as an unpredictable ontological category and spontaneous act—is but one more thing to imagine, design, extract, harness, and militarize on the emerging pharmacological battlefield as a way to somehow fix the future. Military performance enhancement is fundamentally a discussion about distrust: the military cannot trust that the soldier will be good enough, strong enough, fast enough, tough enough, brave enough, resilient enough, durable enough, willing to shoot and kill or be shot and killed. Performance enhancement is a way to make sure these things happen, to assuage military/political uncertainty about the possibly cowardly, possibly frail soldier and the mission. Performance enhancement is not only a "force multiplier" but a policy multiplier and anxiolytic as well.

Projects like Idiophylaxis, the Objective Force Warrior, the Future Force Warrior, and Inner Armor are concerned with the direct intervention in the biology of the soldier to minimize or eliminate weakness. Weakness and frailty are openings to imagine humans who can rise above their innate shortcomings (from a military standpoint) and perform deeds that most others cannot perform. Without a conception of weakness or cowardice, there would be no heroes. But, through this appreciation of cowardice, how do we try to imagine or standardize "heroism" and make it more accessible to the "normal," frail human, to make Clausewitz's "boldness" the norm? Can we train for it, put it in a syringe or a pill, or perhaps even change our DNA to make it something innate and heritable? In the dreams and imaginations of US military researchers, the world of military performance enhancement is the domain and dominion of the postcoward.

Strange Love, Enhanced Soldiers, and Heroism

In the United States, we like to believe in the myth of the citizen-soldier, of citizens rising up to defend the nation in times of war, citizen-soldiers fully prepared and capable of combat. Soldiers are citizens first, but they must be made into soldiers, designed and made and prepared before they are soldiers. And in the high-tech world of modern combat, soldiers must be carefully designed and made, often requiring years of training and preparation before they can be sent into battle; the citizen-soldier Minuteman of the Revolutionary War era is a thing of the past, at least in terms of actual military usefulness and effectiveness (though the Minuteman is still useful as an ideological Everyman in conservative American politics). And in the current military-security-economic context of the United States, and the pronounced civil-military gap, not all citizens have to rise up to become soldiers.

Some might say "support the troops" at any cost but not really think through what that might ultimately mean above and beyond protecting soldiers. On the one hand, we love and venerate our soldiers—particularly in the United States of the Global War on Terrorism era—and we want to do everything in our power to make sure they are safe and protected. To do so, we imagine all sorts of ways we can make them into superheroes: drugs, technologies, science fiction–like applications of technology to turn the soldier into the ultimate cyborg warrior, unstoppable and unkillable. But there is a fundamental tension in all this, a certain palpable fear: we are also afraid of our own creations, of the Frankenstein soldiers we might be on the verge of creating.

Just as dead soldiers have come to represent the "will" or the "soul" of the nation (Gilpin-Faust 2008; Mosse 1990; Ohnuki-Tierney 2002; Wagner 2019; Wagner and Matyók 2018)—the will and the soul of the imagined community of the sticky sweet blood of sacrifice, the ultimate feeling of collective sacrifice and the willingness to give one's all, "the last full measure of devotion," as Abraham Lincoln said at Gettysburg—so too do living soldiers represent "us" as we prepare to shed our blood and the blood of our children and loved ones, and the blood of others, to cement our bond. We might think of soldiers representing us in a variety of ways— the obvious ones, like wearing a US flag on their uniforms, or simply "US Army" on their pocket patch, or as the "best of America"—but they represent us in ways we often fail to recognize, and we often fail to think about what it means to "prepare." Each soldier is a kind of congealed representation of how we think about life and death, risk and reward, heroism and cowardice, and, increasingly, how we think about biomedical "fixes" to seemingly insurmountable ethical and cultural problems. We might not think about medicine and biomedical technology when we look at soldiers, but the last few decades have seen a dramatic increase in the ways in which medicine "makes" the modern soldier. This preparation is to ensure that the soldier gives a healthy measure of devotion but not necessarily the full. That is for the other poor bastard.

You can try to make soldiers brave and fearless, to make them desire a heroic death on the battlefield. You can drill it in to kids when they are young through stories and films. You can venerate soldiers and the military, and even celebrate soldiers and the military at sporting events. And once in the military, you can teach soldiers about other soldiers who were heroes. You can even train soldiers to desire death. The Wehrmacht practiced soldier funerals as a way to convince soldiers that they would be venerated after death in combat, and to make them desire a *Heldentod*—a hero's death (Hafeneger and Fritz 1993), and the Japanese military celebrated dead soldiers as so many cherry blossoms falling to the earth in a beautiful, slow motion, fluttering death (Ohnuki-Tierney 2002).

In "Mourning Rights: *Beowulf*, the *Iliad*, and the War in Iraq," Robin Norris writes that "transmitting sorrow through the technology of poetry is an experience unique to human beings" (2007, 277). But what about the transmission of sorrow through the language and framing of skin-in technologies like military biotechnology and performance enhancement? Thinking about military performance enhancement through the optics and language of superheroes gives us a vocabulary to talk about war and killing as clean and devoid of death and trauma, much like Cohn's (1987) US defense intellectuals and nuclear war. But perhaps we should resist this language and easy characterization of war play and remain in the earthly and the real.

As Mosse (1990) described it, the cult of the fallen soldier is an important part in constructing the myth of the heroic soldier, and death—a glorious, meaningful, useful death—is an essential part of this myth. But what if the old myths no longer work, either culturally or politically? What if dead soldiers on the battlefield are seen less as a heroic triumph of the state and more as a political mistake and horrible spasm of wasted lives? What if you want war and heroism without death and blood and remorse? That seems to be where we are in the US today.

Transhuman, All Too Human: Being All You Might Be Allowed to Become

The idea of drugging and/or enhancing soldiers to make them better fighters in combat is not new. But we really do not think of the practical, real-world attempts and implications of changing the biology of the soldier, and what this means not just for the soldier but potentially for all of us, for everyday life as civilians. Performance enhancements promise to change the nature of military service as well as military recruiting and the political economy of soldiering. By making it seem like you can become a superhero, an enhanced military offers not just a job but a chance to expand your abilities. US Army recruiting slogans like "Army Strong" and "An Army of One" hint at the desire to have enhanced supersoldiers who are better than unenhanced soldiers and who have the firepower and combat capabilities of entire companies of soldiers: this could be "you." This same "body" could then be used for recruiting/promotional purposes to entice people—or potentially, only certain types of people—to enlist in the military. Volunteering for the military—or being in a position where one "must" volunteer to get ahead or at least stay afloat—means committing to the complete giving over of one's labor power to the military (Bailey 2013). Having volunteered to give all of one's labor power to the military, the military, through performance enhancing drugs, will make sure it gets every ounce of what it was promised through the enlistment contract.

Performance enhancement drugs, if given to widespread use in the military, will have significant impacts on the role of the military as a rung up the class ladder in the United States. Fundamentally, who will be allowed to enlist and become the enhanced soldier/hero, and who will be prohibited? While all of this is by necessity speculative, some of the most troubling aspects of the potential future of military performance enhancement lie with issues of race, class, and recruitment. If the military has been seen as an avenue of advancement for minority/disadvantaged groups in the United States, what will happen to recruitment and enlistment if permanent performance enhancements become part of the standard enlistment contract and package? Enhancements might solve some military recruiting issues by allowing the military to do more with fewer soldiers (Schachtman 2009), but this elides the question of who the military will actually take into its ranks. Will the military continue to allow people from low-income communities to join? Will the military remain an equal opportunity employer and continue to accept almost everyone who wishes to join its ranks? Military enhancements could also help fuel class antagonisms and be seen as a new kind of internal security issue: for a potential soldier, whose "life chances and life choices" in many ways compel or funnel him to join the "all-volunteer" force, enhancements could be seen as possible compensation or as a way to right structural and economic wrongs and level the playing field with those in a different class stratum. But "enhanced" military service for members of low-income groups could possibly be seen as dangerous by the military or the government, as the creation of a class of citizen-soldiers who could pose a long-term threat to the status quo; these enhanced former soldiers might not be content with equaling the playfield but desire to plow it up completely and replant it. The current all-volunteer force in the United States firewalls the experience of war and trauma to a small sample of the overall population; but because of the potential fear around enhanced soldiers and veterans, it is not outside the realm of possibility that a limited form of the draft could one day be reinstated. While the military already applies certain screens to enlistment and maintains certain enlistment standards—criminal background checks and aptitude tests, for example—a draft based on both genomics and an assessment of one's ideological and class reliability is not necessarily that far-fetched.

I am not convinced that the "enhanced" soldier represents or will represent the transhuman soldier. They may be "enhanced" humans, but they are and will be human nonetheless, and will possibly continue to be humans drawn from disadvantaged or disenfranchised groups in the US. To say that they are more than human runs the risk of removing them from considerations of what it means to be human, just as "war" in military discourse often seems to be removed from human agency and endeavor and simply is, has been, and always will be. As the "soldier system of systems" and like the fetishism of commodities, we run the risk of masking origins and histories of potential supersoldiers. As such, these moves remove the potential soldier from the political economy of soldiering, from the processes and politics of enhancement and becoming. Reflections on transhumanism in a military sense become a kind of trauma-blocking drug at the national level, a way to ignore or forget where soldiers come from and why. When we think of enhanced soldiers as "supersoldiers," as soldiers always capable of heroic acts, we are thinking of them in the terms the military wants us to think of them as: capable of the seemingly impossible, no worse the wear for their service, as entities that came from a blank past and will return to an unproblematic personal future. We are to forget about it just as they are to forget about it and not question what they did or what was done "in our name." The soldier becomes a kind of unmarked "super" category that does not need to be debated or considered—they are above it all, above the fray in the worse way possible.

We want our soldiers to survive combat, and we are afraid of not giving them every form of protection and every kind of advantage on the battlefield that will allow them to survive in combat. But we are also afraid of what we might have to do to them in order to help them survive. The idea of soldiers with computer chips in their brains fills us with a certain kind of dread—while also serving as profitable clickbait because it is frightening and tantalizing—because we are stuck between wanting this and fearing it, finding it both cool and frightening, amazing and off-putting at the same time. This will demand a different notion of the "full measure of devotion": not of death but of the full commitment to a biomedical future possibly antithetical to our ideas of the human.

Armored Life

Advances in military medicine and military biotechnology make war much more survivable than it was even twenty years ago (Davis, Johnston, and Khalili 2018), but this increase in survivability leads some in various military and policy circles to the belief that war—at least for US soldiers—is somehow "clean" and almost nonlethal, a new kind of military ethics based on technological advances that promise certainty. These pharmacological and biotechnical "skin-in solutions" produce a kind of "armored life": biotechnology, psychopharmacology, and military medicine used not necessarily to restore or maintain the well-being of the soldier but to make the individual more effective in combat, and (theoretically) less of a burden in terms of medical and financial care after combat. It is a way of preventing experiences of trauma and preventing the causes of war trauma from having to be addressed after war and combat. It is also concerned with making war more easily tolerated by civilians, by creating soldiers who—at least theoretically—will have greater chances of surviving combat and injury. In this conception of soldiering, the natural resilience of the soldier is seen as insufficient and lacking. Only by reconfiguring the soldier internally can the soldier be made tough enough to withstand modern combat; the soldier will be made to fit the war. And through the portrayal, imagination, and deployment of these technologies and interventions, civilians may learn to accept and support what is done to the soldier in the name of survivability and protection. In this conception of the soldier, the health and armoring of the individual is analogous to the health and armoring of the state; the internally armored body of the soldier is the internally armored body politic. In essence, this dynamic is the medicalization of national security concerns, played out in and on the bodies of soldiers.

Performance enhancements might not promote boldness only in soldiers on the battlefield; they might also promote a kind of policy boldness as well, an enhanced politics and foreign policy. If successful, military performance enhancement technologies would allow for increased deployment: both by making the individual soldier more lethal and "protected" and by lowering the number of soldiers actually required. Universal conscription or a larger military means that war and combat become a concern for a higher number of families and friends; this raises concern and interest in what the military does with its members. A smaller, more lethal military enhances deployability while reducing accountability: the fewer people who are emotionally or politically connected to the military will reduce awareness or concern for military action. In other words, the fewer the soldiers, the less the risk of fallout on the "home front." Technology therefore allows for increased deployment, and makes warfare more politically palatable for civilians and easier to undertake for politicians, both by making the individual soldier more lethal and protected and by lowering the number of soldiers actually required. Of course, the recent wars in Iraq and Afghanistan, with deployment levels in the hundreds of thousands, and the concomitant costs and logistical strains, only serve to underline the desire for doing more with less.

The fundamental paradox of military performance enhancements is this: they might actually save soldiers' lives, but they might also make soldiers more easily deployable and thus increase the risk to their lives; you might be "kill-proof" for only so long. Soldiers who can operate effectively at sixteen thousand feet without going through months of acclimatization stand a better chance of surviving combat at those heights than the nonenhanced soldier. But that also makes it easier to deploy a soldier into those conditions and opens up the possibility of deployment into these environments without the exploration of nonmilitary solutions to a problem or a threat. If we believe our soldiers are somehow "kill-proof," why necessarily pursue a diplomatic solution to a problem when we might not have to worry about setbacks to military intervention? Environmental barriers to combat are no longer barriers but opportunities to exploit to best the enemy, but each new pharmacological battlefield is another new opportunity for soldiers to be killed and wounded.

Old Myths in New Syringes: The Once and Future Soldier-Hero

The US military's vision of the supersoldier—a biomedical chemical hero—is the desire to be the hero, to imagine yourself into a future where you can withstand and conquer all foes and threats. As Gorman sings the praises of the lone Objective Force Warrior, standing guard on the frontier, it is not too great of a leap of imagination to consider that he is imagining himself as the OFW soldier. "Be All That You Can Be" and "An Army of One" mean imagining yourself as more than you are: you can be the hero, and the military wants to help you imagine being that hero and help turn you into that hero. And by becoming that hero, you are the Force that ensures that no bad or ill can come to your homeland, your family, or yourself.

But superheroes need supervillains, or at least threats that imperil the very existence of the nation-state. As such, the supersoldier is always on watch, always anxious, always in a state of readiness. Because ontopower works at the level of preemption and the "unknown unknowns," it is always operative; as Massumi writes, "Even if a threat did not eventuate into an actual danger, it always could have, so preemptive action will always have been right. This is a tautological logic, but one that does not self-destruct. Instead, it produces: affective facts" (2015, 240). And because threats will always be there lurking in the new environment of war, they will require constant vigilance and response, and no enhancement will ever be good enough to stand up to the new and ever-increasing threats of the military imaginary. As General Schoomaker said of the Future Combat System, there is no end point, and in the logic of preemption, there can never be an end point, just constant beginnings and endless fractals of emergent threats.

The supersoldier brings this endless future anxiety—a certain sort of perpetual risk society—into the present, or at least an idea or "vision" into the future, where all conflict and threats are known, preemption is constant, and the soldier stands a constant, deathless watch. Biotechnology and psychopharmacology anchor the future in the present body of the soldier: "you might encounter X—we don't know, but you will encounter something—so these technologies will protect you when you do." The future soldier is designed and made in the present to protect against future threats conceived of in the present. It is a future made present through chemical compounds that change perceptions and understandings of time, the marking of time, what is possible in time, what can be remembered and recollected, recalled and analyzed, for the enhanced soldiers, the military, and civilians.

The military, perceiving and feeling the future to be one of myriad, unknown threats, produces the enhanced soldier as a biological affective fact. Failing to produce supersoldiers is to surrender the future; if you do not produce heroes, you lose the future to the fires others have set. The chemical hero is preemption personified—he can protect and defend against any and all future threats and is there to stand guard against a dangerous and unknown future, a future unknown except for the knowledge that it is dangerous: Buck Rogers and Captain America and the Future Force Warrior to the rescue, and always to the rescue, now and forevermore. It is an imagined future made present in the body of the soldier through the biomedical manipulation of the soldier's biology; and by anchoring it in biology, we make it both real and seem real. And through this manipulation of the soldier, anything becomes possible—even cheating death—and the supersoldier takes on the qualities of the superhero or the Jedi. Preemption is the Force: all-knowing, flowing in and through everyone. The net-centric power of the Future Force provides real-time intelligence to the soldier so that she can predict and preempt a threat before it has a chance to strike or occur. This, combined with the idiophylactic and skin-in "inner armor" protection afforded the soldier, makes them something more than the normal, average, soldier. Through this ability to interdict the future and survive, the supersoldier takes on the qualities of a superhero. You Are One with the Force.

Despite the plethora of allusions to Achilles one finds in analyses of soldiering, Achilles never existed. As the first supersoldier, Achilles was nothing but a dream, an illusion, a vision of the supersoldier, a mythic construction of the anxiety of anticipation and preemption. While Achilles is of course interesting and instructive to think about as the first enhanced soldier in Western thought, the US supersoldier will not be Achilles, or Gilgamesh, or Cú Chulainn, or Beowulf, or a Jedi Knight caught up in the strange techno-time-loop of Star Wars and medieval chivalry that some in the US military seem to imagine (and desire). As with all mythic representations of the supersoldier, they are a kind of wish/desire fulfillment—a cry for solace and succor against the terrors of war and killing—that in many ways recognize the horrors of war, the humanity of soldiers, and the fact that most people do not want to kill. We must draw on Achilles and superheroes to imagine and talk about new forms of war magic in the forms of military technology, killing, and death; imagining the superheroic is a way for civilians who are to become soldiers to imagine not having to think or worry about killing or being killed. It is a modern dream of perfect control and ultimate victory on the battlefield. It is a kind of biomedical war-magic as illusion (G. Jones 2017).

Military performance enhancements might create soldiers who can physically and mentally act like heroes or perform what might have been called pre-enhancement as "heroic," but they might not be seen as heroes, or at least heroes as we currently conceptualize them. If the concerns raised by bioethicists around enhancements and heroism are taken seriously, we might achieve a kind of performative heroism without the cultural component: in other words, they might be heroes in deed but not be seen as heroes. It will potentially be one Medal of Honor–worthy heroic act after another but with an asterisk, just as they used to designate US baseball players in the 1990s who broke countless records but who were suspected of using performance enhancing drugs at the same time. But will this really matter? Unlike fairness in sports, the military does not care about fairness on the battlefield when it is in our favor. Will the military actually care about cultural constructions of the hero, as long as soldiers are not weak and cowardly? Will enhancements call for and create new forms of heroism? As Pfaff writes: "If one does not experience fear, it makes no sense to reward one for displays of courage. While enhancing soldier survivability and lethality always makes moral sense, enhancing it to the point of near-invulnerability (or even the perception of invulnerability) will profoundly alter the warrior identity. Soldiers who experience neither risk nor sacrifice are not really soldiers as we conceive of them now and are likely better thought of as technicians than warriors" (2017, 69).

Pfaff is correct about supersoldiers as technicians, but the military will still imagine and portray enhanced soldiers as heroes. Conceived of through a blend of classical literature, science fiction, notions of the New Man, and the hypertechnical focus and fetishism of modern US military doctrine and research, the supersoldier appears as a kind of deathless figure, the autochthonous superhero rising up to protect the homeland from all threats, now and in the future. US supersoldiers are but our images of the eternal hero. And as the US military cancels, refines, and dreams up new images of the "future soldier," the myth goes on and on. Each iteration of the hero is the distillation of hopes and dreams of defense and security, each a kind of imagined form of anthropomorphized preemption, preemption made human, easily understandable, and, perhaps most importantly, lovable. For us, the supersoldier is our mythic hero, a hero we think we can make come to life through the technologies and the ontopower of biomedicine: we really can make a kill-proof Achilles, if only we understand and exploit and tease out the deepest secrets of the soldier's body. And unlike Thetis and Achilles, this time we will get it right. The promise of the US supersoldier is the promise of transcending the horrors of war: "The happy ending of the fairy tale, the myth, and the divine comedy of the soul, is to be read, not as a contradiction, but as a transcendence of the universal tragedy of man. The objective world remains what it was, but, because of a shift of emphasis within the subject, is beheld as though transformed. Where formerly life and death contended, now enduring being is made manifest" (Campbell 1973, 26).

Ultimately, supersoldier projects based on ideas of cowardice, weakness, and frailty force us to think about and question what we want from our soldiers and what we are willing to allow the military to do to them. By examining how the US military imagines future threats and imagines built-in solutions, we can see how the military simultaneously imagines the "component man" as natural coward and emergent chemical hero. To anticipate, preempt, and expunge cowardice is to imagine and try to bring into being a future of perfect war, of soldiers who are no longer the problem in war. In the new bio-imaginary of war, the pharmacological battlefield is a battlefield void of cowardice—at least on our side—and populated only by heroes. It would seem that we are returning to the old myths again.

Works Cited

Abramowitz, Sharon. 2017. "Epidemics (Especially Ebola)." *Annual Review of Anthropology* 46:421–45.

Adams, Bryn L. 2016. "The Next Generation of Synthetic Biology Chassis: Moving Synthetic Biology from the Laboratory to the Field." *ACS Synthetic Biology* 5 (12): 1328–30.

Adams, Vincanne, Michelle Murphy, and Adele Clarke. 2009. "Anticipation: Technoscience, Life, Affect, Temporality." *Subjectivity* 28 (1): 246–65.

Altman, Howard. 2014. "MacDill Matters: Iron Man Suit Out at SOCom, but New Innovations Still Needed for Commandos." *Tampa Bay Times*, February 12.

Anderson, Sulome. 2015. "These Are the People Making Captagon, the Drug ISIS Fighters Take to Feel 'Invincible.'" *New York Magazine*, December 9.

Annas, Catherine L., and George J. Annas. 2009. "Enhancing the Fighting Force: Medical Research on American Soldiers." *Journal of Contemporary Heath and Law Policy* 25 (2): 283–308.

Appel, J. M. 2009. "Is All Fair in Biological Warfare? The Controversy over Genetically Engineered Biological Weapons." *Journal of Medical Ethics* 35 (7): 429–32.

Archer, T. C. R. 1958. "Medical Problems of the Operational Infantry Soldier in Malaya." *Journal of the Royal Medical Corps* 104 (1): 1–13.

Armstrong, Robert E., Mark D. Drapeau, Cheryl A. Loeb, and James J. Valdes. 2010. *Bio-inspired Innovation and National Security*. Washington, DC: National Defense University Press.

"Army Medical Science and Technology Initiatives in Advanced Biotechnology Briefing." 2004. United States Department of Defense, Washington, DC.

Aronova, Elena. 2014. "Big Science and 'Big Science Studies' in the United States and the Soviet Union during the Cold War." In *Science and Technology in the Global Cold War*, edited by Naomi Oreskes and John Krige, 393–431. Cambridge, MA: MIT Press.

Arrington, Yolanda R. 2017. "Future Defense Scientists Take on Challenge of Synthetic Biology." *DoD News, Defense Media Activity*, May 4.

Asad, Talal. 1983. "Notes on Body Pain and Truth in Medieval Christian Ritual." *Economy and Society* 12 (3): 287–327.

Ashcroft, Richard Edmund. 2008. "Regulating Biomedical Enhancements in the Military." *American Journal of Bioethics* 2 (2): 47–49.

Association of the United States Army Magazine (AUSA). 2016. "1956 AUSA Story Is Inspiration for Mad Scientist Contest." November 29.

Austin, J. L. 1975. *How to Do Things With Words*. Cambridge, MA: Harvard University Press.

Bacevich, Andrew J. 2013. *Breach of Trust: How Americans Failed Their Soldiers and Their Country*. New York: Metropolitan Books.

Back, Les. 2015. "Why Everyday Life Matters: Class, Community, and Making Life Livable." *Sociology* 49 (5): 820–36.

Bailey, Beth. 2013. "Soldiering as Work: The All-Volunteer Force in the United States." In *Fighting for a Living: A Comparative History of Military Labour 1500–2000*, edited by Erik-Jan Zürcher, 581–612. Amsterdam: Amsterdam University Press.

Banzhaf, H. Spencer. 2014. "The Cold-War Origins of the Value of Statistical Life." *Journal of Economic Perspectives* 28 (4): 213–26.

Basulto, Dominic. 2015. "Trends in Synthetic Biology Include Military, Space Issues." *Washington Post*, October 8.

Beam, Thomas E. 2003. "Medical Ethics on the Battlefield: The Crucible of Military Medical Ethics." In *Military Medical Ethics*, vol. 2, edited by Thomas E. Beam and Linette R. Sparacino, 369–402. Falls Church, VA: Office of the Surgeon General, United States Army.

Beard, Matthew, Jai Gailliott, and Sandra Lynch. 2016. "Soldier Enhancement: Ethical Risks and Opportunities." *Australian Army Journal* 13 (1): 5–20.

Beidel, Eric. 2010. "Army Makes New Attempt to Field Networked Soldier System." *National Defense* 95 (683): 38–40.

Bell, Joshua A., Briel Kobak, Joel Kuipers, and Amanda Kemble. 2018. "Unseen Connections: The Materiality of Cell Phones." *Anthropological Quarterly* 91 (2): 464–84.

Ben-Ari, Eyal. 2005. "Docile Bodies, Pharmorgs and Military Knowledge: The Regulation of Sleep and Night-Time Combat in the American Army." *Paideuma* 51:165–79.

Benenson, Abram S. 1984. "Immunization and Military Medicine." *Reviews of Infectious Diseases* 6 (1): 1–12.

Ben-Ghiat, Ruth. 2004. *Fascist Modernities: Italy, 1922–1945*. Berkeley: University of California Press.

Benjamin, Walter. 1968. "The Work of Art in the Age of Mechanical Reproduction." In *Illuminations*, edited by Hannah Arendt, 217–52. New York: Schocken Books.

Benjamin, Walter. 2019. *The Storyteller Essays*. New York: New York Review of Books.

Bergen-Cico, Dessa K. 2012. *War and Drugs: The Role of Military Conflict in the Development of Substance Abuse*. Boulder, CO: Paradigm.

Berman, Marshall. 1975. *All That Is Solid Melts into Air: The Experience of Modernity*. New York: Penguin.

Besnier, Niko, and Susan Brownell. 2012. "Sport, Modernity, and the Body." *Annual Review of Anthropology* 41:443–59.

Bess, Michael D. 2008. "Icarus 2.0: A Historian's Perspective on Human Biological Enhancement." *Technology and Culture* 49 (1): 114–26.

Besteman, Catherine, and Hugh Gusterson. 2019. *Life by Algorithms: How Roboprocesses Are Remaking Our World.* Chicago: University of Chicago Press.

Bickford, Andrew. 2008. "Skin-in Solutions: Militarizing Medicine and Militarizing Culture in the United States Military." *North American Dialogue* 11 (1): 5–8.

Bickford, Andrew. 2010. "Triumph of the Pill: Armored Life, Biotechnology, and Health in the United States Military." Invited Keynote Talk, "Are Soldiers Human?" Workshop, the Humanitarian and Conflict Response Institute, the Post Structural Research and Thought Cluster, and the British International Studies Association Post-Structural Politics Group, University of Manchester, September 24.

Bickford, Andrew. 2011. *Fallen Elites: The Military Other in Post-Unification Germany.* Palo Alto, CA: Stanford University Press.

Bickford, Andrew. 2015. "Anthropology, the Anthropocene, and the Military." *EnviroSociety,* January 31. http://www.envirosociety.org/2015/01/anthropology-the -anthropocene-and-the-military.

Bickford, Andrew. 2018. "From Idiophylaxis to Inner Armor: Imagining the Self-Armoring Soldier in the United States Military from the 1960s to Today." *Comparative Studies in Society and History* 60 (4): 810–38.

Bigo, Didier. 2008. "Globalized (In)Security: The Field and the Ban-Opticon." In *Terror, Insecurity, and Liberty: Illiberal Practices of Liberal Regimes after 9/11,* edited by Didier Bigo and Anastassia Tsoukala, 10–48. New York: Routledge.

Biljan, Darko, Roman Pavić, and Mirna Šitum. 2008. "Dermatomycosis, Hyperhydrosis, and Mechanical Injury to Skin of the Feet in Croatian Soldiers during War in Croatia 1991–1992." *Military Medicine* 173 (8): 796–800.

Biro, Matthew. 1994. "The New Man as Cyborg: Figures of Technology in Weimar Visual Culture." *New German Critique,* no. 62 (Spring/Summer): 71–110.

Boldt, Joachim. 2014. "Synthetic Biology." In *Bioethics,* edited by Victor W. Sidel, 3051–57. 4th ed. Farmington Hills, MI: Macmillan Reference USA.

Bolton, Claude M., Jr. 2004. "ASA (ALT) Perspective: Military Medicine: Ready and Relevant." The Honorable Claude M. Bolton Jr., Assistant Secretary of the Army (Acquisition, Logistics and Technology) and Army Acquisition Executive, February 10.

Bonsignore, Ezio. 2009. "A Technology Too Far: 'Reviewing' (or Terminating?) the FCS Programme." *Military Technology* 33 (7): 12–14.

Boscagli, Maurizia. 1996. *Eye on the Flesh: Fashions of Masculinity in the Early Twentieth Century.* Boulder, CO: Westview Press.

Bourke, Johanna. 1999. *An Intimate History of Killing: Face-to-Face Killing in Twentieth-Century Warfare.* New York: Basic Books.

Brady, Jenna. 2016. "Game-Changing Synthetic Biology Research May Enable Future Capabilities for Soldiers." Army Research Laboratory, October 16.

Brandler, Philip. 2005. "The United States Army Future Force Warrior—An Integrated Human Centric System." In *Strategies to Maintain Combat Readiness* during *Extended Deployments—A Human Systems Approach*, KN-1–KN-12. Meeting Proceedings RTO-MP-HFM-124, keynote. Neuilly-sur-Seine, France: RTO.

Braudy, Leo. 2003. *From Chivalry to Terrorism: War and the Changing Nature of Masculinity*. New York: Knopf.

Braun, William G., III, Stéfanie von Hlatky, and Kim Richard Nossal. 2017. *Developing the Super Soldier: Enhancing Military Performance*. Carlisle, PA: Strategic Studies Institute, US Army War College.

Breede, H. Christian. 2017. "Capability and Connection: Social Cohesion and Soldier Performance Enhancement in Canada and the United States." In *Developing the Super Soldier: Enhancing Military Performance*, edited by William G. Braun III, Stéfanie von Hlatky, and Kim Richard Nossal, 7–27. Carlisle, PA: Strategic Studies Institute, US Army War College.

Brennan, Fred H., Cody R. Jackson, Cara Olsen, and Cindy Wilson. 2012. "Blisters on the Battlefield: The Prevalence of and Factors Associated with Foot Friction Blisters during Operation Iraqi Freedom." *Military Medicine* 177 (2): 157–62.

Brown, Mark B. 2009. *Science in Democracy: Expertise, Institutions, and Representation*. Cambridge, MA: MIT Press.

Brühl, Annette B., Camilia d'Angelo, and Barbara J. Sahakian. 2019. "Neuroethical Issues in Cognitive Enhancement: Modafinil as the Example of a Workplace Drug?" *Brain and Neuroscience Advances* 3:1–8.

Buchanan, Ian. 1997. "The Problem of the Body in Deleuze and Guattari, Or, What Can a Body Do?" *Body and Society* 3 (3): 73–91.

Buchner, Christina M. 2013. "Biologically Fit: Using Biotechnology to Create a Better Soldier." PhD diss., Naval Postgraduate School, Monterey, CA.

Buck-Morss, Susan. 1992. "Aesthetics and Anesthetics: Walter Benjamin's Artwork Essay Reconsidered." *October* 62 (Fall): 3–41.

Burchell, Mark. 2014. "Skillful Movements: The Evolving Commando." In *Bodies in Conflict: Corporeality, Materiality and Transformation*, edited by Paul Cornish and Nicholas J. Saunders, 208–18. Abingdon: Routledge.

Burgess, Jonathan. 1995. "Achilles Heel: The Death of Achilles in Ancient Myth." *Classical Antiquity* 14 (2): 217–44.

Büscher, Bram. 2018. "From Biopower to Ontopower? Violent Responses to Wildlife Crime and the New Geographies of Conservation." *Conservation and Society* 16 (2): 157–69.

Butts, W. K. 1942. "War: A Challenge to Biology." *Bios* 13 (4): 205–12.

Caduff, Carlo. 2008. "Anticipations of Biosecurity." In *Biosecurity Interventions: Global Health and Security in Question*, edited by Andrew Lakoff and Stephen Collier, 257–77. New York: Columbia University Press.

Caduff, Carlo. 2012. "The Semiotics of Security: Infectious Disease Research and the Biopolitics of Informational Bodies in the United States." *Cultural Anthropology* 27 (2): 333–57.

Caldwell, J. Lynn, and Dennis F. Shanahan. 1992. "Triazolam and Temazepam: Issues and Concerns Relevant to the Army Aviation Community." USAARL Report no. 92-23. Ft. Rucker, AL: US Army Aeromedical Research Library.

Caldwell, John A. 2008. "Go Pills in Combat: Prejudice, Propriety, and Practicality." *Air and Space Power Journal* 12 (3): 97–104.

Caldwell, John A., and J. Lynn Caldwell. 2005. "Fatigue in Military Aviation: An Overview of US Military-Approved Pharmacological Countermeasures." *Aviation, Space, and Environmental Medicine* 76 (7): c39–c51.

Callahan, Michael. 2007. "Inner Armor." DARPATech, DARPA's 25th Annual Systems and Technology Symposium, Teleprompter Script for Dr. Michael Callahan, Program Manager, Defense Sciences Office, August 7, 2007. Anaheim, CA.

Campbell, Joseph. 1973. *The Hero with a Thousand Faces*. Princeton, NJ: Princeton University Press.

Carey, Benedict, and Jennifer Steinhauer. 2019. "Veterans Agency to Offer New Depression Drug, despite Cost and Safety Concerns." *New York Times*, June 21.

Caron, Jean-François. 2018. *A Theory of the Super Soldier: The Morality of Capacity-Increasing Technologies in the Military*. Manchester, UK: Manchester University Press.

Cavanagh, S. A. 2018. "swj Factsheet: The Pharmaceutical Soldier—Performance Enhancing Drugs on the Battlefield—An Open Source Intelligence Study." *Small Wars Journal*. https://smallwarsjournal.com/jrnl/art/swj-factsheet-pharmaceutical -soldier-performance-enhancing-drugs-battlefield-open-source.

Channon, Jim. 1979. *The First Earth Battalion: Ideas and Ideals for Soldiers Everywhere*. Fort Monroe, VA: United States Army Training and Doctrine Command.

Chaput, Catherine. 2017. Review of *Ontopower: War, Powers, and the State of Perception*, by Brian Massumi. *International Journal of Communication* 11:2236–40.

Chen, Nancy N., and Lesley A. Sharp, eds. 2014. *Bioinsecurity and Vulnerability*. Santa Fe, NM: School for Advanced Research Press.

Cheng, Yinghong. 2009. *Creating the "New Man": From Enlightenment Ideals to Socialist Realities*. Honolulu: University of Hawai'i Press.

Cho, Renee. 2014. "How Climate Change Is Exacerbating the Spread of Disease." State of the Planet, Earth Institute, Columbia University, September 4. http://blogs.ei .columbia.edu/2014/09/04/how-climate-change-is-exacerbating-the-spread-of -disease/.

Christensen, Wendy M. 2016. "The Black Citizen-Subject: Black Single Mothers in US Military Recruitment Material." *Ethnic and Racial Studies* 39 (14): 2508–26.

Chua, Jocelyn Lim. 2018. "Fog of War: Psychopharmaceutical 'Side Effects' and the United States Military." *Medical Anthropology* 37 (1): 17–31.

Clarke, Adele E., Laura Mamo, Jennifer Ruth Fosket, Jennifer R. Fishman, and Janet K. Shim. 2010. "Biomedicalization: A Theoretical and Substantive Introduction." In *Biomedicalization: Technoscience, Health, and Illness in the US*, edited by Adele E. Clarke, Laura Mamo, Jennifer Ruth Fosket, Jennifer R. Fishman, and Janet K. Shim, 1–46. Durham, NC: Duke University Press.

Clausewitz, Carl von. 1976. *On War*. Edited and translated by Michael Howard and Peter Paret. Princeton, NJ: Princeton University Press.

Clynes, Manfred E., and Nathan S. Kline. 1960. "Cyborgs and Space." *Astronautics*, September 26–27, 74–76.

CNA Corporation. 2007. *National Security and the Threat of Climate Change.* Alexandria, VA: CNA Corporation.

Cohn, Carol. 1987. "Sex and Death in the Rational World of Defense Intellectuals." *Signs* 12 (4): 687–718.

Committee on Armed Services. 2008. *Military Readiness: Implications for Our Strategic Posture.* Hearing before the Committee on Armed Services, House of Representatives, One-Hundred-Tenth Congress, Second Session. Washington, DC: US Government Printing Office.

Committee on Foreign Affairs. 2008. *Genetics and Other Human Modification Technologies: Sensible International Regulation or a New Kind of Arms Race?* Hearing before the Subcommittee on Terrorism, Nonproliferation, and Trade. House of Representatives, One-Hundred-Tenth Congress, Second Session. Serial no. 110-201. Washington, DC: US Government Printing Office.

Committee on Strategies for Identifying and Addressing Potential Biodefense Vulnerabilities Posed by Synthetic Biology. 2018. *Biodefense in the Age of Synthetic Biology.* Washington, DC: National Academies Press.

Cory-Slechta, Deborah, and Roberta Wedge. 2016. *Gulf War and Health.* Vol. 10, *Update of Health Effects of Serving in the Gulf War.* Washington, DC: National Academies Press.

Courtwright, Andrew. 2014. "What We Talk about When We Talk about Performance Enhancement." *Virtual Mentor, American Medical Association Journal of Ethics* 16 (7): 543–46.

Cowdrey, Albert E. 1994. *Fighting for Life: American Military Medicine in World War II.* New York: Free Press.

Creager Angela N. H. 2014. "Atomic Tracings: Radioisotopes in Biology and Medicine." In *Science and Technology in the Global Cold War,* edited by Naomi Oreskes and John Krige, 31–73. Cambridge, MA: MIT Press.

Davis, Michael R., David S. Johnston, and Ramin A. Khalili. 2018. "Between Yesterday and Tomorrow." *Army AL&T* magazine, April–June.

Deakin, Stephen. 2014. "Naked Soldiers and the Principle of Discrimination." *Journal of Military Ethics* 13 (4): 320–30.

de Almeida, Maria Eneida. 2015. "The Permanent Relation between Biology, Power, and War: The Dual Use of the Biotechnological Development." *Ciênc. Saúde Coletiva* 20 (7).

DeBruyne, Nese F., and Anne Leland. 2015. *American War and Military Operations Casualties: Lists and Statistics.* Washington, DC: Congressional Research Service.

De Castro, Mauricio J., and Clesson E. Turner. 2017. "Military Genomics: A Perspective on the Successes and Challenges of Genomic Medicine in the Armed Forces." *Molecular Genetics and Genomic Medicine* 5 (6): 617–20.

Defense Advanced Research Projects Agency (DARPA). 2008. "The Feedback Regulated Automatic Molecular Release Program (FRAMR)." In *2008 DARPA Fact File: A Compendium of Programs,* 36–37. Accessed April 20, 2020. https://www.theblackvault.com/documentarchive/2008-darpa-fact-file-june-2008/.

DeLanda, Manuel. 1991. *War in the Age of Intelligent Machines*. New York: Swerve Editions.

Deleuze, Gilles. 1966. *Bergsonism*. New York: Zone.

Department of the Army. 1962. "Army Invites 500 Leaders to Biennial Science Conference." *Army Research and Development News Magazine* 3 (4): 1.

Department of the Army. 2015. "ATP 3-34.5/MCRP 4-11B Environmental Considerations." Washington, DC: Headquarters, Department of the Army.

Douglas, Robert, Wayne Downing, Marty Steele, Anthony Hyder, and Charles Otstott. 2001. "The Objective Force Soldier/Soldier Team." Army Science Board.

Dugan, Kerri. n.d. "Battlefield Medicine Program." Defense Advanced Research Projects Agency (DARPA). Accessed October 15, 2019. https://www.darpa.mil/program /battlefield-medicine.

Dumit, Joseph. 2012. *Drugs for Life: Growing Health through Facts and Pharmaceuticals*. Durham, NC: Duke University Press.

Dyvik, Synne L., and Lauren Greenwood. 2016. "Embodying Militarism: Exploring the Spaces and Bodies In-Between." *Critical Military Studies* 2 (1–2): 1–6.

Eagleton, Terry. 1989. "The Ideology of the Aesthetic." In *The Rhetoric of Interpretation and the Interpretation of Rhetoric*, edited by Paul Hernandi, 75–104. Durham, NC: Duke University Press.

Ebert, James R. 1993. *A Life in a Year: The American Infantryman in Vietnam, 1965–1972*. Novato, CA: Presidio Press.

Ebrey, Jill. 2016. "The Mundane and Insignificant, the Ordinary and the Extraordinary: Understanding Everyday Participation and Theories of Everyday Life." *Cultural Trends* 25 (3): 158–68.

Edwards, Brett. 2017. "We've Got to Talk: The Militarization of Biotechnology." *Bulletin of the Atomic Scientists*, August 4.

Edwards, Paul N. 1996. *The Closed World: Computers and the Politics of Discourse in Cold War America*. Cambridge, MA: MIT Press.

Eksteins, Modris. 2000. *The Rites of Spring: The Great War and the Birth of the Modern Age*. Boston: Houghton Mifflin.

Elsey, James, and Merel Kindt. 2016. "Manipulating Human Memory through Reconsolidation: Ethical Implications of a New Therapeutic Approach." *AJOB Neuroscience* 7 (4): 225–36.

Erickson, Paul, Judy L. Klein, Lorraine Daston, Rebecca Lemov, Thomas Sturm, and Michael D. Gordin. 2013. *How Reason Almost Lost Its Mind: The Strange Career of Cold War Rationality*. Chicago: University of Chicago Press.

Erwin, Sandra I. 2007. "Wrangling over Future Combat Systems Raises Larger Questions." *National Defense* 92 (644): 9.

Esposito, Roberto. 2008. *Bios: Biopolitics and Philosophy*. Minneapolis: University of Minnesota Press.

Esposito, Roberto. 2011. *Immunitas: The Protection and Negation of Life*. Cambridge, UK: Polity Press.

Evans, Nicholas G., and Jonathan D. Moreno. 2014. "Yesterday's War; Tomorrow's Technology: Peer Commentary on 'Ethical, Legal, Social, and Policy Issues in the Use of Genomic Technologies by the US Military.'" *Journal of Law and the Biosciences* 2 (1): 1–6.

Farren, Mick. 2010. *Speed-Speed-Speedfreak: A Fast History of Amphetamine*. Port Townsend, WA: Feral House.

Feickert, Andrew. 2005. "The Army's Future Combat System (FCS): Background and Issues for Congress." Congressional Research Service.

Feickert, Andrew. 2008. "The Army's Future Combat System (FCS): Background and Issues for Congress." Congressional Research Service.

Feickert, Andrew. 2009. "The Army's Future Combat System (FCS): Background and Issues for Congress." Congressional Research Service.

Feldman, Allen. 1994. "On Cultural Anesthesia: From Desert Storm to Rodney King." *American Ethnologist* 21 (2): 404–18.

Filkins, Dexter. 2009. *The Forever War*. New York: Vintage.

Finley, Erin P. 2011. *Fields of Combat: Understanding PTSD among Veterans of Iraq and Afghanistan*. Ithaca, NY: Cornell University Press.

Ford, Kenneth, and Clark Glymour. 2014. "The Enhanced Warfighter." *Bulletin of the Atomic Scientists* 70 (1): 43–53.

Foucault, Michel. 1979. *Discipline and Punish: The Birth of the Prison*. New York: Vintage.

Foucault, Michel. 1980. *The History of Sexuality, Volume 1*. New York: Vintage.

Foucault, Michel. 2003. *"Society Must Be Defended": Lectures at the Collège de France, 1975–1976*. New York: Picador.

Friedl, Karl E. 2005. "What Does Military Biomedical Research Contribute to Sustaining Soldier Performance in Cold Environments?" US Army Research Institute of Environmental Medicine Technical Note T07-13, December.

Friedl, Karl E. 2015. "US Army Research on Pharmacological Enhancement of Soldier Performance: Stimulants, Anabolic Hormones, and Blood Doping." *Journal of Strength and Conditioning Research* 29 (Suppl. 11): s71–s76.

Friedl, Karl E. 2018. "Military Applications of Soldier Physiological Monitoring." *Journal of Science and Medicine in Sport* 21 (11): 1147–53.

Friedl Karl E., and Jeffrey H. Allan. 2004. "USARIEM: Physiological Research for the Warfighter." United States Army Research Institute for Environmental Medicine, Natick, MA.

Friedl, Karl E., Stephen Grate, and Susan P. Proctor. 2009. "Neuropsychological Issues in Military Deployments: Lessons Observed in the DoD Gulf War Illnesses Research Program." *Military Medicine* 174 (4): 335–46.

Frisina, Michael E. 2003. "Medical Ethics in Military Biomedical Research." In *Military Medical Ethics*, vol. 2, edited by Thomas E. Beam and Linette R. Sparacino, 533–61. Falls Church, VA: Office of the Surgeon General, United States Army.

Fritz, Stephen G. 1996. "'We Are Trying . . . to Change the Face of the World':
Ideology and Motivation in the Wehrmacht on the Eastern Front: The View from
Below." *Journal of Military History* 60 (4): 683–710.

Fulco, Carolyn, Catharyn T. Liverman, and Harold C. Sox. 2000. "Depleted Uranium,
Sarin, Pyridostigmine Bromide, Vaccines." In *Institute of Medicine (US) Committee
on Health Effects Associated with Exposures during the Gulf War*, edited by Carolyn
Fulco, Catharyn T. Liverman, and Harold C. Sox, 207–66. Washington, DC:
National Academies Press.

Fussell, Paul. 1975. *The Great War and Modern Memory*. London: Oxford University Press.

"Future Combat Systems: Assault on Normandy." Promotional film. Accessed April 20,
2020. https://www.youtube.com/watch?v=X11K35lOWZE.

Gabriel, Richard A. 1987. *No More Heroes: Madness and Psychiatry in War*. New York:
Hill and Wang.

Gadamer, Hans-Georg. 1996. "Apologia for the Art of Healing." In *The Enigma of
Health*, 31–44. Stanford, CA: Stanford University Press.

Galliot, Jai, and Mianna Lotz, eds. 2015. *Super Soldiers: The Ethical, Legal, and Social
Implications*. Burlington, VT: Ashgate.

Garthwaite, Josie. 2016. "US Military Prepares for Gene Drives Run Amok." *Scientific
American*, November 18.

Gaydos, Steven J., Amanda M. Kelley, Catherine M. Grandizio, Jeremy R. Athy, and P.
Lynne Walters. 2015. "Comparison of the Effects of Ketamine and Morphine on
Performance of Representative Military Tasks." *Journal of Emergency Medicine*
48 (3): 313–24.

Gell, Alfred. 1988. *Art and Agency: An Anthropological Theory*. Oxford: Oxford
University Press.

Geroulanos, Stefanos, and Todd Meyers. 2018. *The Human Body in the Age of
Catastrophe: Brittleness, Integration, Science, and the Great War*. Chicago: University
of Chicago Press.

Giddens, Anthony. 1991. *Modernity and Self-Identity: Self and Society in the Late Modern
Age*. Stanford, CA: Stanford University Press.

Gillis, John R., ed. 1989. *The Militarization of the Western World*. New Brunswick, NJ:
Rutgers University Press.

Gilpin-Faust, Drew. 2008. *This Republic of Suffering: Death and the American Civil War*.
New York: Knopf.

Giordano, James. 2014. "Neurotechnology, Global Relations, and National Security:
Shifting Contexts and Neuroethical Demands." In *Neurotechnology in National
Security and Defense: Practical Considerations, Neuroethical Concerns*, edited by
James Giordano, 1–10. New York: CRC Press.

Glannon, Walter. 2006. "Psychopharmacology and Memory." *Journal of Medical Ethics*
32 (2): 74–78.

Global Defense. 2016. "The DoD and Synthetic Biology Milestones." *Global Defense*,
April 12.

GlobalSecurity.org. n.d. Objective Force Warrior (OFW). Accessed April 6, 2020. https://www.globalsecurity.org/military/systems/ground/ofw.htm.

GlobalSecurity.org. n.d. Future Force Warrior (FFW). Accessed April 6, 2020. https://www.globalsecurity.org/military/systems/ground/ffw-program.htm.

Goldsmith, Lowell A. 2003. "Remembering Marion Sulzberger, 1895–1983." *Journal of Investigative Dermatology* 121 (5): v.

Goldstein, Daniel. 2010. "Toward a Critical Anthropology of Security." *Current Anthropology* 51 (4): 487–517.

Gourley, Scott R. 2012. "Nett Warrior." *Army Magazine* (March): 81–82. https://www.ausa.org/sites/default/files/SA_0312.pdf

Gourley, Scott R. 2013a. "Nett Warrior: Mission." *Army Magazine* (June): 24–27. https://www.ausa.org/sites/default/files/Gourley1_June2013.pdf.

Gourley, Scott R. 2013b. "The Rise of the Soldier System." *Defense Media Network*, June 25.

Graeber, David. 2016. *The Utopia of Rules: On Technology, Stupidity, and the Secret Joys of Bureaucracy.* New York: Melville House.

Gray, Chris Hables. 1989. "The Cyborg Soldier: The US Military and the Post-Modern Warrior." In *Cyborg Worlds: The Military Information Society*, edited by Les Levidow and Kevin Robins, 43–71. London: Free Association Books.

Gray, Chris Hables. 1994. "'There Will Be War!': Future War Fantasies and Militaristic Science Fiction in the 1980s." *Science Fiction Studies* 21 (3): 315–36.

Gray, Chris Hables. 1997. *Postmodern War: The New Politics of Conflict.* New York: Guilford Press.

Greene, Marsha, and Zubin Master. 2018. "Ethical Issues of Using CRISPR Technologies for Research on Military Enhancement." *Bioethical Inquiry* 15 (3): 327–35.

Greenough, Paul, Christine Holmberg, and Stuart Blume. 2017. *The Politics of Vaccination: A Global History.* Manchester, UK: Manchester University Press.

Gross, Michael L. 2006. *Bioethics and Armed Conflict: Moral Dilemmas of Medicine and War.* Cambridge, MA: MIT Press.

Gross, Michael L., and Don Carrick. 2013. "Introduction." In *Military Medical Ethics for the 21st Century*, edited by Michael L. Gross and Don Carrick, 1–16. New York: Routledge.

Grosz, Elizabeth. 2006. "Naked." In *The Prosthetic Impulse: From a Posthuman Present to a Biocultural Future*, edited by Marquard Smith and Joanna Mora, 187–202. Cambridge: MIT Press.

Gumilev, Nikolai S. (1916) 1972. *Selected Works of Nikolai S. Gumilev.* Translated by Burton Raffel and Alla Burago. Albany: State University of New York Press.

Guo, Ji-Wei. 2006. "The Command of Biotechnology and Merciful Conquest." *Military Medicine* 171 (11): 1150–54.

Gusterson, Hugh. 1996. *Nuclear Rites: A Weapons Laboratory at the End of the Cold War.* Berkeley: University of California Press.

Gusterson, Hugh. 2016. *Drone: Remote Control Warfare.* Cambridge, MA: MIT Press.

Gusterson, Hugh, and Catherine Besteman. 2019. "Cultures of Militarism: An Introduction to Supplement 19." *Current Anthropology* 60 (Suppl. 19): s3–s14.

Hacking, Ian. 1999. *The Social Construction of What?* Cambridge, MA: Harvard University Press.

Hacking, Ian. 2002. *Historical Ontology.* Cambridge, MA: Harvard University Press.

Hafeneger, Benno, and Michael Fritz. 1993. *Sie starben für Führer, Volk, und Vaterland: Ein Lesebuch zur Kriegsbegeisterung junger Männer.* Vol. 3, *Die Hitlerjugend.* Frankfurt: Brandes and Apsel.

Hagopian, Patrick. 2011. *The Vietnam War in American Memory: Veterans, Memorials, and the Politics of Healing.* Amherst: University of Massachusetts Press.

Halvaksz, Jamon. 2016. "Supermythologies and Superenvironments." *EnviroSociety,* January 11. www.envirosociety.org/2016/01/supermythologies-and-superenvironments.

Hammes, Thomas X. 2010. "Biotech Impact on the Warfighter." In *Bio-inspired Innovation and National Security,* edited by Robert E. Armstrong, Mark D. Drapeau, Cheryl A. Loeb, and James J. Valdes, 1–7. Washington, DC: National Defense University Press.

Hardon, Anita, and Emilia Sanabria. 2017. "Fluid Drugs: Revisiting the Anthropology of Pharmaceuticals." *Annual Review of Anthropology* 46:117–32.

Harrison, Mark. 2010. *The Medical War: British Military Medicine in the First World War.* Oxford: Oxford University Press.

Haug, Wolfgang Fritz. 1986. *Critique of Commodity Aesthetics.* Cambridge, UK: Polity Press.

Hautzinger, Sarah, and Jean Scandlyn. 2014. *Beyond Post-traumatic Stress: Homefront Struggles with the Wars on Terror.* New York: Left Coast Press.

Hayden, Cori. 2007. "A Generic Solution? Pharmaceuticals and the Politics of the Similar in Mexico." *Current Anthropology* 48 (4): 475–95.

Hayden, Cori. 2012. "Population: A Chemical Device." In *Inventive Methods: The Happening of the Social,* edited by Celia Lury and Nina Wakeford, 172–184. London: Routledge.

Haynes, John. 2003. *New Soviet Man: Gender and Masculinity in Stalinist Soviet Cinema.* Manchester, UK: Manchester University Press.

Heath, Deborah, Rayna Rapp, and Karen-Sue Taussig. 2007. "Genetic Citizenship." In *A Companion to the Anthropology of Politics,* edited by David Nugent and Joan Vincent, 152–67. Malden, MA: Blackwell.

Henry, Michael, Jennifer R. Fishman, and Stuart J. Youngner. 2007. "Propranolol and the Prevention of Post-Traumatic Stress Disorder: Is it Wrong to Erase the 'Sting' of Bad Memories?" *American Journal of Bioethics* 7 (9): 12–20.

Herzfeld, Michael. 2001. *Anthropology: Theoretical Practice in Culture and Society.* Malden, MA: Blackwell.

Hoffman, Nancy Yanes. 1983. "Marion Sulzberger, M.D.: 'Mr. Dermatology.'" *Journal of the American Medical Association* 249 (10): 1243–49.

Hogle, Linda F. 2005. "Enhancement Technologies and the Body." *Annual Review of Anthropology* 34:695–716.

Howe, Edmund G. 1986. "Ethical Issues Regarding Mixed Agency of Military Physicians." *Social Science and Medicine* 23 (8): 803–15.

Howe, Edmund G. 2013. "Medical Education: Teaching Military Medical Ethics at the Uniformed Services University of the Health Sciences." In *Military Medical Ethics for the 21st Century*, edited by Michael L. Gross and Don Carrick, 279–96. New York: Routledge.

Howe, Edmund G., and Edward D. Martin. 1991. "Treating the Troops." *Hastings Center Report*, March–April.

Howell, Alison. 2014. "Resilience, War, and Austerity: The Ethics of Military Human Enhancement and the Politics of Data." *Security Dialogue*, November 7.

Howell, Alison. 2015. "Resilience as Enhancement: Governmentality and Political Economy beyond 'Responsibilisation.'" *Politics* 35 (1): 67–71.

Howell, Alison. 2017. "Neuroscience and War: Human Enhancement, Soldier Rehabilitation, and the Ethical Limits of Dual-Use Frameworks." *Millennium: Journal of International Studies* 45 (2): 133–50.

Huebner, Andrew J. 2008. *The Warrior Image: Soldiers in American Culture from the Second World War to the Vietnam Era.* Chapel Hill: University of North Carolina Press.

Hunter, John A. A., and Karl Holubar. 1984. "Sulzberger! Biography, Autobiography, Iconography: A Posthumous Festschrift." *American Journal of Dermapathology* 6 (4): 344–70.

Huyssen, Andreas. 1995. *Twilight Memories: Marking Time in a Culture of Amnesia.* New York: Routledge.

Jablonski, Nina. 2004. "The Evolution of Human Skin and Skin Color." *Annual Review of Anthropology* 33:585–623.

Jablonski, Nina. 2011. "Evolving Skin." Interview by Beth Herbert. *The Helix*, September 16.

Jacobsen, Annie. 2015. *The Pentagon's Brain: An Uncensored History of DARPA, America's Top-Secret Military Research Agency.* New York: Little, Brown.

Jancin, Bruce. 2019. "Single-Dose Propranolol Tied to 'Selective Erasure' of Anxiety Disorders." *Clinical Psychiatry News*, January 3.

Jarvis, Christina. 2004. *The Male Body at War: American Masculinity during World War II.* DeKalb: Northern Illinois University Press.

Jasanoff, Sheila. 2015. "Future Imperfect: Science, Technology, and the Imaginations of Modernity." In *Dreamscapes of Modernity: Sociotechnical Imaginaries and the Fabrication of Power*, edited by Sheila Jasanoff and Sang-Hyun Kim, 1–33. Chicago: University of Chicago Press.

Jasanoff, Sheila, and Sang-Hyun Kim, eds. 2015. *Dreamscapes of Modernity: Sociotechnical Imaginaries and the Fabrication of Power.* Chicago: University of Chicago Press.

JASON. 2008. *Human Performance.* McLean, VA: MITRE Corporation.

JASON. 2010. *The $100 Genome: Implications for the DoD.* McLean, VA: MITRE Corporation.

Jauregui, Beatrice. 2015. "World Fitness: US Army Family Humanism and the Positive Science of Persistent War." *Public Culture* 27 (3): 449–85.

Jenkins, Amy. n.d. In Vivo Nanoplatforms Program. Defense Advanced Research Projects Agency (DARPA). Accessed October 15, 2019. https://www.darpa.mil/program /in-vivo-nanoplatforms.

Jones, Ann. 2013. *They Were Soldiers: How the Wounded Return from America's Wars— The Untold Story*. Chicago: Haymarket Books.

Jones, Graham. 2014. "Secrecy." *Annual Review of Anthropology* 43:53–69.

Jones, Graham. 2017. *Magic's Reason: An Anthropology of Analogy*. Chicago: University of Chicago Press.

Juengst, Eric. 1998. "What Does *Enhancement* Mean?" In *Enhancing Human Traits: Ethical and Social Implications*, edited by Erik Parens, 29–47. Washington, DC: Georgetown University Press.

Jünger, Ernst. (1920) 2003. *Storm of Steel*. Translated by Michael Hofmann. London: Penguin Books.

Jünger, Ernst. (1922) 1994. "Fire." In *The Weimar Republic Sourcebook*, edited by Anton Kaes, Martin Jay, and Edward Dimendberg, 18–20. Berkeley: University of California Press.

Jünger, Ernst. (1922) 2012. *Der Kampf als inneres Erlebnis*. Berkeley: University of California Press.

Kahn, Jonathan. 2014. "Privatizing Biomedical Citizenship: Risk, Duty, and Potential in the Circle of Pharmaceutical Life." *Minnesota Journal of Law, Science, and Technology* 15 (2): 791–896.

Kamieński, Łukasz. 2012. "Helping the Postmodern Ajax: Is Managing Combat Trauma through Pharmacology a Faustian Bargain?" *Armed Forces and Society* 39 (3): 395–414.

Kamieński, Łukasz. 2016a. "The Drugs That Built a Super Soldier." *The Atlantic*, April 8.

Kamieński, Łukasz. 2016b. *Shooting Up: A Short History of Drugs and War*. Oxford: Oxford University Press.

Kan, Paul Rexton. 2009. *Drugs and Contemporary Warfare*. Dulles, VA: Potomac Books.

Kass, Leon. 2003. *Beyond Therapy: Biotechnology and the Pursuit of Happiness*. Washington, DC: President's Council on Bioethics.

Kelley, Amanda M., Catherine M. Webb, Jeremy R. Athy, Sanita Ley, and Steven Gaydos. 2010. "Cognition-Enhancing Drugs and Their Appropriateness for Aviation and Ground Troops: A Meta-Analysis." United States Army Aeromedical Research Laboratory, Warfighter Performance and Health Division.

Kelley, Amanda M., Catherine M. Webb, Jeremy R. Athy, Sanita Ley, and Steven Gaydos. 2012. "Cognition Enhancement by Modafinil: A Meta-Analysis." *Aviation, Space, and Environmental Medicine* 83 (7): 685–90.

Kelly, Catriona. 2016. "The New Soviet Man and Woman." In *The Oxford Handbook of Modern Russian History*, edited by Simon Dixon. Oxford: Oxford University Press.

Kelly, S. H. 1996. "The Common Thread for 30 Years: Taking Care of Soldiers." *NCO Journal* 6 (4): 10–16.

Killion, Thomas H., Stephen J. Bury, Rene de Pontbriand, and James Belanich. 2009. "United States Army Science and Technology: Sustaining Soldier Performance." *Military Psychology* 21 (1): S9–S22.

King, James. 2017. "The Overweight Infantryman." *Modern War Institute at West Point*, January 10.

Kinzer, Stephen. 2019. *Poisoner in Chief: Sidney Gottlieb and the CIA Search for Mind Control*. New York: Henry Holt.

Knickerbocker, Brad. 2002. "Military Looks to Drugs for Battle Readiness." *Christian Science Monitor*, August 9.

Kohn, Richard. 2009. "The Danger of Militarization in an Endless 'War' on Terrorism." *Journal of Military History* 73 (1): 177–208.

Kostadinov, Rostislav. 2009. "Medical Intelligence as a Tool Enhancing Situational Awareness." NATO RTO-MP-HFM-181.

Krishnan, Armin. 2018. *Military Neuroscience and the Coming Age of Neurowarfare*. New York: Routledge.

Kuiken, Todd. 2017. "DARPA's Synthetic Biology Initiatives Could Militarize the Environment." *Future Tense*, May 3.

Lakoff, Andrew. 2015. "Global Health Security and the Pathogenic Imaginary." In *Dreamscapes of Modernity: Sociotechnical Imaginaries and the Fabrication of Power*, edited by Sheila Jasanoff and Sang-Hyun Kim, 300–320. Chicago: University of Chicago Press.

Lakoff, Andrew. 2017. *Unprepared: Global Health in a Time of Emergency*. Berkeley: University of California Press.

Lakoff, Andrew, and Stephen J. Collier. 2008. *Biosecurity Interventions: Global Health and Security in Question*. New York: Columbia University Press.

Landsberg, Alison. 2004. *Prosthetic Memories: The Transformation of American Remembrance in the Age of Mass Culture*. New York: Columbia University Press.

Latiff, Robert H. 2017. *Future War: Preparing for the New Global Battlefield*. New York: Knopf.

Latour, Bruno. 1992. "Where Are the Missing Masses? The Sociology of a Few Mundane Artifacts." In *Shaping Technology / Building Society: Studies in Sociotechnical Change*, edited by Wiebe E. Bijker and John Law, 225–58. Cambridge, MA: MIT Press.

Latour, Bruno. 1994. *The Pasteurization of France*. Cambridge, MA: Harvard University Press.

Leder, Drew. 1990. *The Absent Body*. Chicago: University of Chicago Press.

Lederer, Susan E. 2003. "The Cold War and Beyond: Covert and Deceptive American Medical Experimentation." In *Military Medical Ethics*, vol. 2, edited by Thomas E. Beam and Linette R. Sparacino, 507–31. Falls Church, VA: Office of the Surgeon General, United States Army.

Lentzos, Filippa. 2015. "Synthetic Biology's Defense Dollars: Signals and Perceptions." *Center for Genetic and Society* (blog), December 24. https://www.geneticsandsociety.org/article/synthetic-biologys-defense-dollars-signals-and-perceptions.

Lin, Patrick, Maxwell Mehlman, and Keith Abney. 2013. "Enhanced Warfighters: Risk, Ethics, Policy." Report prepared for the Greenwall Foundation, California Polytechnic State University, San Luis Obispo, CA.

Lin, Patrick, Max Mehlman, Keith Abney, Shannon French, Shannon Vallor, Jai Galliott, Michael Burnam-Fink, Alexander R. LaCroix, and Seth Schuknecht. 2014. "Super Soldiers: The Ethical, Legal and Operational Implications (Part 2)." In *Global Issues and Ethical Considerations in Human Enhancement Technologies*, edited by Steven J. Thompson, 139–60. Hershey, PA: IGI Global.

Lin, Patrick, Max Mehlman, Keith Abney, and Jai Galliot. 2014. "Super Soldiers: What Is Military Human Enhancement? (Part 1)." In *Global Issues and Ethical Considerations in Human Enhancement Technologies*, edited by Steven J. Thompson, 119–38. Hershey, PA: IGI Global.

Linke, Uli. 1998. *German Bodies: Race and Representation after Hitler*. New York: Routledge.

Lo, Chris. 2014. "Blue Angel: DARPA's Vaccine Manufacturing Challenge." *Pharmaceutical Technology*, February.

Lutz, Catherine. 2007. "Militarization." In *A Companion to the Anthropology of Politics*, edited by David Nugent and Joan Vincent, 318–31. Malden, MA: Blackwell.

Lutz, Catherine. 2009. "The Military Normal: Feeling at Home with Counterinsurgency in the United States." In *The Counter-Counterinsurgency Manual*, edited by the Network of Concerned Anthropologists, 23–38. Chicago: Prickly Paradigm Press.

MacKee, George Miller. 1955. "Dr. Marion B. Sulzberger." *Journal of Investigative Dermatology* 24:141–42.

MacLeish, Kenneth. 2012. "Armor and Anesthesia: Exposure, Feeling, and the Soldier's Body." *Medical Anthropology Quarterly* 26 (1): 49–68.

MacLeish, Kenneth. 2015. *Making War at Fort Hood: Life and Uncertainty in a Military Community*. Princeton, NJ: Princeton University Press.

Mailer, Norman. 1948. *The Naked and the Dead*. New York: Holt, Rinehart and Winston.

Malet, David. 2016. *Biotechnology and International Security*. New York: Rowman and Littlefield.

Malinowski, Bronisław. 2014. *Argonauts of the Western Pacific*. New York: Routledge.

Mangan, James A. 1999. *Shaping the Superman: Fascist Body as Political Icon*. Vol. 1, *Aryan Fascism*. New York: Routledge.

Mann, Michael. 2004. *Fascists*. Cambridge: Cambridge University Press.

Manzocco, Roberto. 2019. *Transhumanism: Engineering the Human Condition*. Chichester, UK: Praxis Publishing.

Maradin, Nicholas R., III. 2013. "Militainment and Mechatronics: *Occultatio* and the Veil of Science Fiction Cool in United States Air Force Advertisements." *Ethics and Information Technology* 15 (2): 77–86.

Marinetti, Filippo Tommaso. 1971. *Marinetti: Selected Writings*, edited by R. W. Flint. New York: Farrar, Straus and Giroux.

Martinez-Lopez, Lester. 2004. "Biotechnology Enablers for the Soldier System of Systems." *The Bridge: Linking Engineering and Society* 34 (3): 17–25.

Marzec, Robert P. 2015. *Militarizing the Environment: Climate Change and the Security State*. Minneapolis: University of Minnesota Press.

Masco, Joseph. 2006. *The Nuclear Borderlands: The Manhattan Project in Post–Cold War New Mexico*. Princeton, NJ: Princeton University Press.

Masco, Joseph. 2014. *The Theater of Operations: National Security Affect from the Cold War to the War on Terror*. Durham, NC: Duke University Press.

Massumi, Brian. 2014. *What Animals Teach Us about Politics*. Durham, NC: Duke University Press.

Massumi, Brian. 2015. *Ontopower: War, Powers, and the State of Perception*. Durham, NC: Duke University Press.

Mbembe, Achille. 2003. "Necropolitics." *Public Culture* 15 (1): 11–40.

McCallum, Claire E. 2018. *The Fate of the New Man: Representing and Reconstructing Masculinity in Soviet Visual Culture, 1945–1965*. DeKalb: Northern Illinois University Press.

McElya, Micki. 2016. *The Politics of Mourning: Death and Honor in Arlington National Cemetery*. Cambridge, MA: Harvard University Press.

McManus, John, Sumeru G. Mehta, Annette R. McClinton, Robert A. De Lorenzo, and Toney W. Baskin. 2005. "Informed Consent and Ethical Issues in Military Medical Research." *Academic Emergency Medicine* 12 (11): 1120–26.

McNeill, J. R. 2010. *Mosquito Empires: Ecology and War in the Greater Caribbean, 1620–1914*. Cambridge: Cambridge University Press.

McSorley, Kevin. 2012. "Doing Military Fitness: Physical Culture, Civilian Leisure, and Militarism." *Critical Military Studies* 2 (1–2): 103–19.

McSorley, Kevin. 2014. "Towards an Embodied Sociology of War." *Sociological Review* 62 (Suppl. 2): S107–S28.

Mehlman, Maxwell J. 2004. "Cognition Enhancing Drugs." *Milbank Quarterly* 82 (3): 483–506.

Mehlman, Maxwell J. 2012. *Transhumanist Dreams and Dystopian Nightmares: The Promise and Peril of Genetic Engineering*. Baltimore: Johns Hopkins University Press.

Mehlman, Maxwell J. 2014. "Soldier Enhancement." In *Bioethics*, edited by Victor W. Sidel, 3176–79. 4th ed. Farmington Hills, MI: Macmillan Reference USA.

Mehlman, Maxwell J., and Stephanie Corley. 2014. "A Framework for Military Bioethics." *Journal of Military Ethics* 13 (4): 331–49.

Mehlman, Maxwell J., and Tracy Yeheng Li. 2014. "Ethical, Legal, Social, and Policy Issues in the Use of Genomic Technology by the US Military." *Journal of Law and the Biosciences* 1 (3): 244–80.

Mehlman, Maxwell J., Patrick Lin, and Keith Abney. 2013. "Enhanced Warfighters: A Policy Framework." In *Military Medical Ethics for the 21st Century*, edited by Michael L. Gross and Don Carrick, 113–26. New York: Routledge.

Mereu, Maddelena, Antonello Bonci, Amy Hauck Newman, and Gianluigi Tanda. 2013. "The Neurobiology of Modafinil as an Enhancer of Cognitive Performance and a Potential Treatment for Substance Abuse Disorders." *Psychopharmacology (Berl)* 229 (3): 415–34.

Messelken, Daniel, and Hans Ulrich Baer. 2013. "Hovering between Roles: Military Medical Ethics." In *Military Medical Ethics for the 21st Century*, edited by Michael L. Gross and Don Carrick, 261–78. New York: Routledge.

Messinger, Seth. 2010. "Getting Past the Accident: Explosive Devices, Limb Loss, and Refashioning a Life in a Military Medical Center." *Medical Anthropology Quarterly* 24 (3): 281–303.

Military Technology. 2006. "Army's 'Future Force Warrior' Passes Major Milestone." *Military Technology* 30 (10): 102–3.

Miller, Clark A. 2015. "Globalizing Security: Science and the Transformation of Contemporary Political Imagination." In *Dreamscapes of Modernity: Sociotechnical Imaginaries and the Fabrication of Power*, edited by Sheila Jasanoff and Sang-Hyun Kim, 277–99. Chicago: University of Chicago Press.

Moreno, Jonathan D. 2012. *Mind Wars: Brain Science and the Military in the 21st Century*. New York: Bellevue Literary Press.

Morgan, Charles A., Sheila Wang, Steven M. Southwick, Ann Rasmusson, Gary Hazlett, Richard L. Hauger, and Dennis S. Charney. 2000. "Plasma Neuropeptide-Y Concentrations in Humans Exposed to Military Survival Training." *Biological Psychiatry* 47 (10): 902–9.

Mosse, George. 1990. "The Political Culture of Italian Futurism: A General Perspective." *Journal of Contemporary History* 25 (2/3): 252–68.

Mosse, George. 1996a. "Fascist Aesthetics and Society: Some Considerations." In "The Aesthetics of Fascism," special issue, *Journal of Contemporary History* 31 (2): 245–52.

Mosse, George. 1996b. *The Image of Man: The Creation of Modern Masculinity*. New York: Oxford University Press.

Mukunda, Gautam, Kenneth A. Oye, and Scott C. Mohr. 2009. "What Rough Beast? Synthetic Biology, Uncertainty, and the Future of Biosecurity." *Politics and Life Sciences* 28 (2): 2–26.

Murray, Thomas H. 2008. "Sports Enhancement." In *From Birth to Death and Bench to Clinic: The Hastings Center Bioethics Briefing Book for Journalists, Policymakers, and Campaigns*, edited by Mary Crowley, 153–58. Garrison, NY: Hastings Center.

Nail, Thomas. 2017. "What Is an Assemblage?" *SubStance* 46 (1): 21–37.

Nardulli, Bruce R., and Thomas L. McNaugher. 2002. "The Army: Toward the Objective Force." In *Transforming America's Military*, edited by Hans Binnendijk, 101–28. Washington, DC: National Defense University Press.

National Human Genome Research Institute (NHGRI). n.d. Accessed April 8, 2020, https://www.genome.gov.

National Research Council. 2001. *Opportunities in Biotechnology for Future Army Applications*. Washington, DC: National Academies Press.

National Research Council. 2008. *Emerging Cognitive Neuroscience and Related Technologies*. Washington, DC: National Academies Press.

National Security Directorate, Oak Ridge National Laboratory. 2001. *Objective Force Warrior: "Another Look—The Art of the Possible . . . A Vision."* Report prepared for the Deputy Assistant Secretary of the Army (Research and Technology), December.

New Scientist. 1991. "Drugged Troops Could Soldier on without Sleep." February 9, 18.

New Scientist. 2003. "Molecular Secrets of Special Forces Toughness." February 18, 17.

Nguyen, Viet Thanh. 2017. *Nothing Ever Dies: Vietnam and the Memory of War*. Cambridge, MA: Harvard University Press.

Niler, Eric. 2017. "The Pentagon Ponders the Threat of Synthetic Bioweapons." *Wired*, July 10.

Niruthan, Nilanthan. 2018. "Beyond Human: Rise of the Super-Soldier—A Primer." *Small Wars Journal*, August 27. https://smallwarsjournal.com/jrnl/art/beyond-human-rise-super-soldiers-primer.

Norris, Robin. 2007. "Mourning Rights: *Beowulf*, the *Iliad*, and the War in Iraq." *Journal of Narrative Theory* 37 (2): 276–95.

Ohler, Norman. 2017. *Blitzed: Drugs in the Third Reich*. New York: Houghton Mifflin Harcourt.

Ohnuki-Tierney, Emiko. 2002. *Kamikazes, Cherry Blossoms, and Nationalisms: The Militarization of Aesthetics in Japanese History*. Chicago: University of Chicago Press.

Oreskes, Naomi. 2014. Introduction to *Science and Technology in the Global Cold War*, edited by Naomi Oreskes and John Krige, 11–30. Cambridge, MA: MIT Press.

Orr, Jackie. 2004. "The Militarization of Inner Space." *Critical Sociology* 30 (2): 451–81.

Outram, Simon. 2013. "Discourses of Performance Enhancement: Can We Separate Performance Enhancement from Performance Enhancing Drug Use?" *Performance Enhancement and Health* 2 (3): 94–100.

Parasidis, Efthimios. 2016. "The Military Biomedical Complex: Are Service Members a Vulnerable Population?" *Houston Journal of Health Law and Policy* 16:113–61.

Pearn, John. 2000. "Medical Ethics Surveillance in the Armed Forces." *Military Medicine* 165 (5): 351–54.

Pearn, John. 2004. "Civilian Legacies of Army Health." *Health and History* 6 (2): 4–17.

Pellerin, Cheryl. 2014. "Medical Research Institute Contributes to Vaccine Development Effort." US Department of Defense, *DoD News*, October 28.

Peltier, Chad, and Kyle Pettijohn. 2018. "The Future of Steroids for Performance Enhancement in the US Military." *Military Medicine* 183 (7/8): 151–53.

Perez, Gina. 2006. "How a Scholarship Girl Becomes a Soldier: The Militarization of Latina/o Youth in Chicago Public Schools." *Identities* 13 (1): 53–72.

Perkins, Edward J., and Jeffrey A. Steevens. 2015. "Future Applications of Biotechnology." *Small Wars Journal*. http://smallwarsjournal.com/jrnl/art/future-applications-of-biotechnology.

Pernin, Christopher G., Elliot Axelband, Jeffrey A. Drezner, Brian B. Dille, John Gordon IV, Bruce J. Held, K. Scott McMahon, Walter L. Perry, Christopher Rizzi, Akhil R. Shah, Peter A. Wilson, and Jerry M. Sollinger. 2012. *Lessons from the Army's Future Combat Systems Program*. Santa Monica, CA: RAND.

Petraeus, General David H., and General James F. Amos, USMC. 2009. *U.S. Army and U.S. Marine Corps Counterinsurgency Field Manual.* Kissimmee, FL: Signalman Press.

Petryna, Adriana. 2003. *Life Exposed: Biological Citizenship after Chernobyl.* Princeton, NJ: Princeton University Press.

Petryna, Adriana, Andrew Lakoff, and Arthur Kleinman, eds. 2006. *Global Pharmaceuticals: Ethics, Markets, Practices.* Durham, NC: Duke University Press.

Pfaff, C. Anthony. 2017. "Moral Autonomy and the Ethics of Soldier Enhancement." In *Developing the Super Soldier: Enhancing Military Performance*, edited by William G. Braun III, Stéfanie von Hlatky, and Kim Richard Nossal, 65–80. Carlisle, PA: Strategic Studies Institute, US Army War College.

Picano, James J. 2017. "Soldier Resilience: Lessons Learned from the Assessment and Selection of High-Risk Operational Personnel." In *Developing the Super Soldier: Enhancing Military Performance*, edited by William G. Braun III, Stéfanie von Hlatky, and Kim Richard Nossal, 47–64. Carlisle, PA: Strategic Studies Institute, US Army War College.

Piehler, G. Kurt. 1995. *Remembering War the American Way.* Washington, DC: Smithsonian Institution Press.

Poggi, Christine. 2009. *Inventing Futurism: The Art and Politics of Artificial Optimism.* Princeton, NJ: Princeton University Press.

Poggi, Christine. 2014. "Science in the Origins of the Cold War." In *Science and Technology in the Global Cold War*, edited by Naomi Oreskes and John Krige, 11–30. Cambridge, MA: MIT Press.

Povinelli, Elizabeth A. 2011. *Economies of Abandonment: Social Belonging and Endurance in Late Liberalism.* Durham, NC: Duke University Press.

Price, David. 2013. *Anthropology and Militarism.* Oxford: Oxford University Press.

Pugh, James. 2017. "'Not Like a Rum-Ration': Amphetamine Sulphate, the Royal Navy, and the Evolution of Policy and Medical Research during the Second World War." *War in History* 24 (2): 498–519.

Rabinbach, Anson. 1992. *The Human Motor: Energy, Fatigue, and the Origins of Modernity.* Berkeley: University of California Press.

Rabinow, Paul. 1996. "Artificiality and Enlightenment: From Sociobiology to Biosociality." In *Essays on the Anthropology of Reason*, 91–111. Princeton, NJ: Princeton University Press.

Rabinow, Paul, and Gaymon Bennett. 2009. "Synthetic Biology: Ethical Ramifications 2009." *Systems and Synthetic Biology* 3 (1–4): 99–108.

Radin, Joanna. 2017. *Life on Ice: A History of New Uses for Cold Blood.* Chicago: University of Chicago Press.

Rardin, Donald R., Thomas R. Lawson, and John A. Rush Jr. 1973. "Drug Use by American Soldiers in Europe." *Social Work* 18 (1): 34–41.

Rasmussen, Nicolas. 2011. "The Allies' Use of Amphetamine during World War II." *Journal of Interdisciplinary History* 42 (2) 205–33.

Regalado, Antonio. 2018. "US Military Wants to Know What Synthetic Biology Weapons Could Look Like." *MIT Technology Review*, June 19.

Rainey, Lawrence, Christine Poggi, and Laura Wittman. 2009. *Futurism: An Anthology.* New Haven, CT: Yale University Press.

Revision Military. 2015. "Exoskeleton Integrated Soldier Protection System." Accessed April 8, 2020. https://www.youtube.com/watch?v=RKcqHaPhkkM.

Rheinberger, Hans-Jörg. 2017. "Cultures of Experimentation." In *Cultures without Culturalism: The Making of Scientific Knowledge,* edited by Karine Chemla and Evelyn Fox Keller, 276–95. Durham, NC: Duke University Press.

Rigg, Robert B. 1956. "Soldier of the Futurarmy." *Army,* November, 25–37.

Rigg, Robert B. 1958. *War—1974.* Harrisburg, PA: Military Service Publishing.

Robbins, Lauren R. 2013. "Refusing to Be All That You Can Be: Regulating against Forced Cognitive Enhancement in the Military." In *Military Medical Ethics for the 21st Century,* edited by Michael L. Gross and Don Carrick, 127–38. New York: Routledge.

Robin, Ron. 2001. *The Making of the Cold War Enemy: Culture and the Military-Intellectual Complex.* Princeton, NJ: Princeton University Press.

Robson. Sean. 2014. *Psychological Fitness and Resilience: A Review of Relevant Constructs, Measures, and Links to Well-Being.* Santa Monica, CA: RAND.

Romano, James Jr., Colonel. 2004. "Army Medical Sciences and Technology Initiatives in Advanced Biotechnology." Roundtable for Bio-Supported Products and Systems for National Defense, Durham, NC, September 16–17, 2004.

Ronson, Jon. 2009. *The Men Who Stare at Goats.* New York: Simon and Schuster.

Rose, Nikolas. 2007. *The Politics of Life Itself: Biomedicine, Power, and Subjectivity in the Twenty-First Century.* Princeton, NJ: Princeton University Press.

Rose, Nikolas, and Carlos Novas. 2005. "Biological Citizenship." In *Global Assemblages: Technology, Politics and Ethics as Anthropological Problems,* edited by Aihwa Ong and Stephen Collier, 439–63. Malden, MA: Blackwell.

Sabban, Esther L., and Lidia I. Serova. 2018. "Potential of Intranasal Neuropeptide Y (NPY) and/or Melanocortin 4 Receptor (MC4R) Antagonists for Preventing or Treating PTSD." *Military Medicine* 183 (Suppl. 1): s408–s12.

Saletan, William. 2013. "The War on Sleep: There's a Military Arms Race to Build Soldiers Who Fight without Fatigue." *Slate,* May 29.

Sartin, Jeffery S. 1993. "Infectious Diseases during the Civil War: The Triumph of the Third Army." *Clinical Infectious Diseases* 16 (4): 580–84.

Scarry, Elaine. 1985. *The Body in Pain: The Making and Unmaking of the World.* Oxford: Oxford University Press.

Schachtman, Noah. 2007. "'Kill Proof,' Animal-Esque Soldiers: DARPA Goal." *Wired,* August 7. https://www.wired.com/2007/08/darpa-the-penta/.

Schachtman, Noah. 2009. "The Army's New Land Warrior Gear: Why Soldiers Don't Like It." *Popular Mechanics,* October 1. https://www.popularmechanics.com /military/a1590/4215715/.

Scharre, Paul. 2018. *An Army of None: Autonomous Weapons and the Future of War.* New York: Norton.

Scharre, Paul, and Lauren Fish. 2018. "Human Performance Enhancement." Center for a New American Century, November 7. https://www.cnas.org/publications /reports/human-performance-enhancement-1.

Scharre, Paul, Lauren Fish, Katherine Kidder, and Amy Schafer. 2018. "Emerging Technologies." Center for a New American Century, October 23. https://www.cnas.org/publications/reports/emerging-technologies-1.

Schivelbusch, Wolfgang. 1992. *Tastes of Paradise: A Social History of Spices, Stimulants, and Intoxicants.* New York: Vintage.

Schneider, Angela J. 2004. "Sports, Bioethics of." In *Bioethics*, edited by Stephen G. Post, 2461–69. 3rd ed. New York: Macmillan Reference.

Scott, James C. 1998. *Seeing Like a State: How Certain Schemes to Improve the Human Condition Have Failed.* New Haven: Yale University Press.

Seck, Hope Hodge. 2017. "Super SEALS: Elite Units Pursue Brain-Stimulating Technologies." Military.com, April 2. https://www.military.com/daily-news/2017/04/02/super-seals-elite-units-pursue-brain-stimulating-technologies.html.

Segel, Harold B. 1998. *Body Ascendant: Modernism and the Physical Imperative.* Baltimore: Johns Hopkins University Press.

Shabro, Luke, and Allison Winer. 2018. "U.S. Army Mad Scientist Sci-Fi Stories." *Small Wars Journal.* https://smallwarsjournal.com/jrnl/art/us-army-tradoc-mad-scientist-sci-fi-stories.

Shapiro, Nicholas, and Eben Kirksey. 2017. "Chemo-Ethnography: An Introduction." *Cultural Anthropology* 32 (4): 481–93.

Shaughnessy, Larry. 2012. "One Soldier, One Year: $850,000 and Rising." *CNN Security Clearance* (blog), February 28. http://security.blogs.cnn.com/2012/02/28/one-soldier-one-year-850000-and-rising/.

Shay, Jonathan. 1995. *Achilles in Vietnam: Combat Trauma and the Undoing of Character.* New York: Simon and Schuster.

Sheehan, Paul. n.d. Biological Control Program. Defense Advanced Research Projects Agency (DARPA). Accessed October 20, 2019. https://www.darpa.mil/biological-control.

Sherman, Nancy. 2015. *Afterwar: Healing the Moral Wounds of Our Soldiers.* Oxford: Oxford University Press.

Shils, Edward. 1962. "Minerva [Editorial]." *Minerva* 1 (1): 5–17.

Shils, Edward. 1972. "Minerva: The Past Decade and the Next." *Minerva* 10 (1): 1–9.

Shinseki, Eric K. 2001. *Concepts for the Objective Force.* US Army White Paper. Washington, DC: United States Government Printing Office.

Si, Tong, and Huimin Zhao. 2016. "A Brief Overview of Synthetic Biology Research Programs and Roadmap of Studies in the United States." *Synthetic and Systems Biotechnology* 1 (4): 258–64.

Sidel, Victor W., and Barry S. Levy. 2004. "Physician-Soldier: A Moral Dilemma?" In *Textbooks of Military Medicine: Military Medical Ethics*, vol. 1, edited by Edmund D. Pelegrino, Anthony E. Hartle, Edmund G. Howe, and Walter Reed, 293–329. Falls Church, VA: Office of The Surgeon General Department of the Army.

Sidel, Victor W., and Barry S. Levy. 2014a. "Chemical and Biological Weapons." In *Bioethics*, edited by Victor W. Sidel, 3169–76. 4th ed. Farmington Hills, MI: Macmillan Reference USA.

Sidel, Victor W., and Barry S. Levy. 2014b. "Medicine and War." In *Bioethics*, edited by Victor W. Sidel, 3159–65. 4th ed. Farmington Hills, MI: Macmillan Reference USA.

Simmons, Angela, and Linda Yoder. 2013. "Military Resilience: A Concept Analysis." *Nursing Forum* 48 (1): 17–25.

Sinclair, Robert R., and Thomas W. Britt, eds. 2013. *Building Psychological Resilience in Military Personnel*. Washington, DC: American Psychological Association.

Singer, Peter W. 2008. "How to Be All That You Can Be: A Look at the Pentagon's Five Step Plan for Making Iron Man Real." Brookings Institution, May 2.

Singleton, Jeffrey D. 2014. "Army Basic Research." NDIA Science Engineering and Technology Conference, Army Science and Technology Program Session, Hyattsville, MD, April 9.

Singer, Peter W., and August Cole. 2016. *Ghost Fleet: A Novel of the Next World War*. Boston: Mariner Books.

Skradol, Natalia. 2009. "Homo Novus: The New Man as Allegory." *Utopian Studies* 20 (1): 41–74.

Slotten, Hugh Richard. 2014. "War and Medicine." In *The Oxford Encyclopedia of the History of American Science, Medicine, and Technology*, edited by Hugh Richard Slotten. Oxford: Oxford University Press. Accessed November 1, 2020, https://search.credoreference.com/content/entry/ouposmat/war_and_medicine/.

Smith, Frank L., III. 2014. "We Have Military Research to Thank for Ebola Vaccines." *The Week*, November 3.

Snoek, Anke. 2015. "Among Super Soldiers, Killing Machines, and Addicted Soldiers: The Ambivalent Relationship between the Military and (Synthetic) Drugs." In *Super Soldiers: The Ethical, Legal, and Social Implications*, edited by Jai Galliot and Mianna Lotz, 95–106. Burlington, VT: Ashgate.

Soboleva, Maja. 2017. "The Concepts of the 'New Soviet Man' and Its Short History." *Canadian-American Slavic Studies* 51 (1): 64–85.

Social Science for Emergency Response. n.d. "Ebola Response Anthropology Platform." Accessed April 4, 2020. http://www.ebola-anthropology.net.

Soeter, Marieke, and Merel Kindt. 2011. "Disrupting Reconsolidation: Pharmacological and Behavioral Manipulations." *Learning and Memory* 18 (6): 357–66.

SoldierMod.com. 2019. "Programmes at a Glance: January 2019." Accessed April 26, 2020. https://www.soldiermod.com/volume-22/pdfs/articles/programmes-overview-jan-2019.pdf.

Soldiers. 2006. "The Army's Future Combat Systems." *Soldiers* 61 (1): 34–37.

Speckhard, Anne, and Ahmet S. Yayla. 2015. "Eyewitness Accounts from Recent Defectors from Islamic State: Why They Joined, What They Saw, Why They Quit." *Perspectives on Terrorism* 9 (6): 95–118.

Spotts, Frederic. 2004. *Hitler and the Power of Aesthetics*. Woodstock, NY: Overlook.

Stahl, Roger. 2006. "Have You Played the War on Terror?" *Critical Studies in Media Communication* 23 (2): 112–30.

Stand-To! The Official Focus of the U.S. Army. 2015. "Force 2025 and Beyond." March 27. https://www.army.mil/standto/archive_2015-03-27/.

Stanton, Shelby L. 1992. *Rangers at War: Combat Recon in Vietnam*. New York: Orion Books.

Starn, Orin. 1991. "Missing the Revolution: Anthropologists and the War in Peru." *Cultural Anthropology* 6 (1): 63–91.

Steinkamp, Peter. 2003. "Pervitin (Methamphetamine) Experiments and Its Use in the German Wehrmacht." Published abstract for symposium *Man, Medicine, and the State: The Human Body as an Object of Government Sponsored Research, 1920–1970*. Reichspräsident-Friedrich-Ebert-Gedenkstätte, Heidelberg, October 9–10.

Steinkamp, Peter. 2006. "Pervitin (Methamphetamine) Tests, Use, and Misuse in the German Wehrmacht." In *Man, Medicine, and the State: The Human Body as an Object of Government Sponsored Medical Research in the 20th Century*, edited by Wolfgang U. Eckart, 61–71. Stuttgart: Franz Steiner Verlag.

Stewart, Andrew. 1997. *Art, Desire, and the Body in Ancient Greece*. Cambridge: Cambridge University Press.

Stoller, Paul. 1997. *Sensuous Scholarship*. Philadelphia: University of Pennsylvania Press.

Stouder, Richard L. 2002. "Inventing the 21st-Century Soldier: Battle Suit 2010." *World and Information* 17 (5): 140–47.

Sulzberger, Marion B. 1962a. "Body Armor." January 30. Papers of Marion B. Sulzberger, M.D. Technical Director of Research, US Army Medical Research and Development Command, Office of the Surgeon General.

Sulzberger, Marion B. 1962b. "Progress and Prospects in Idiophylaxis (Built-in Individual Self-Protection of the Combat Soldier)." *Proceedings of the 1962 Army Science Conference, United States Military Academy, West Point, N.Y., 20–22 June 1962*, vol. 2, 316–31. Headquarters, Department of the Army, Washington, DC: Office of the Chief of Research and Development.

Sulzberger, Marion B. 1981. "Contemporaries: Marion B. Sulzberger, M.D." *Journal of the American Academy of Dermatology* 4 (4): 500–504.

Sund, Christine. n.d. Biological Robustness in Complex Settings (BRICS). Defense Advanced Projects Agency (DARPA). Accessed May 23, 2020. https://www.darpa .mil/program/biological-robustness-in-complex-settings.

Sunder Rajan, Kaushik. 2006. *Biocapital: The Constitution of Post-Genomic Life*. Durham, NC: Duke University Press.

Sunder Rajan, Kaushik. 2017. *Pharmocracy: Value, Politics, and Knowledge in Global Biomedicine*. Durham, NC: Duke University Press.

Swets, John A., and Robert A. Bjork. 1990. "Enhancing Human Performance: An Evaluation of 'New Age' Techniques Considered by the US Army." *Psychological Science* 1 (2): 85–96.

Swofford, Frank. 2004. "Interview with Arthur K. Cebrowski, Director, Office of Force Transformation." *Defense AT&L* March-April: 2–9.

Taraska, Philip Andrew. 2017. "How Can the Use of Human Enhancement (HE) Technologies in the Military Be Ethically Assessed?" PhD diss., Duquesne University, Pittsburgh, PA.

Taussig, Karen-Sue, Klaus Hoeyer, and Stefan Helmreich. 2013. "The Anthropology of Potentiality in Biomedicine: An Introduction to Supplement 7." *Current Anthropology* 54 (Suppl. 7): s3–s14.

Taylor, Charles. 2004. *Modern Social Imaginaries*. Durham, NC: Duke University Press.

Terry, Jennifer. 2017. *Attachments to War: Biomedical Logics and Violence in Twenty-First-Century America*. Durham, NC: Duke University Press.

Theweleit, Klaus. 1987–89. *Male Fantasies*. 2 vols. Minneapolis: University of Minnesota Press.

Thompson, Mark. 2015. "Pentagon Taps Crowdsourcing to Chart Future Threats." *Time*, August 15.

Thompson, Mike. (2008) 2019. "Killing in the Name Of: The US Army and Video Games." *Ars Technica*, January 1.

Tilghman, Andrew. 2015. "DoD Launches 'Crowdsourcing' Portal to Meet Warfighter Needs." *Military Times*, October 17.

Timmerman, Frederick W., Jr. 1987. "Future Warriors." *Military Review*, September, 46–55.

Tolzmann, Michael. 2012. "Developing Capabilities for a 21st Century Army." *Soldiers* 67 (1): 20–25.

Tracy, Irene, and Rod Flower. 2014. "The Warrior in the Machine: Neuroscience Goes to War." *Nature Reviews: Neuroscience* 15:825–34.

Tucker, Patrick. 2015. "Military's Ebola Vaccine Tests Safe." *Defense One*, April 1.

Tucker, Patrick. 2019. "The US Military Is Chopping Up Its Iron Man Suit for Parts." *Defense One*, February 7.

Ulrich, Andreas. 2005. "Hitler's Drugged Soldiers." *Der Spiegel*, May 6.

United States Africa Command Instruction. 2019. "Force Health Protection Requirements and Medical Guidance for Entry into the US Africa Command Theater." Document ACI 4200.09A.

United States Army. 1998. *Army Science and Technology Master Plan*. Washington, DC: Department of the Army.

United States Army. 2005. "They Have the Will . . . We Have the Way." Program Executive Office Soldier Portfolio, October.

United States Army Center for Promotion and Preventive Medicine (USACHPPM). 1998. "Force Medical Protection Strategy, January 1998," 41–44.

United States Army Medical Research and Materials Command (USAMRMC). n.d. Military Operational Medicine Research Program (MOMRP) Overview: Science to Service Member. Accessed April 9, 2020. https://momrp.amedd.army.mil /overview/program-overview.

United States Army Medical Research and Materials Command (USAMRMC). n.d. Military Operational Medicine Research Program Frequently Asked Questions. Accessed April 9, 2020. https://momrp.amedd.army.mil/about/FAQs.

United States Army Medical Research and Materials Command (USAMRMC). 2004. Military Operational Medicine Research Program Info Paper, October 21.

United States Army Natick Soldier RD&E Center (NSRDEC). 2014. "Warfighter Directorate" (WD). June 5.

United States Army Natick Soldier RD&E Center (NSRDEC). 2009. "Future Soldier 2030 Initiative: Future Soldiers Need to Own the Fight!" February.

United States Army Research Laboratory. 2014. "Army Research Laboratory Technical Strategy 2015–2035." United States Army Medical Research and Development Command (USAMRDC).

United States Army Training and Doctrine Command (TRADOC). 2005. "Military Operations: Force Operating Capabilities." TRADOC Pamphlet 525-66. Department of the Army, Headquarters, July 1.

United States Army Training and Doctrine Command (TRADOC). n.d. "About." *Mad Scientist Laboratory* (blog). Accessed November 1, 2019. https://madsciblog.tradoc .army.mil/about/.

United States Department of the Army/Department of the Navy. 2014. Joint Publication 2-01.3, Joint Intelligence Preparation of the Operational Environment. Washington, DC.

United States Deparament of Defense. 1997. Department of Defense Instruction Number 6490.3, August 7, "Implementation and Application of Joint Medical Surveillance for Deployments," 16.

United States Navy. 2000. "Performance Maintenance during Continuous Flight Operations." NAVMED-6410.

United States Navy. 2010. "US Navy Climate Change Roadmap." Task Force Climate Change / Oceanographer of the Navy, Washington, DC.

US Army Medical Research Institute of Infectious Diseases (USAMRIID). 2014. "USAMRIID Fact Sheet." December. https://www.usamriid.army.mil/docs /RIIDFactSheet_Dec2014.pdf.

US Military HIV Research Program. 2016. "Walter Reed Army Institute of Research Begins Phase 2 Clinical Trial of Ebola Vaccine." Press release, January 6.

Virilio, Paul. 1975. *L'insécurité du territoire*. Paris: Stock.

Vujošević, Tijana. 2017. *Modernism and the Making of the Soviet New Man*. Manchester, UK: Manchester University Press.

Wagner, Sarah E. 2019. *What Remains: Bringing America's Missing Home from the Vietnam War*. Cambridge, MA: Harvard University Press.

Wagner, Sarah E., and Thomas Matyók. 2018. "Monumental Change: The Shifting Politics of Obligation at the Tomb of the Unknowns." *History and Memory* 30 (1): 40–75.

Waite, Robert G. L. 1952. *Vanguard of Nazism: The Free Corps Movement in Post-War Germany, 1918–1923*. New York: Norton.

Walter Reed Army Institute of Research (WRAIR). 1962. "Idiophylaxis: Biological Armor for the Soldier." *Army Research and Development Newsmagazine*, September, 3, 27.

Walter Reed Army Institute of Research (WRAIR). U.S. Army Medical Research Directorate-Africa. Accessed April 4, 2020. https://www.wrair.army.mil/sites /default/files/2019-06/USAMRD-A.pdf.

Walsh, Chris. 2014. *Cowardice: A Brief History*. Princeton, NJ: Princeton University Press.

Wang, Lei. 1998. "Development of Biological Detecting Technology by the U.S. Military." *Beijing Renmin Junyi (People's Military Surgeon)* 41 (2).

Weber, Max. 1978. *Economy and Society: An Outline of Interpretative Sociology*. Berkeley: University of California Press.

Webster, Jamieson. 2018. "The Psychopharmacology of Everyday Life." *New York Review of Books*, November.

Wegryzn, Renee. n.d. Safe Genes Program. Defense Advanced Research Projects Agency (DARPA). Accessed October 20, 2019. https://www.darpa.mil/safe-genes.

Weil, Simone, and Rachel Bespaloff. 2005. *War and the Iliad*. New York: New York Review of Books.

Weinberg, Alvin M. 1996. "Edward Shils and the 'Governmentalisation' of Science." *Minerva* 34:39–43.

Weinberger, Sharon. 2017. *The Imagineers of War: The Untold Story of DARPA, the Pentagon Agency That Changed the World*. New York: Knopf.

West, Paige. 2016. *Dispossession and the Environment: Rhetoric and Inequality in Papua New Guinea*. New York: Columbia University Press.

Wheelis, Mark. 2004. "Will the 'New Biology' Lead to New Weapons?" *Arms Control Today* 34 (6): 6–13.

Wheelis, Mark, and Malcolm Dando. 2005. "Neurobiology: A Case Study of the Imminent Militarization of Biology." *International Review of the Red Cross* 87 (859): 553–71.

White House. 2015. "National Security Strategy of the United States of America: February 2015." Washington, DC: White House Office.

White House. 2017. "National Security Strategy of the United States of America: December 2017." Washington, DC: White House Office.

Winsor, Morgan. 2015. "China to Mass Produce Ebola Vaccine Developed by Chinese Military Scientists." *International Business Times*, October.

Winter, Jay. 2014. *Sites of Memory, Sites of Mourning: The Great War in European Cultural History*. Cambridge: Cambridge University Press.

Wolfe, Audra. 2013. *Competing with the Soviets: Science, Technology, and the State in Cold War America*. Baltimore: Johns Hopkins University Press.

Wolfendale, Jessica. 2008. "Performance-Enhancing Technologies and Moral Responsibility in the Military." *American Journal of Bioethics* 8 (2): 28–38.

Wolfendale, Jessica, and Steve Clarke. 2008. "Paternalism, Consent, and the Use of Experimental Drugs in the Military." *Journal of Medicine and Philosophy* 33 (4): 337–55.

Wong, Wilson W. S. 2013. *Emergent Military Technologies: A Guide to the Issues*. Santa Barbara, CA: Praeger.

Wool, Zoe. 2015. *After War: The Weight of Life at Walter Reed*. Durham, NC: Duke University Press.

Wright, Evan. 2008. *Generation Kill: Devil Dogs, Ice Man, Captain America, and the New Face of American War*. New York: Berkley Caliber.

Wurzman, Rachel, and James Giordano. 2014. "'NEURINT' and Neuroweapons: Neurotechnologies in National Intelligence and Defense." In *Neurotechnology in National Security and Defense: Practical Considerations, Neuroethical Concerns*, edited by James Giordano, 79–114. New York: CRC Press.

Zehr, E. Paul. 2018. "Captain America on Mars." *Scientific American*, August 3. https://blogs.scientificamerican.com/observations/captain-america-on-mars/.

Index

Page numbers in italics refer to figures.